rayo

An Imprint of HarperCollins*Publishers*

Girl Trouble

The True Saga of Superstar Gloria Trevi
and the Teenage Sex Cult That Stunned the World

Christopher McDougall

HarperCollins books may be purchased for educational, business, or sales promotional use. For information, please write: Special Markets Department, HarperCollins Publishers Inc., 10 East 53rd Street, New York, NY 10022.

FIRST EDITION

Designed by Leah Carlson-Stanisic

Printed on acid-free paper

Library of Congress Cataloging-in-Publication Data
McDougall, Christopher.
Girl trouble: the true saga of superstar Gloria Trevi
and the teenage sex cult that stunned the world/
Christopher McDougall.
p. cm.
ISBN 0-06-053662-4
1. Trevi, Gloria.   2. Singers—Mexico—Biography.   I. Title.
ML420.T805M33 2004
782.42164'092—dc22   2004049185
[B]

04 05 06 07 08 DIX/RRD 10 9 8 7 6 5 4 3 2 1

Especially now, this book is dedicated
to all those who have the power to hurt, and don't.

CONTENTS

ACKNOWLEDGMENTS

*W*ithout Claudia Kolker's generosity, great reporting, and humbling ability with a story, I would never have started on the trail of Gloria and Sergio in the first place. I'm grateful as well to Dean Robinson of the *New York Times Magazine* for calming the breathlessness of my first take on the tale, and to the always-for-you Boyans for that indispensable assist into a jail cell in Brazil. Dan Mandel was an agent clever enough to make this a book, for which I'm thankful, and René Alegria always valued courtesy over deadlines, by which I'm astonished.

The sad failings of the families in this tragedy remind me continually of the love and guidance of mine. Most of all, though, this is for Mica, Maya, and Sophie, girls who wouldn't know the meaning of trouble.

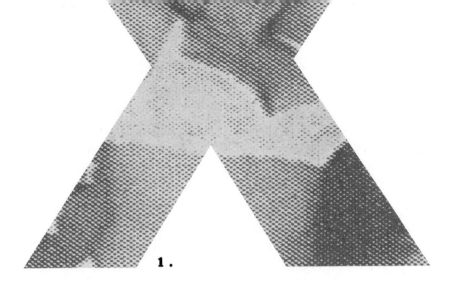

Gloria, Live

On a Sunday night in December 1989, eighteen-year-old Gloria Trevi was staring at a backstage curtain and contemplating the end of her show business career. In a few minutes, she'd be stepping onto the stage of the wildly popular Mexican variety show *Siempre en Domingo* to sing a song she'd written about a girl much like herself: young, beautiful, creative—and absolutely desperate.

"Two minutes now . . ."

Gloria stood quietly as a makeup team bustled around her in a final frenzy of preparation, dabbing her already glossy lips, smoothing a strand of her always rebellious hair, lacquering her into the perfect porcelain image of a singing Lladró. This wasn't her lucky break, she knew.

"One minute . . ."

She'd already gotten her lucky break in 1985, when she was barely fifteen and charmed her way into the fifth and final spot on a new girl group, Boquitas Pintadas ("Little Painted Mouths"). Now *that* was lucky. Gloria had never played an instrument in her life at that point, or sung a note in public, and yet somehow she lucked into a chance that far more experienced singers would have killed for. The Boquitas were the latest creation of Sergio Andrade, the hot young record producer who'd been nicknamed "Mr. Midas" for his remarkable ability to match unknown artists with star-making material. He'd had tremendous success with the lovely young chanteuse Lucerito (now known as Lucero), the beautiful blind singer Crystal, and the rock band Grupo OkiDiki.

With Boquitas Pintadas, Sergio was trying his hand at rock-and-roll girl groups, a genre that was catching fire in the United States and seemed custom-made for his talents. After all, Bananarama was earning gold records for basically looking good standing next to each other, while The Go-Gos and The Bangles were selling out arenas because they could pluck a few rudimentary chords. That's why Sergio, a classically trained pianist, knew he could do better. Instead of just jiggling guitar twangers, he'd turn his girls into serious musicians. He handpicked five Boquitas and sequestered them for a year, teaching them keyboards and harmonics and creating their neat, office-girl look. He worked them hard—maybe too hard: The girls bickered, and Boquitas Pintadas folded in less than a year.

"Thirty seconds, Miss Trevi."

That's how, at age sixteen Gloria ended up out of work and out on the street. She'd come to Mexico City three years before on a TV talent scholarship, but her talent hadn't landed her more than a few soap opera walk-ons. Just as her money and confidence were running out, she got her lucky break with the Boquitas. That one year as a Boquita gave her a glimpse at what a pop singer's life could be, and now she was desperate for one last shot—but on her own this time, without having to rely on such undependables as squabbling bandmates and a phony prefab image. She dreaded the alternative: a grim, fourteen-hour bus trip back home to Monterrey, the smog-hazed factory town hard on the Texan border. So after the Boquitas folded, Gloria begged her mother for money to live on while she wrote songs and courted record companies, but her mother refused—no way she was letting her daughter live alone in the lethal labyrinth of Mexico City without at least a recording company or TV training program to look out for her.

"OK, Miss Trevi, on my count. Five . . ."

Gloria defied her family and basically disappeared. Very few people know where sixteen-year-old Gloria went after she vanished or what she did to survive. Afterward, those lost years would become the basis of her legend. Teenage girls across the world would hear Gloria tell stories of how she was evicted from her boardinghouse and lived on the streets, singing for coins at bus stops and begging on the streets.

"Four . . ."

Gloria would turn the story of her lost years into a teenybop adventure, spinning epic tales of begging dowagers for coins and scrubbing toilets for rent. She was thrilled, she'd say, when she got the chance to strip off her rubber scrub gloves and teach aerobics for slave wages. After twelve straight hours of classes a day, Gloria would recount, she barely had enough to pay for a few street vendor tacos and cover her weekly boardinghouse bill. Whatever she was actually doing during her post-Boquita years, it had the ironic side effect of making her more glamorous than she'd ever been as an aspiring pop star. If she truly had been eating as miserably and exercising as endlessly as she'd say, it made Gloria's body simultaneously trimmer and bustier. She couldn't afford to have her hair cut, so she let it go long and loose. She couldn't buy clothes, so she paid more attention to the few she had, assembling them in a far more daring and artful style, mimicking the breakthrough popularity of Madonna and Cyndi Lauper to create her own Latin-style, trash-chic look.

She was also writing furiously in her notebooks, making use of the breaks between aerobics sessions to jot down the rhymes and melodies she'd come up with during class. In a way, the job was perfect for an aspiring pop star—Gloria was being paid to rehearse dance moves and let her mind run free, all to a steady techno backbeat. She'd been writing verses since she was five years old, and had learned to read and arrange music during her year with the Boquitas. Her tough new life, meanwhile, was giving her plenty of hard-knocks and girl-alone material to draw on for lyrics.

"Three . . ."

One year after the Boquitas' final concert, as Gloria would tell the story, she was back in Sergio Andrade's office, this time carrying a scrawled collection of nearly thirty songs. Mr. Midas rarely made a mistake, and never twice. He liked Gloria, and he'd been impressed with her raw intelligence and willingness to work during Boquitas rehearsals (one observer called her the "sharpest little devil" in the group), but he was reluctant to take another chance on a singer he'd struck out with before. Besides, Sergio was having troubles of his own by then and was in the midst of his own sabbatical from the record industry. Even if he were willing to reemerge and gamble on a new singer, Gloria was still way too inexperienced to be more than a backup vocalist.

Still, Sergio agreed to read her songbook and let her peck out a few of her tunes on the piano. He was surprised to find they were catchy and quite polished. They could be hits, he speculated—but not sung by someone as green as Gloria. Maybe she could sell them to another singer, someone established and unquestionably bankable, and use the money to live on until she was established enough to sing her own material.

At that moment, Gloria faced the same dilemma that a bankrupt young actor named Sylvester Stallone had faced a few years earlier, when he was offered ten thousand dollars for the rights to his first script about a hard-knocks boxer. And Gloria made exactly the same choice as Stallone—even though she was broke, she decided to hold out until she could do the songs her way. Sergio might not have faith enough to bankroll her dream, but he might at least have the confidence to help her if Gloria found a way to pay for the record herself. With barely enough money to live on, let alone buy pricey recording time in a California studio, Gloria decided to make another appeal to her mother. This time she went for broke, adding an all-or-nothing offer: If her mother paid the recording fees and the record failed, Gloria would come home to Monterrey.

"I showed up at her door, crying, and I knew how hard it would be, because I had basically run away from home," she'd recall. "I had a microphone in my hand and said, 'Mom, this is my last chance. Look at me with this microphone—this is what I'm dying to do. And if I don't achieve it, I'll do as you say.' And because my mother had received a small inheritance, she gave me that ultimate opportunity." Since all he had to do was produce, Sergio agreed to help create Gloria's first solo album.

After her attempts to break into television and a girl group, Gloria was getting her last chance at stardom—for the last time.

"*Two . . .*"

The prerelease single was "¿Qué hago aquí?" ("What Am I Doing Here?"), but that title track proved to be less popular than another cut, a much darker song called "Dr. Psiquiatra" ("Dr. Psychiatrist"). It was cleverly written, but surprisingly violent for the debut album of a pretty pop singer. "Dr. Psiquiatra" is about a girl who is dragged off to an insane asylum and put in the care of a leering, leg-ogling psychiatrist. The metaphoric similarities to Gloria's own life were striking, though nimbly fictionalized—like the thwarted protaganist of her "Dr. Psiquiatra," Gloria saw herself as misunderstood and underappreciated, desperate to change her life but boxed in by societal forces that demeaned her as nothing more than a sex object and belittled her exuberance and creativity as "nutty."

Luckily for Gloria, however, a more subtle subtext was never picked up by entertainment executives: The song describes the horror and frustration of a young woman who goes to men of authority for help and finds herself chased, groped, and, ultimately, locked up for not playing along. In Gloria's case, the lock was turned from the inside—before her mother agreed to finance her album, Gloria complained that she couldn't break back into the music industry without throwing her body into the bargain. "I would knock on doors and demonstrate one of my songs, and the director of the company would want to take me to dinner at the restaurant of a hotel," Gloria would later recall.

"I preferred not to go."

"*One . . .*"

Because he was also the host of his own radio show, Sergio was able to give "Dr. Psiquiatra" a little air time. He also got Gloria a few minutes on some of the late-night TV shows. Her song started to catch some ears and climb the charts. Sergio was also sort of an at-large talent scout for Televisa, Mexico's only television network. It was a power he used sparingly—he couldn't risk diluting his credibility by shoehorning all his new hopefuls onto Televisa's programs. But a buzz was starting to circulate about this beautiful young girl and her disturbing new song, so Sergio decided to take the risk. He got her on *Siempre en Domingo,* Televisa's premiere showcase, hosted by courtly old Raúl Velasco, the Ed Sullivan of the Latin airwaves.

Gloria knew exactly what she was supposed to do—Sergio had worked with her on every syllable of her song, every dance step, every throwaway gesture to either include for charm's sake or discard as a distraction. Her mind was fuzzy with detail, but she felt surprisingly calm, almost transcendentally removed from the moment. Years later, she'd recall those final minutes before she went through the curtain very vividly and say she hadn't felt like a performer—she felt more like a cliff diver who was risking disaster but understood that nervousness would guarantee it.

"Ladies and gentlemen . . ."

What was so thrilling and dreadful about this performance was its intimacy—*this was all about her!* She had created this opportunity with her persistence, her talent, and her ability to win over doubters. She now had to win over many more: Right now, she thought, millions are watching me, most of Mexico and Latin America and people overseas. This is it, my one true shot. By "true" she meant that if she didn't wow the world tonight, well . . . what else did she have to offer? This was the best Gloria had. She'd tried subjecting herself to someone else's design and that had failed. This time, she was basing her whole appeal on her natural appearance and ability. There couldn't be another attempt, because she couldn't be another Gloria.

"Stay calm," Sergio kept telling her. "Relax, and breathe."

"Please welcome . . ."

Gloria relaxed . . . then came out screaming. "I felt like I was exploding," is how she'd describe the show later—much later, that is, because most of that performance would be a blank to her. She'd have to be told what she did, and even then she wouldn't believe it till she saw the tape. "I stretched, I jumped, I dropped and rolled around, I tore my stockings so my panties were showing," Gloria says, still a bit incredulous herself. "I even yanked the glasses off the presenter."

Yanked the glasses off poor Raúl Velasco! This was *not* how the venerable Mr. Sunday Night was treated. And this was certainly not how serious Mexican performers—especially young ladies!—behaved in public. Look at Lucerito, Sergio's most famous protégé—she stood tall and elegant, usually in a long gown or folkloric ranchero getup. Once she'd raised the mike to her mouth, that was about it: Little moved but her lips. Her panties were definitely not part of the show.

But Gloria was electrified. She doesn't recall making the decision consciously, but in that performance she shut down her self-censor and acted on any impulse that popped into her head. Even that thick, long mane of hers, so carefully coiffed on the album cover, had burst free and seemed to be writhing from her scalp. The camera crew were given urgent orders from the control room to keep their lenses as tight as possible on this wild thing's face and, by all means, to avoid showing her from the rear or give any hint of what she was doing when her hands dropped below her waist.

Meanwhile, the song Gloria had recorded as a growling lament came out, this time, as a screaming anthem of feminist independence:

Doctor Psychiatrist
don't keep staring at my legs. . . .
NO, NO, NO, NO, NO, NO
I'M NOT CRAZY!

By the time she finished, the studio audience was on its feet, screaming for more. Gloria had come prepared to perform three songs—but she was quickly ushered offstage. "Most singers get to do two, three songs," she would later complain. "As soon as I finished 'Doctor Psiquiatra," they got me right off. I couldn't even hear what they were telling me, the applause was so loud. I just knew they wanted me to go, right away. So I left."

X   X   X

The next day, Sergio got word from Televisa: Gloria Trevi was banned. Not just from *Siempre en Domingo,* but from every program on Televisa, meaning she was off the Mexican airwaves for good. The verdict was unappealable, Sergio was told: It had come down directly from

Emilio Azcárraga Milmo, the owner of Televisa, a man known as "the Rupert Murdoch of Mexico," for his tremendous multimedia power, but more colloquially as "The Tiger," for his white-streaked hair and ferocious temper.

Azcárraga had been hosting a dinner party that Sunday night, and one of his guests was Cardinal Ernesto Ahumada Corripio, the seventy-year-old archbishop of Mexico City. Ordinarily, Azcárraga would have left the television off while entertaining, but *Siempre en Domingo* was his special baby—he had created the show himself and personally selected Raúl Velasco as host. *Siempre en Domingo* meant a lot to Azcárraga; it was the first Mexican-generated show to challenge the dominance of imported TV fare, and as such Azcárraga saw it as a model of what Mexican programming should be. He rarely missed it.

So as The Tiger and the archbishop watched, Gloria Trevi was busy making a statement of her own. The archbishop, needless to say, was appalled. "He said I looked like a French whore," Gloria would later recount. She tells the story with pleasure, because two months after Gloria's startling debut appearance on *Siempre en Domingo* in December 1989, Azcárraga had to reverse his decision and remove the ban.

Seven days after the album had its nationwide release, "Dr. Psiquiatra" became the No. 1 single in the country. It would remain there for nearly three months, only dropping to No. 2 when another song from the same album, "¿Qué Voy a Hacer Sin Él?" ("What Will I Do Without Him?"), replaced it. One month later, a third song from the album—"El ultimo beso" ("The Last Kiss")—leapfrogged to the top spot. Gloria's songs were Nos. 1, 2, and 3 on Mexico's hit parade. With her debut album, she'd become the Mexican Elvis.

Gloria's forced exile from television made a delicious accompanying story—the press soon took up her cause, putting the controversial new sensation on magazine covers with headlines like "The Unsinkable Gloria Trevi." Azcárraga had thought that by pretending Gloria didn't exist, he could make her disappear. In most cases he'd have been right. But for Gloria, Televisa's hostility played perfectly into the rebel-outcast image she was creating for herself. The longer she was kept out of the public eye, the more authentic and enticing she became.

"She was so spontaneous, both on stage and in person," says Humberto Leal Valenzuela, the news director for Juárez's RadioNet radio station who, in the dawn of Gloria's career, was often sent on assignment to cover this new phenomenon. At her first concert in Juárez, Valenzuela recalls, she sparked the audience into an uproar by pretending to get angry and dumping her can of Coke on the heads of some fans in the front row. She then walked off the stage in a huff, only to bound back on again with a delighted grin when the crowd started to roar. "Gotcha!"

No other sex symbol—no other singer, for that matter—seemed to have Gloria's sense of humor and natural flair for endearing, self-deprecating silliness. Madonna had been a Latin idol even before she curtsied southward with "La Isla Bonita," and Tina Turner had won millions of Latin fans as much for her hard-stomping pop as her image as a sexy survivor of hard times, but they were both so . . . *self-impressed*. Madonna's wit was as spiky as her brassiere, her mockery pointed outward at a world that would never approach her lofty hipness. Tina's raspy laugh, on the other hand, always carried an echo of bitter memories. Cyndi Lauper, for all her cutesy contralto clowning, never radiated raw heat.

But Gloria, Mexico's own homegrown sensation, had something none of these American imports could match: raw beauty, a flair for storytelling, and uninhibited sex appeal coupled with a genuinely funny sense of the absurd. And because she was *theirs*, one of their own daughters, Gloria's audacity was simultaneously more shocking and more endearing; she wasn't some Hollywood gringa shoving Hollywood sin in their faces, but a real Latina who'd sprung from their culture and shared their treasured traditions, even when, with a half-penitential shrug, she was making fun of them. If Madonna stripped naked and posed with a Pancho Villa sombrero on her head and bullet belts barely covering her nipples, she'd look ridiculous or despicable. Gloria did it and looked cute and ravishing, like a prematurely well-developed girl playing dress-up in granddad's old army uniform. That unforgettable pinup poster also made a subtle artistic statement, one immediately recognizable despite the distraction of her jutting breasts: Madonna might rule the army of foreign pop culture invaders, but Gloria Trevi was leader of the local underground rebellion.

In her battle against Madonna and other more heavily promoted superstars for dominance in the Latin pop market, Gloria had a weapon that none of her rivals could match: She was truly funny. Gloria had a natural, rapid-fire wit and a different kind of shamelessness—one that allowed her to slash back and forth from silly to sexy. She made fun of macho men and Barbie doll blondes and Catholic sexual absurdities, but she made fun of herself just as much. Her press conferences were always a hit, not just because they were guaranteed to provide some new outrage for the next morning's headlines, but also because they were rapidly becoming the best stand-up act in the country: Give Gloria a microphone and some questions, and she'd keep her audience in stitches.

By her own predisposition, she had hit on the natural, subliminal connection between laughter and lust; when you laugh, you relinquish control, you breathe heavily, you convulse—much like sex (consider how often "sense of humor" is listed as the most attractive quality in the opposite sex). By not taking herself seriously, by letting her own impromptu prankishness erupt, Gloria had found another way—besides her naughty schoolgirl outfits and flat-out graphic raunchiness—to turn on her audience. Finally, here was a bombshell who would really let her hair down, in every sense.

But if there was anything calculated in Gloria's approach, she kept it invisible. That's what made her so irresistible. "She'd come into my office, throw her feet up on my desk, and just start talking about anything that crossed her mind," says RadioNet's Valenzuela. "You have to understand how incredibly unusual that was for a young entertainer. First, to be so relaxed with someone who is going to review your work and could hurt your career. And secondly, she would talk about things other singers would never mention. It was never about hairstyles, or any of that silly nonsense," Valenzuela continues. "She would dive right into politics, sociology, drugs, abortion—whatever was the hot topic of the moment. Her positions were pretty well thought out, I have to say, and no one could ever tell how serious *really* she was about her political ambitions. She wasn't talking yet about being the first female president of Mexico—that would come later. Back then, she just wanted to be the first pop singer to be elected mayor of Monterrey."

Sales of *¿Qué Hago Aquí?* were shooting through the roof. School-girls were fashioning themselves into "mini-Trevis" and adopting Gloria's trademark clunky boots, while young women in nightclubs were nicking imitative holes in their nylons. Within months, the homeless street girl from Monterrey had become the most imitated woman in Latin America. Sergio, meanwhile, was getting urgent calls from concert pro-moters in Venezuela, Puerto Rico, Argentina, and Spain, and even from Portuguese-speaking Brazil and Spanish-speaking corners of the United States. Gloria might be banned from the airwaves in her own country, but that didn't mean she couldn't become a sensation everywhere else. If Sergio took Gloria on tour, the promoters promised, she'd become as fa-mous for her outlaw status as she was for her music: Fans would flock to see the singer who was so dangerous she had to go into exile to perform.

Faced with such staggering public acclaim, The Tiger relented and made Sergio an offer: Gloria could return to television, but only if she combed her hair and covered her underwear. "And make sure she wears nylons without holes," Azcárraga added. "We can't have all that leg skin." But Gloria refused. "Everyone thought that without television, I'd be nothing, but my songs were selling like hotcakes," Gloria says. "This was coming from my heart, and people were reacting to my heart, so I couldn't just change."

Azcárraga bristled—and surrendered. The Tiger may have been a re-spectful son of the Church, but he was also a tough-minded media mogul, and he could sense where this trend was heading. He understood that Gloria wasn't putting on schtick but had tapped into a creative force that was not only natural to her, but seemed to express sentiments shared by millions of her fellow Mexicans. Azcárraga could try to ignore what was stirring in his viewing public—but he knew it would only get bigger.

Social rebellion and franker sexuality were brewing in Mexico, rat-tling the constrictions of a Roman Catholic clergy that was still insisting that women were partly to blame for rape because they wore miniskirts. It was no secret that a revolution was gathering momentum—the only mys-tery was, where had this new teenage revolutionary come from?

Because for all Gloria's audacity, she was deftly and extraordinarily evasive about her personal life. That's not to say she was reclusive; from the start, Gloria was a delightful interview—unless you pushed too far. That's what happened when Gloria made an early appearance on a talk show hosted by Veronica Castro, one of the country's most revered actresses and television personalities. According to a Televisa producer who was on the set at the time, the trouble began when the new star made a quip about prostitution.

"But surely you agree that prostitution is terrible," Veronica Castro said, eager to find some safe, common ground so she could move the conversation off this extremely non-Televisa topic and get back to her real interest, which was Gloria's life and the inspiration for her music.

"Prostitutes are all around us," Gloria rebutted. That should have given Castro a whiff of danger, but she pressed on.

"Well, I believe they should be taken off the streets," Castro replied.

"At least they do it for food and for their families," Gloria retorted. "Not to get their own talk shows." While Veronica Castro was gasping in astonishment, a grinning Gloria raised her fist in the air and shouted toward the camera, *"Viva la prostitución!"*

In less combative moments, however, she was witty and quick to share emotionally riveting tales about her early struggles. Or so it seemed. But when various versions of her life story were compared, it became apparent that Gloria—the woman who'd become a superstar by telling it "straight from the heart"—was playing with the facts. Certain key anecdotes such as the explanation for why she never seemed to have a romantic partner, or what really happened back home in Monterrey, were never honestly addressed. Gloria's answers would always be long and colorful, but they'd also be contradictory—her own stories didn't add up.

Gloria was hiding something. Despite her uninhibited flamboyance onstage, the so-called "intellectual honesty" that had won her the acclaim of even esteemed Mexican cultural critics like Carlos Monsiváis and Elena Poniatowska would vanish when attention turned toward her offstage life. It took a while before the press and her public began to pick up on this; for those first few thrilling years, Gloria was making enough news and commotion to prevent anyone from looking any deeper.

But eventually, inevitably, the questions started to arise. It took a few years, but by 1998 Gloria's fans and the celebrity gossip magazines were wondering with increasing persistence how a woman who made such an issue out of sex didn't seem to be having any herself. When asked about love interests in the first few years of her career, Gloria could get away with the stock reply that touring and recording left her no time for romance. But after nearly eight years, that story had worn impossibly thin. Wasn't it odd, the gossip mags wondered, that she was *still* not only single, but free of any emotional involvement that anyone was aware of? Why was she never seen in public with anyone but the young girls in her band, who surrounded her at all times like a platoon of petite, ponytailed bodyguards? Something about her isolation was strange—and at the same time, rumors were starting to grow about Gloria's unusual behavior when she wasn't in the public eye. As soon as the stage lights were dimmed, backstage producers whispered, Gloria Trevi turned into an astonishingly different person.

Of course, that made her all the more attractive. As much as Gloria revealed, as much as she bared her body and her opinions, there was always the thrilling suggestion that the *real* excitement was yet to come. But Gloria also turned out to be exceedingly shrewd at misdirection: As interest continued to grow about her current life, she steered the questions instead toward the one she'd left behind, by hinting at hidden scars. The best way to distract attention from the present, she'd found, was to mystify people with her past.

It was only later, after Gloria had disappeared, that anyone realized that all along her secret had been playing out right before their eyes.

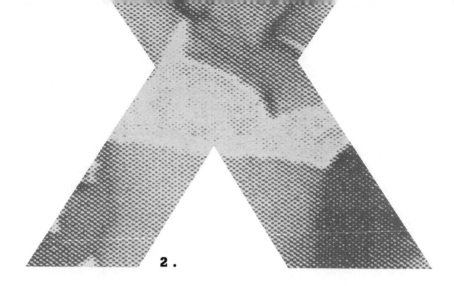

2 .

From Little Monster to the Big Monster

*H*er real name is Gloria de los Ángeles Treviño Ruiz. She was born . . . when? Even this, the very first fact of Gloria Trevi's life, is a mystery.

In every official biography, in every newspaper article written about her Gloria's birth date is given as February 15, 1970. She certainly looked that young, and because she had dropped out of school in her early teens and lived off her wits, there was no circulating written record—no school reports, no university applications, no payroll documents—that could pop up and challenge her age. It was only after she was arrested in Brazil that police seized her passport and found yet another new puzzle: Gloria's birth date was listed as February 15, 1968.

"That's a confusion," Gloria would tell me, during a three-hour conversation we had while she was a prisoner in Brazil. "There was a problem with my birth documents." It was the only one-on-one interview she would give after her first year in custody, and she wanted to use it to set the record straight about her life. She had granted very few interviews after her strange and sudden disappearance in September 1998 and subsequent arrest in Rio de Janeiro in January 2000. And then, as Mexico stepped up efforts to bring her home on charges of rape, kidnapping, and corruption of minors, gearing up for what would surely be its version of the O. J. Simpson Trial of the Century, she stopped talking altogether.

But as Gloria maintained her silence behind prison walls, rumors began to spread: Stories swirled of her involvement in Satanism and sex cults, of torture, kidnapping, child abandonment, and the mysterious disappearance of her child. Two young women accused her of recruiting them off the street and subjecting them to expert and irresistible brainwashing. Gloria's own cousin said the singer watched from a doorway while she was raped. "You know, when I was a nine-year-old girl going to see my favorite music star," one of Gloria's teenage backup singers would later declare, "I never thought that one day I'd be helping her hide a corpse."

Once Gloria was behind bars, her former friends and band members added their tales of depravity. Even the Brazilian police contributed to the frenzy, accusing Gloria of masterminding a cunning plan to escape prison by secretly inseminating herself with bags of sperm smuggled to her in glasses of warm milk from a notorious Brazilian gangster. It was becoming impossible to tell what was fact and what was fiction in the ever-stranger life of Gloria Trevi—especially since much of the confusion was deliberately sown by Gloria herself.

By February of 2002, Gloria was facing imminent extradition to Mexico, where her life, she claimed, was in danger. She insisted that the powerful Mexican politicans were afraid of what she had discovered about their dealing with the television industry and wanted her dead. She issued a statement comparing herself to Digna Ochoa, the Mexican human rights lawyer who was shot to death in October 2001 for attacking government abuse. Gloria said she was the Digna Ochoa of Mexican entertainment.

Then, on February 5, 2002, Mario Escobedo Anaya was gunned down in Juárez. Escobedo was another crusading attorney, shot to death by Chihuahua State Judicial Police—the same law enforcement body that was helping pursue Gloria's extradition. The police said it was a case of mistaken identity; civil rights activists said Escobedo had been murdered by a police force that was out of control. While it was impossible to take seriously Gloria's previous assertion that dark government forces were out to get her because she was a crusading voice of the people, like Ochoa, this new outrage lent some weight to her reluctance to come home and publicly prove her innocence: If the Chihuahua police really were as murderous and out of control as Escobedo's death suggested, then maybe a high-profile suspect like Gloria was better off staying out of their hands.

But true to the unpredictability that had helped make her a star, Gloria soon reversed course. Whether from true fear of what could happen to her in the isolation of a news blackout or from the shrewd public relations calculation of building anticipation by first saying no, Gloria decided to break her silence and told her lawyers she wanted to make sure her version of what had really happened with the "Trevi-Andrade clan" was on record before she was returned to Mexico. She agreed to one interview: She would speak with me, with no holds barred, for a lengthy article for the *New York Times Magazine*. We would have several hours alone in her room in the heavily guarded hospital where she was being held while she prepared to give birth.

When I arrived at the Hospital Regional da Asa Norte, in the center of Brazil's remote inland capital of Brasilia, I was braced to see another example of what the horrible Brazilian prisons typically produce: a haggard, frightened woman aged beyond her years. I'd been warned in advance by Gloria's attorney. "It's crazy, but they've put Mexico's most famous entertainer in the same jail as two of the most dangerous criminals in Brazil," attorney Otavio Bezerra Neves had complained. "And if you've seen *Midnight Express*, you know what kind of conditions she's been living with. When it comes to incarceration, Brazil unfortunately lives up to its reputation as a Third World country."

Gloria confirmed the horrible conditions herself, in a published account of her first days behind bars. As she was being locked in, Gloria says, a fellow prisoner called, "I heard you molested more than one hundred little girls. Better watch out—the women in here are out for you. A lot of them are mothers, and for them, that's the one thing that's unforgivable." Gloria was locked in protective custody with a light burning overhead all night and no air conditioning in the brutal Brazilian summer. "The heat was infernal," Gloria wrote. "The clanging of the keys, of the chains, of the barred doors, were all pounding in my head . . . the guard told me we'd be sharing a cell with a murderer who'd just been jailed while they evaluated her."

It didn't get any better. According to Gloria, she would soon endure rats, bedbugs, prison riots, a cell fire, and death threats. She would spend twenty-three hours a day in a small cement cell with a hole in the floor for a toilet and a knee-high, cold water spigot for a shower. Most of the news from home detailed what would happen to her and Sergio if they were ex-tradited: If the courts didn't get them, the press kept predicting, their fellow prisoners would.

It was a terrible end to a story that had begun so wonderfully, the story of a talented young girl who'd charmed and seduced a continent with, more than anything, her courage and imagination. I steeled myself, hoping to keep my objectivity and not be overwhelmed by sympathy at the miserable sight of the fallen beauty. But I was still shocked.

Gloria looked magnificent. She was propped up in bed, flanked by enormous bouquets of lush red roses. She gave me a smile and a small girlish wave. For a woman who had just spent the last two years in one of the worst prison systems in the industrialized world, Gloria was radiant. Her eyes were lightly shadowed, her lips were subtly glossed, and the trademark mane that had inspired the title of her No. 1 hit single and her box-office smash movie, *Pelo Suelto (Untamed Hair)*, was fanned forward over her shoulder, the faint gold strands catching the gold flecks in her eyes. Except for the very pregnant belly beneath her blue print maternity dress, she could have been ready to strip down for one of her near-nude, million-selling calendar shoots.

Her room was as much a study in contrasts as Gloria herself. On the table to the right of her bed were more than a dozen images of the Virgin Mary. On the table to the left, however, was propped a large photo of Gloria and another attractive woman, both with their prison-issue denim shirts knotted above their navels. In the photo Gloria is leaning vampishly against a tall, very handsome man, her lips slightly puckered at the camera.

"Who's that?" I asked. "The man?" she replied. "He's a prison guard. The woman is Mary Raquenel." María Raquenel Portillo, otherwise known as Mary Boquitas, Gloria's former bandmate from Boquitas Pintadas and until recently her cell mate. There was no further explanation of this odd photo, which looked more like three friends off to the beach rather than a portrait of a federal guard and his two notorious prisoners. In another corner of the room was a new crib with a few stuffed animals inside and a photo book of animal kingdom mommies entitled *Querida Mamãe: Obrigada por tudo (Dear Mommy: Thanks for everything)*. In a few days, Gloria would be bringing her own child into this world she had created for herself.

Gloria got up from the bed, swung her bare feet to the floor, padded over to her second-floor window, and pulled back the curtains a crack. The news cameras that had been staking out the hospital around-the-clock were still trained on her window. She treated the cameramen to a little wave, and then began dragging a steel straight-backed chair out of the corner toward the window. The faint screech of the chair across the hard tile floor caught the attention of the two federal police officers guarding the door. They immediately came inside.

"*Oi, menina, o que estás fazendo?*" one of the officers asked in Brazilian Portuguese. "Hey, girl, what are you doing?"

"*Não é nada,*" answered Gloria in faultlessy accented Portuguese. "It's nothing." One of the officers took the chair from her, setting it down in a nice patch of afternoon sun.

"How's this?" he asked.

"Perfect," Gloria replied. The officer held the back of the chair courteously while Gloria sat and settled herself. She threw back her hair, then changed her mind and fanned it forward again across her chest. Hair, lighting, makeup—perfect. "Thanks for coming to my aid," she said, rewarding and dismissing the officer with a smile. The officer grinned, then returned to his post by the door.

Now, for the first time in over a year, Gloria would have a chance to defend herself to the world, to describe the horrible prison conditions her lawyers have said she'd endured, the disease and death threats and repeated sexual abuse by predatory prison officials—but instead she launched into a defense of Sergio. Even though her situation was by far the more dire, Gloria's immediate concern was making sure that Sergio wasn't misunderstood. She wanted to put Sergio's brilliant methods in their true, blameless perspective, she said, so she began with a little story.

"Once, at a concert in Chihuahua, I was singing 'Los borregos' ('The Lambs'), and because I was dancing so much, my voice started to give out," Gloria said. Thinking quickly, she came up with a solution: She managed to hide her cracking voice by pointing the mike toward the crowd and having them chant back the chorus. It worked. "When I came off stage," Gloria recalled with a smile, "everyone was shouting, '*Bravo! Bravo!* You are *la maxima!*' "

Everyone, that is, except Sergio. "He looked at me and shook his head," Gloria recalled. "He said, 'It's shameless, to be the highest-paid female performer in Latin America and have your voice go out during a song about lambs.' I thought he couldn't tell. But he knew." At dawn the next morning, Sergio rousted her out of bed with only a few hours' sleep and told her to put on sneakers. He took her down to the Cathedral, which is surrounded by a public square at least a quarter-mile long. "Now run," Sergio ordered her. And Gloria ran—around and around the Cathedral, while early-risers arriving for morning Mass stared in astonishment as Mexico's biggest star, the uncontrollable wild child, sweated and ran and grimaced and her heavyset manager leaned silently against a wall with his arms folded across his chest.

"People were watching me, and they were all whispering, 'What an inhuman man, making Gloria Trevi run like that,' " Gloria said. "But I did it." Sergio made her run twenty laps, the equivalent of five miles, before allowing her to stop. "Sergio told me to and I obeyed, because I knew it would make me a better artist," Gloria said. With that, she sat up straight and threw back her hair. "Sergio was a very demanding producer," she said, her voice so forceful it bordered on anger, "but they have misinterpreted that brutally. They have converted him into a kind of hypnotizer. Him into a hypnotizer, and me into some dumb cow. It's all so false. Anything I did, I did because I wanted to. That was the price to be great. Ever since I was seven years old I wanted to be great. I knew what I had to do."

She fell back in her chair with a small, expectant smile, as if to say, "So there!" She awaited my reaction. It was an astonishing performance, as astonishing to me as her appearance. At this critical moment, it was so obvious what Gloria should have said, what she *had* to say, to free herself and protect her child: She had to distance herself from Sergio and claim that she, too, was his victim. Privately, I knew that some members of her legal team had been urging her in that direction for months. They'd told her, confidentially, that it didn't matter what she might later say in court if forced to testify; once she was free, she could claim a faulty memory, or fudge her account, or passively reassert her loyalty to Sergio in any way she liked. But for now, they told her, it was imperative that she cut herself loose. Sergio was lost; there was no way he could avoid deportation and a criminal trial back in Mexico. But Gloria—Gloria had a chance. She had a strong humanitarian appeal pending in the courts, plus several highly respected advocates on her side, including an outspoken politician, a priest, and a revered nun. The way her advisers saw it, if Gloria could only convince the world that she was a two-time victim—first at the hands of Sergio, then at the hands of her Brazilian jailers—she could very well win humanitarian asylum and walk out the hospital door with her baby in her arms, a free and still wealthy woman.

But instead of pleading for herself, Gloria came out with that perplexing tale of cruelty. As an apology for Sergio's managerial methods, it made no sense: There is absolutely no connection between cardiovascular fitness and a healthy larynx. In fact, the opposite is true—exposing a raw throat to cold morning air would only aggravate her already strained voice. If anything, the story only seemed to confirm what people were whispering about Sergio—that he was a sadist who indulged his taste for torture on the girls in his control.

Gloria didn't see it that way. To her it made perfect sense that she should be punished for her shortcomings, even if the punishment was absurd. And that's when it began to dawn on me that of all the girls, Gloria could be the most damaging witness against Sergio, even in her efforts to defend him. She not only had been obeying his orders for more than a decade, but she also had been absorbing their rationale. Gloria was the first of Sergio's disciples, and the most deeply conditioned; consequently, she now seemed incapable of distinguishing between acceptable discipline and pure cruelty. I'd feared that Gloria would be closemouthed or deceptive, but I now saw that in many areas she couldn't be: She didn't know what should be hidden, so she wouldn't try to hide anything.

"So," Gloria continued, "what is it you would like to know about me?" She would answer any question, she promised, about any part of her life. Only one topic was off limits: She would not explain how, as the most scrutinized prisoner in a video-monitored jail, she had somehow gotten pregnant, without a boyfriend, a behind-bars romance, or a conjugal visit. But as it turned out, the answer to that final mystery would soon arrive from another source.

"Well," I replied, "Let's start with your birth date. How old are you *really?*"

"I am thirty-two years old," she answered. "I will be thirty-three next week." Seeing the doubt in my eyes, she laid a hand on my arm and said, very softly, "Believe me. I am who I tell you I am."

X   X   X

Gloria was the first daughter of Manuel Treviño, a recent architecture graduate, and Gloria Ruiz, an eighteen-year-old aspiring dancer. Three younger brothers soon followed. Her father had been orphaned at an early age and raised by relatives, so as a young architect trying to support a rapidly growing family, he didn't have parents to fall back on for a financial boost. Money was tight, and design jobs were not easy to find for an untested architect in those pre-NAFTA days in Monterrey, in the state of Nuevo León.

When Gloria was just a few years old, her father decided to try job hunting in Ciudad Victoria, a smaller city in the neighboring northern Mexican state of Tamaulipas. For reasons Gloria never understood—or preferred not to—she was left behind with her great-grandparents. She later romanticized that first separation from her parents as one of the great memories of her childhood, a time when she was surrounded by nothing but love and approval. Years later, when she was struggling to make it as a Boquita, she enjoyed dwelling on those memories. Ironically, the person she shared them with was Rubén Aviña, Sergio Andrade's publicist at the time and the same man who later heard the confidences of Andrade's ex-wife, Aline Hernández. Back then, Aviña was working in a small office in Sergio's studio where Gloria often went to study her Boquitas sheet music.

"It was fantastic!" Gloria told Aviña, as she began another exuberant bout of reminiscing. "It was like living in Disneyland, because they agreed with whatever I said and let me do whatever I wanted! So, imagine how I couldn't have been the happiest girl in the world, living with my great-grandparents!" Those stories of a young girl left behind by her parents obviously touched Aviña, because they lodged in his memory long before Gloria was anything more than just another young hopeful crowding Sergio Andrade's busy office. Despite the role he later played in Gloria's downfall, Aviña would always remember her with affection.

Rather than being traumatized by the separation from her parents, Gloria was more frightened by the reunion. One morning, her great-grandmother said Gloria's father was coming by for a visit. When he arrived, Gloria didn't recognize him anymore. They got in the car for a drive, but as they traveled farther and farther, Gloria realized she was being taken away from her great-grandparents. She became hysterical. "It was horrible! I wanted to die!" she said later. "I felt like I was being kidnapped." The situation only got worse when they arrived in Ciudad Victoria: Instead of bringing Gloria home to live with the rest of the family, her father dropped her off with the aunt and uncle who had raised him when he was orphaned. Why she was once again being farmed off to relatives, she was never told. She hated it there, and apparently her relatives were no more pleased to be stuck with her. A few nights later, she says, she was awakened when a screaming fight broke out between Gloria's mother and her in-laws. Soon afterward her mother took her out of the house and finally brought her home.

Because Gloria's father was still out of a job, Gloria's mother had begun trying to earn a little money by giving dance lessons. Despite the rigors of trying to find enough food for four children, Gloria Ruiz was still a stunningly beautiful woman, a platinum blonde with the brassy allure of a Las Vegas showgirl. She was also a lively, enthusiastic teacher, and she soon had a following of devoted, adoring young students. It wasn't long before she managed to transform her few amateurish classes into a thriving dance studio of her own.

The studio was where Gloria spent all her time outside of school. She started dancing with her mother at three and was studying ballet by age five. She was also composing her own songs, printing them in block letters in a notebook that she illustrated with self-portraits of doll-like girls with enormous round eyes. Twenty years later, when she released her second album, *Tu Ángel de la Guarda (Your Guardian Angel)*, Gloria decorated the back cover with cartoons that looked strikingly like the images she'd made of herself at age seven.

Although Gloria's mother had become the family's major breadwinner, her father was the only steak eater. "When there wasn't enough to go around, my father always got a decent piece of meat, and the rest of us ate whatever was left," Gloria said. "Usually it was a little chopped beef with a lot of potatos." A *lot* of potatoes, she added. When she later swelled into a chubby adolescent, Gloria blamed it on years of living on little more than potatoes, flour, and cooking oil. "My mother adored my father, so she also saw to it that he had the best, even if we did without."

Manuel's hold on the family wasn't restricted to the dinner table: He also demanded that his wife hurry home from her last dance class each night and be in the door no later than 8:00 P.M. Gloria recalls walking home with her mother one December night, the two of them feeling an increasing sense of dread as they realized they were going to be late, gradually increasing their pace until they were running. They arrived panting, hoping they'd made it before Manuel had gotten home.

They hadn't. Even though it was just a few minutes after the curfew, Manuel was very angry. According to Gloria, he wouldn't let his wife in the home. "If you like walking the streets so much, then stay there!" she recalls him shouting. "Then, he slammed the door shut and locked it. And this was in the middle of December, when it was freezing outside." Gloria and one of her brothers climbed out a window and ran to keep their mother company. How long the three of them sat there crying in the cold before her father finally let them back in the house, Gloria can't remember.

Gloria Ruiz finally gathered up her children and walked out on Manuel when Gloria was ten. If she thought escaping her husband would win her any sympathy from her family, she was in for a big letdown. As Gloria later told Rubén Aviña, Gloria Ruiz brought the kids to her mother and asked for help. Instead of taking them in, Gloria's grandmother said they should accept Manuel's machismo brutishness and go home. "That's just one of the crosses that God has put in your path," Gloria's grandmother told her daughter. Gloria also says that when her mother asked for a little food to feed the kids, her grandmother refused. "My grandmother wouldn't give us a thing! Not a tortilla! Not a glass of water!"

Gloria Ruiz refused to return to Manuel, however, and set out to make a living on her own. It was a hard and precarious life for a single mother in Monterrey—Gloria tells of living in a tiny, unfurnished apartment, and of a New Year's Eve when the entire family of five had only one scrawny chicken to divide. Gloria got used to doing her schoolwork by candlelight after the electricity was shut off, and to hiding in the bathroom with her mother and brothers when the landlord came knocking at the door demanding overdue rent.

She didn't see her father for more than a year. For the second time in the first ten years of Gloria's life, Manuel was turning into a distant, frightening stranger. But it wasn't long before there were other men around the house, vying to become Gloria's new father. Gloria Ruiz was only twenty-eight years old and still model thin from her hours of daily dance instruction. And just the way she would later romanticize what it was like to be left behind as a little girl when her family moved to Ciudad Victoria without her, Gloria likes to remember her mother's return to the singles market as less of a trauma and more of a madcap, romantic adventure.

"A very rich doctor had fallen in love with her, and he used to give me little gifts so I would help convince my mother to marry him," Gloria would recall. Gloria was all for it; although she still wanted her parents to get back together, that hope seemed more a desire to avoid the stigma of divorce than any real affection for her father. In the meantime, this doctor with deep pockets and a desperate desire for Gloria Ruiz seemed like just the guy to help the struggling family. "Well," Gloria continues, "my mother had to go in for a hernia operation, and I guess the surgeon who was treating her fell in love with her while she was on that table." According to Gloria, her mother ended up marrying this second doctor in secret, and claims she only found out later, when her mother told her twelve-year-old daughter to pack up and get ready to move in with her new mystery dad.

There's something suspiciously sunny about this tale: about the way wealthy men tumble over each other to throw riches at virtuous children, and a lucky meeting ends in a surprise marriage, and a nasty, penniless man is replaced by a kind, rich one. It sounds like a soap opera; actually, it sounds exactly like the kind of romantic comedies Gloria would later star in. Perhaps it's just a case of pop art imitating life; but more likely, both her films and her happily-ever-after memories are rooted in the same thing: This is the way Gloria wants to see her world, and her imagination is powerful enough to make it real—at least for her. On the other hand, while she may have prettied up the details, by all accounts her stepfather was a decent man and was quite devoted to his new family. "He was very good to us," Gloria recalls fondly. "I even called him 'Papa.' "

Her mother, however, was a different story. Gloria Ruiz had to abandon her own dreams of an entertainment career when she became pregnant with Gloria at age seventeen, but she never abandoned the dream of becoming famous. If she couldn't storm Hollywood herself, there was always her namesake daughter. She had Gloria dancing in theater productions by the time she was seven and was horrified when her daughter—who now had access to a fully stocked fridge for the first time in her life—started putting on preteen pudge.

"My mother was always super-thin from dancing and had a really nice body," Gloria confessed to Aviña, "and she wanted her only daughter to be thin as well." Gloria, however, couldn't stop indulging; in secret she would devour chocolates and canned, syrupy fruit. When her mother caught her, she humiliated Gloria by pinning a paper pig's tail to her skirt. Gloria reacted to this kind of Mommy Dearest discipline in a curious way: Instead of making her hate hating her mother, it seemed to create a lifelong need for her approval, as if Gloria somehow believed she de-

served her punishments. When the press later began digging up unflatter-
ing stories about Gloria Ruiz's questionable child rearing, no one was
quicker to defend her than her wayward child.

School life for thirteen-year-old Gloria was no better. She was pudgy
and shy, and her darting imagination made it difficult for her to focus in
class. Every time she brought home a poor grade, Gloria claimed, her
mother would spank her. When she flunked eight subjects, Gloria was so
terrified of the whipping to come that she considered killing herself and
hid a rope outside her house. When she wasn't in terror of her mother or
her teachers, the future pinup girl was taunted by her classmates: To keep
her rambunctious hair under control, Gloria always wore it in a tight
braid down her back, leading her classmates to mock her with the nickname "Squaw Treviño."

She was miserable—until one day an older friend took Gloria under
her wing and gave her an after-school makeover. She helped Gloria brush
out her hair and experiment with lipstick and eyeliner. Gloria looked in
the mirror and was delighted with what she saw. She was immediately inspired to start dieting. It didn't take long for her to burn off the weight,
and as soon as she'd slimmed down, Gloria began leading what she'd
later call her "double life."

"I'd leave for school in the morning in my uniform, with my hair back
in my nice schoolgirl's braid," she'd say. "But in the afternoon I'd put on
some short-shorts or a miniskirt, shake my hair out, and put on makeup."
The transformation was devilishly effective: The boys who'd been teasing her just months before were now doting on her. "Every boy in the
neighborhood was after me," Gloria says with a smirk. "But I didn't date
any of them," she hastens to add. "To go out with someone, you really
have to like them a lot and, well—well, no, I didn't like any of them
enough to fall in love."

Fall in love? She was barely fourteen years old! It was an unusually
strict self-imposed guideline for any girl to set for her first boyfriend, but
it's apparently one that Gloria kept: Unlike other stars who are dogged by
the returning ghosts (and photos) of boyfriends past, Gloria has had no
one come forward with a convincing story of a teenage romance with the
wild-haired Monterrey teenager in the short-shorts.

With her daughter newly slim and stylish, and obviously no longer shy, Gloria Ruiz decided to enter her in a nationwide contest to select the girl who looked most like "Chispita," the young soap opera darling played by Lucerito. Although she was only a year older than Gloria, Lucerito was physically outgrowing the role and had already recorded a hit album with Sergio Andrade. She was getting ready to leave Chispita behind and move up to films and full-time singing, so Televisa needed to get a Chispita backup on the lot as soon as possible.

First prize in the Chispita look-alike contest was a new wardrobe, a little dog like Chispita's, and a one-year scholarship to Televisa's young-talent training school, formally known as El Centro de Capacitación de Televisa. Gloria's mother mailed in a photo, and Gloria was invited to come to the capital for the final selection round. So in 1985, Gloria and her mother boarded a bus to ride the six hundred miles from "The Little Monster," as Monterrey is known, to "The Big Monster"—Mexico City.

It's hard to see the resemblance now, ever since the girlish "Lucerito" became the elegant "Lucero" and transformed her long brown curls into a slick blond fall, but as a young teen her resemblance to Gloria was astonishing. "When I lined up for the final judging round, some of the contestants came up to me and asked for autographs," Gloria says. "They were that sure I was going to win." They were right—Gloria was selected from the final ten contestants and was awarded a year's study in the Televisa school. Still, she was disappointed. "I really wanted the dog, and they never gave it to me."

Her mother stayed around long enough to show her how to ride the Mexico City buses, Gloria says, and that was it: At fifteen, she was on her own in one of the largest and most dangerous cities on the planet, setting out to make a name for herself in one of the most competitive professions in the world. "It was marvelous!" Gloria says, her eyes glowing years later at the memory. "It was a challenge, too, because every few months or so they [El Centro] gave you tests, and if you didn't pass, you were gone, but I loved it." It's a true sign of Gloria's fierce competitive nature that she thrilled to an environment that caused many other young hopefuls to crack. While it might seem like pure glamour, Mexico's television training academies are a severe test of self-confidence; they gather the most attractive and talented young performers in the country for what is essentially a star-quality face-off.

"Mexico is probably unlike any other country in the way it develops entertainers," says author Sam Quiñones, who examined the Mexican television industry in his cultural study *True Tales from Another Mexico*. Young talent is recruited in the provinces, then brought to Mexico City for years of training at the TV network's "star factories." Because Televisa was the only network for decades, the competition for a spot in one of its performance schools was intense. After TV Azteca was launched in 1996, the talent wars changed: The two networks began trying to outscout each other by signing up younger and younger performers.

"You don't freelance," Quiñones explains. "You don't scrounge around like Madonna, hanging out at clubs and hoping for a record deal. The Televisa method for creating stars is to seclude young girls in singing and dancing schools, then have them emerge a few years later with a new name and appearance. That's the only way to make it."

Not surprisingly, it's a system ripe for abuse by the men who run it, says Judith Enriqueta Chávez-Parks Flores, the former singing star known as "Ga-Bí." As a fifteen-year-old backup singer for a local orchestra in the mid-seventies, she was offered a weekly spot on a Sunday variety show. While her mother waited outside on her first day of rehearsal, teenage Ga-Bí was raped by one of the producers inside his office. "That was my first experience as a show business professional," says Chávez-Parks, who would later describe the attack in her memoir *Como Carne de Cañón (Like Cannon Fodder)*.

"Like thousands of other girls in Mexico, I kept my mouth shut, because that is what we were always taught to do," says Chávez-Parks Flores, now forty-two. The girls were also assured that reporting the attacks would end their careers. "My first boss told me, 'You're disposable. There are a thousand "Marias" out there ready to take your place.' "

According to Gloria, she never had a problem with predatory talent scouts. In fact, her problem was they didn't notice her *enough*. During her year at the star factory, she only landed small walk-on parts in a few soap operas. When it came time for her scholarship to end, Gloria wasn't granted the Chispita role she'd been recruited for. She wasn't given any other on-screen job, or even an extension of her Televisa talent scholarship (a decision, it's assumed, that the Televisa talent scouts must later have seriously regretted).

"I was scared, panicking," Gloria says. "I was sure they were going to send me home to Monterrey, and I hadn't achieved anything yet. I was walking around, trying to figure out what to do, and I happened to run into Ricky Luis, a very good singer and a friend of mine from home."

"So what are you going to do?" Ricky asked.

"It looks like I'm going home," Gloria said.

"Hey, why don't you come with me?" Ricky asked. He had just signed to cut his first album with Sergio Andrade, and he offered to arrange an introduction. Maybe she could audition for the new girl group Sergio was forming.

"Let's go, let's go!" Gloria erupted. "This has to be destiny!"

She soon learned her destiny was operating on a different schedule. She and Ricky arrived at Sergio's studio at four in the afternoon and took a seat in the lobby. There was a steady stream of young musicians filing through; word about Sergio's new project had spread fast. Gloria kept trying to angle her way into the back office for an interview, but she was sent back to wait. Several hours later, Ricky got hungry and left. Gloria remained. Girls kept going in and coming out, but Sergio never left the back office.

Finally, at two o'clock in the morning, Gloria was shown in. Behind a piano was a scowling man whose voice seemed to bristle as much as the thick stubble covering his broad cheeks and fleshy neck. When he stood up, Gloria was surprised; he looked broad and powerful when there was a Steinway between them, but once Sergio slid off the bench and approached her, she saw he was actually not much taller than she was and kind of . . . sort of . . . It was hard to believe, but she had to admit that the swaggering power broker of Mexican music was a little chubby.

Sergio looked her over in return. He had Gloria sing a few songs. He was concerned about her height; Gloria was taller than the other four girls who had already been selected. He figured it might be all right as long as she never wore heels. Would she mind not wearing heels?

Absolutely not.

Hmmm . . . Sergio was giving it some more thought. He'd been looking at girls nearly around the clock for days now, and none of them was right. This one—she had something. He saw it the instant she came in the room: Other girls walked in, ducked in, minced in, but this Treviño girl, she *burst* in. At two o'clock in the morning, after waiting on a bench for ten hours without any food, she was still ablaze with energy. Besides, she looked a hell of a lot like Lucerito—that couldn't hurt.

Sergio had one more question. "Can you learn to play the piano in two months?"

Gloria had never touched a piano key in her life. The Boquitas were scheduled to begin live rehearsals in two months. "It's going to mean practicing eighteen hours a day," Sergio warned her. "The piano isn't a toy."

"I'll do whatever it takes," Gloria answered.

x   x   x

If she had hesitated at that moment, if she had gotten tired and discouraged a few hours earlier while waiting on that bench by herself, it's very likely she wouldn't be telling this story fifteen years later, under police guard in a shabby Brazilian maternity ward. But if the bitter irony ever crossed her mind, that running into Ricky that afternoon had truly started her on the path that would lead her here, she never showed it. Instead, a look of scorn curled her face.

"There was no way I was going to tell him, 'Um, maybe, I'll try, I'm not sure,'" Gloria says in a mock girly tone, grimacing with remembered distaste for all the girls she had competed with for that spot with the Boquitas and vanquished. "That's why those other girls didn't make it. They weren't sure. I *was* sure. I would do whatever it took to become a success."

It was the right answer. Sergio Andrade would accept nothing less.

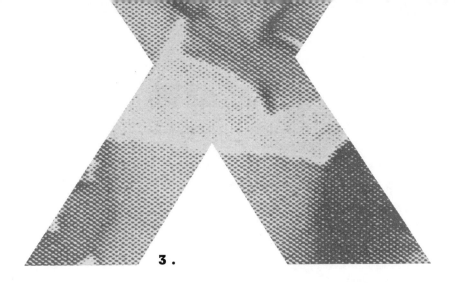

Magic Hands

*D*on't take this as a lack of modesty, but I consider myself one of the most talented musicians, composers and producers in many years," Sergio Andrade wrote to me in a hand-printed letter from prison on April 20, 2002. "And that's something indisputable even among my 'enemies.' "

Perhaps that's a shade overstated, but even Patricia Chapoy, the veteran TV executive who was the first media sleuth to start investigating the Gloria Trevi saga and remains the most dogged to this day, is quick to acknowledge Sergio's talent. "It's undeniable that Sergio Andrade is an outstanding musician and composer," Paty, as she's known, told me one afternoon in April 2003 during a long chat in her TV Azteca office about her own involvement in the case.

"I met Sergio Andrade when he started out as a star maker," Paty recalls. It was at the OTI International Festival in Puerto Rico 1981, where he'd gone to present young Olga Maria, daughter of the famous cat-eyed Cuban singer Olga Guillot, "Queen of the Bolero." Paty was impressed with the tremendously thorough job Sergio had done for such a young manager; he'd not only coached Olga Maria on voice and presentation, but also had done all her song arrangements and written her showcase number. Soon after, he did the same with Crystal, the blind Mexican singer who became a finalist at OTI and hit No. 1 in the charts with "Suavemente," one of Sergio's finest songs. (Years later, when Sergio was despised in Mexico, Crystal would quietly insist on including that song on her latest greatest-hits albums. "I couldn't imagine representing myself without 'Suavemente,'" Crystal says. Of course, one of Sergio's former lovers angrily claims "Suavemente" is rightfully *her* song—but that's another story.)

"Sergio started out as a great composer and as the creator of many young stars," Paty agrees. Over the years, Paty's and Sergio's careers— and so their private lives, Sergio would allege—would continually inter-twine: Paty was a raw talent booker when Sergio was just handling his first clients, and as she jetted up through the executive ranks and gained more control over selecting performers, Sergio was swiftly evolving into the most reliable source to provide them. "You could see that he was going to make it big," Paty says, "because he was highly intelligent and willing to work hard."

"I have a great natural talent improved through years of serious musi-cal study," Sergio's letter continues. His blunt self-promotion hits an odd, jangling note: Of *course* he was extraordinary successful; if he weren't, he wouldn't be in this predicament. That's why, under most circumstances, his insistence on proclaiming his own fame would sound ludicrously shrill, like Jennifer Lopez reminding autograph hounds that she's a star. Except, as Sergio adds in a revealing comment later in the letter, there have been so many people trying to define who he is and what he's done, so many truths, half-truths, and lies told about him, that even he's begin-ning to have trouble getting a grip on who he really is:

> *I'm trying to see myself in the mirror—but of course, that's only a figure of speech—we [the prisoners] are not allowed to have a mirror. I haven't seen myself in a mirror for more than a year.*
>
> *But I do know this—Many, many things are dramatically and completely distorted.*

For more than a year, Sergio had been locked in virtual isolation in his small cell in the dreaded Papuda Correctional Facility, deep in the Brazilian interior. He was so cut off from the outside world, it took three months for him to get that letter to me, after I'd first written to ask to see him. Papuda's closest neighboring city is Brasilia, the capital, which is as isolated in its own way as the prison. Set inland, Brasilia is hundreds of miles from the glamorous Brazilian coast and most of Brazil's major cities. The only way in or out of Brasilia is either by air or an excruciatingly long overland drive, which is why, when the door slams shut behind you in Papuda, you can look forward to very few visitors.

But it wasn't the distance that isolated Sergio; it was suspicion and high-level governmental humiliation. In the first months after he was arrested, Sergio was able to give a few short interviews, enough to declare his innocence and begin explaining how all these accusations—all the stories that he and Gloria had used her concert tours to abduct more than a hundred girls from a half-dozen countries, that they'd beaten and brainwashed them into sex slaves and prostitutes—all this was not about *him*, but about his *brother*. The shocking accusations, he said, were part of a plot to destroy his brother, Eduardo Andrade Sánchez, the powerful Mexican senator who had created bitter enemies when he tried to torpedo the presidential candidacy of Vicente Fox.

Eduardo's opposition had failed, and now, Sergio claimed, President Fox was determined to crush Eduardo as a political threat. Just consider how curiously convenient the sequence has been, Sergio insisted; the timing and circumstances couldn't be more revealing. For Eduardo's enemies, the ideal place to aim the blade would not be directly at Eduardo—no, that would be too transparent. Better to target his family: That way, they could shame Eduardo into silence, yet cover their tracks and avoid any counterattacking charge of foul play and undemocratic intimidation. Sergio was the perfect fall guy: Not only was he already linked in the public eye to the "immorality" and "decadence" of rock singers and film stars, but better yet, he had helped create the most irreverent one of all, that body-baring, *machismo*-hating, Church-defying wild woman, Gloria Trevi.

It's odd, though, that Eduardo would never say a word about this. Revealing such a plot, after all, would help him as much as Sergio; if his brother really was being ruined just to stifle Eduardo, wouldn't Eduardo go back to his friends at Televisa (where he'd worked for years before entering politics) and use its airwaves to expose Sergio's persecution as a dirty political trick? Certainly Televisa would go along; besides its loyalty to Eduardo and years of success with Gloria and Sergio, a tale like that—of sex, intrigue, and power—would make for some killer TV programs.

But Eduardo said nothing. The only time he ever breathed a word about his brother's plight was when one of Paty Chapoy's hard-charging camera crews doorstopped Eduardo as he was leaving his home one morning and jammed a mike in his face. According to a TV Azteca source, Eduardo was going to storm right on by in silence, as he had every other time, but changed his mind when a quick-thinking Azteca producer made him an on-the-spot deal: Speak now, and we'll never ambush you again. Eduardo agreed—and said basically nothing. He urged his brother to come home and be heard in a court of justice, he reminded the public that nothing had been proven yet, he offered sympathy for any young girls who might have been wronged. He never suggested Sergio's problems had anything to do with anyone except Sergio.

"I have proof," Sergio's letter to me insists. "I have letters, documents, photographs. I can prove that what I am saying is the truth. Please, come to talk personally with me," Sergio urges. "See the proof, 'feel' the truth in the real story. And don't let me be forgotten. I know the dimension of the people who have put us in this mess, the way they are, the power they handle. You know the political system there, the 'suicides' that occur in jail . . ."

But getting a chance to "feel the truth" would be extremely tricky, if not impossible. "We've been trying for months," Sergio's lawyers assured me. "But Sergio has become a problem that Brazil just wants to get rid of as quickly—and as quietly—as possible. They don't want him talking to anybody until he's off their hands."

Ever since Gloria's mysterious pregnancy was revealed in October 2001, the Brazilian Justice Ministry had cut off Sergio's access to the press and held him virtually incommunicado. The episode had shaken the

Brazilian penal system from top to foundation: It was not only a bizarre mystery, but a political hot button and a strain on diplomatic relations. With one of Latin America's biggest stars in its custody, the Brazilian prison system had either failed to control her by letting her frolic as she pleased in a maximum-security lockdown, or it had failed to protect a vulnerable Mexican citizen, letting her fall prey to sex crimes.

Gloria's lawyers were calling for her release, claiming that even though Gloria, Sergio, and Mary were supposedly being held in a special wing of a new, modernized, and video-monitored prison, supervision was so lax that even a celebrity prisoner could be raped by her guards without any prison officials finding out. Prison administrators were responding with their sperm-in-a-baggy theory. Even though Gloria refused to talk, or even confirm that she'd been raped, the aftershock of the scandal kept spreading: The justice minister and the chief of federal police lost their jobs over it. The opposition party used "The Trevi Scandal" to make prison conditions a key issue in the subsequent elections. Human rights organizations were demanding a full investigation. Nearly a hundred guards volunteered their DNA to prove that they were not the star's rapist.

And behind all the turmoil, the Brazilian authorities suspected, behind all the political furor and penal system upheaval, was Sergio. As yet no one knew quite why, or even how, he could have conspired with Gloria to get her pregnant. But from what they knew of Sergio, there had to be some gain in it, and of the three jailed stars, he was the one clever enough both to see the long-term benefit and to design the strategy. After so many years by Gloria's side, after so many risky adventures in so many countries (and the still unresolved question of what happened to the infant Gloria said she'd had, and lost, in Rio), it was impossible to believe that Sergio didn't know exactly what Gloria was up to.

Sergio, on the other hand, wasn't doing a lot to relieve suspicion: Even behind bars, his reputation as an inventive and unstoppable lady's man was soaring to legendary heights. First, there were the kids. Back home in Mexico, the girls he'd trained as singers continued having babies in the months after his arrest until the most reliable estimates were that he had fathered at least nine children by six different women, including Gloria

Trevi; then fourteen-year-old Karina Yapor; a woman he somehow managed to marry in Mexico while he was on the run in Spain; and two sisters who conceived within months of each other.

Then there was "The Book." At the same time that he was declaring himself an innocent victim of poisonous minds and trying to convince the world that the very notion that Sergio Andrade had ever raped or corrupted a minor was "absolutely absurd and surreal," Sergio released a book of erotic stories and love poems called *Revelaciones,* and subtitled *Una inquietante colección de historias eróticas, poemas y un alegato contra el linchamiento (Revelations: An Unsettling Collection of Erotic Stories, Poems and an Allegation of Lynching).* Never one to suffer from modesty or undue delicacy, Sergio didn't just give his book a name that alluded to the Bible: No, he settled for the book that contains both the revealed wisdom of Jesus Christ and the glorification of his persecution ("Behold, he cometh with clouds; and every eye shall see him, and they also which pierced him: and all kindreds of the earth shall wail because of him. Even so, Amen" [Rev. 1:7 KJ]).

If that wasn't bold enough, Sergio's book also made legal history: It's quite likely the first time an accused rapist has declared his innocence from behind bars while also telling smutty stories. Among the selections from *Revelaciones:* "I am God" and "The crazy whores, hores, horses." Another story, called "*Private* Caligula," opens with this passage: "The following morning, they got up late. The man and ten women had decided to spend the night together. . . . The girls who'd lost the dance and striptease contests the night before got up a little earlier." Most of the poems were dedicated to the young women who'd disappeared with him or to his illegitimate children.

Add to the book and the babies the whispers: not just vague, easily deniable little rumors passed along by gossip and tabloids, but specific, salacious tales told by Sergio's own close acquaintances. One of Sergio's own lawyers was whispering, confidentially, that after seeing Sergio on television and falling in love with him, several wealthy American women had traveled to Brasilia and waited for hours under the blazing summer sun in hopes of getting a glimpse of the prisoner. The attorney also swore that at least one Brazilian woman had managed to have sex with Sergio during visiting hours in hopes of raising his paternity totals to ten children by seven women. "It's amazing the way women respond to him," the attorney said in a voice that combined admiration for the feats with frustration over a self-destructive client.

Finally, there was the fiancée.

x   x   x

A fifty-four-year-old legal assistant assigned to courier documents back and forth between Sergio's cell in Papuda and his attorneys back in Rio had not only fallen in love with Sergio, but announced their engagement. After decades in the business, tough-talking, no-nonsense, chain-smoking Silvia Beeg had been jolted from her professional equilibrium for the first time in her career and found herself all giggles in the middle of a jailhouse romance.

"He's so incredibly *romantic*," Silvia gushes, and after spending her life working with oilmen, prisoners, and con men, she's not a woman who gushes lightly. We met one evening in her small, tidy bungalow in a suburb of Brasilia about an hour's drive from Papuda. She had just gotten back from her regular Wednesday visit with Sergio and was relaxing in jeans and a T-shirt, her legs folded up under her on the sofa and reading glasses folded onto her shirt collar. While talking, she stroked the back of her hand, unconsciously caressing the spot where he had last touched her.

"And he has such a sense of humor!" she suddenly continues, breaking out of her reverie. "Do you know what he wanted to call his book? Instead of *Revelaciones*, he wanted the title to be either *The Sultan of Copacabana* or *How to Make Women Your Slaves, From an Expert*. See, he really has a Brazilian sense of humor—and a great head for marketing!" She erupts into laughter, then slowly quiets. "But I don't think that plays very well in Mexico. That has always been Sergio's problem—he's too brilliant for many people to understand." Not that she's a genius, Silvia hastens to add; it's just that she recognizes his boyishness, and everything flows from there. She knows when he's joking even if she doesn't get the joke.

Sergio himself called their relationship "clean and pure," which Brazilian journalists were quick to agree was very believable: Since Sergio's sexual tastes ran exclusively to skinny thirteen-year-olds, they joked, it was hard to imagine he was suddenly enjoying a healthy romance with a chain-smoking, bespectacled, raspy-voiced grandmother with a mannish bob and body. Nevertheless, Sergio held up his engagement to Silvia as proof that any reckless dalliances he might have indulged in with girls of a questionable age had come to an end; as Sergio told a Brazilian journalist soon after Silvia announced their engagement, "This woman appeared in the most difficult time of my life, and I have the right, even though everyone may attack me and the world may oppose us, to re-make my life, even behind bars."

But what about Gloria? Hadn't she and Sergio just had a child together before their capture—the infant Ana Dalay, who somehow vanished? Wasn't Gloria just then reversing years of public denials to call Sergio the "love of her life"? Wouldn't this be a crushing blow for her, to discover that at the most needy time in her life, her man was abandoning her for a prison romance with their errand woman? Curiously, though, even Gloria took pains to publicly bless Sergio's new relationship, saying, "Sergio needs someone tender and loyal right now," which only made people more suspicious: It smelled like some kind of scam was afoot to win Sergio Brazilian citizenship and help him dodge extradition. Once again, perhaps, Gloria was following Sergio's lead to help him out of a jam.

Silvia, however, would have none of it. "He has the most sensual, magical hands," Silvia says with a smile." And when he speaks about love, he knows what he's talking about." Silvia had originally worked as a petroleum company wrangler, helping foreign oil workers who'd been hired by Brazil's offshore rigs get their work visas. Thanks to her experience with foreign clients and her mastery of Brazil's bureaucracy, she eventually branched out and found plenty of business working with prisoners facing extradition. Because the phrase "running away to Rio" had become embedded in the world lexicon, criminals kept falling for the fantasy that they could escape the law by slipping into Brazil (even the most sophisticated fugitives have been known to fall for that myth; one of Sergio's neighbors in Papuda was the wealthy American Peter Paul Franklin, who had slept in the Lincoln bedroom and donated more than

$2 million to Hillary Clinton's Senate campaign before fleeing charges that he'd manipulated stock prices).

When the law firm she works with in Rio asked her to take on Sergio, Gloria, and Mary, she showed up to see them with a supply of food and clothes and was surprised by what she found. "Really, I was shocked," Silvia says. "I'd been hearing so much about what horrible villains they are, but here are three people with nothing of the bandit about them. They appeared totally normal and intelligent. I thought, Something is really wrong here. Why are these people in prison? So I decided to investigate on my own."

Even though she's not a lawyer, her friends in the Brazilian Justice Ministry helped her get her hands on background documents on the extradition petition, and during her logistical support visits with Sergio, she began asking him specific questions about the accusations. At first, it was Gloria who impressed Silvia the most. "From the beginning, this woman who everyone says is such a monster, she struck me as very sincere and natural. She didn't come across as either a star or a criminal—just a polite, pleasant young woman," Silvia says. "As time went on—I'm talking months and years, now—I became convinced from seeing her nearly every week, under the most terribly stressful conditions, that here is a very humane, good-hearted lady who would give you the clothes off her back and make you feel proud while she did it."

Once word got around that Silvia was Sergio's go-to gal, something curious began to occur. "Every day in the newspaper I'm reading statements from these little girls back in Mexico accusing him of the most terrible things. They're saying he beat them, starved them, forced them to eat shit off the floor—well, not *shit*, just his scraps and garbage. And then these same girls are calling me on the phone, *crying*, saying they can't live without him. I saw Liliana crying for Sergio, Karina crying for Sergio, Karla de la Cuesta crying for Sergio . . .

"Well," Silvia continues, a small smile curling her lips, "that naturally excited my woman's curiosity. I had to ask myself, 'What kind of man is this?'" What she discovered, however, was not what she expected. "All my girlfriends were joking about his sexual prowess," Silvia says. "But as I got to know Sergio, I learned what *really* makes a man sexy." It was about that time that a cancerous polyp was discovered in Silvia's breast. Whenever she went to visit Sergio in prison, that was the first thing he'd want to hear about: Was she getting good care, shouldn't she be taking care of herself instead of bothering with him, was there anything he could do—sing her a song, tell her a story—to make her feel better?

"He was very caring, very tender and sensitive," Silvia says. More so, in fact, than any man she had ever known. If her ex-husband had been remotely as compassionate as Sergio, she says, she'd still be married. If her ex-boss had shared Sergio's kindness, she'd still be working for him. In fact, Sergio was partially her inspiration to quit: When she asked the attorney she worked for to help her out with an advance so she could pay for chemotherapy in a private hospital, he turned her down. "You know how it works, dear," she says he told her. "You get paid when the job is done. Tell that to the hospital—they'll understand." Instead, she told him what he could do with his "dears" and his job: She quit. "All these macho men I've been surrounded by my entire life," she says in disgust. "And then I meet Sergio, and I finally see it doesn't have to be that way."

Though she was no longer being paid for it, Silvia continued to visit "her famous new family." It was a "point of honor," she says. "They had no one else they could trust, and it was frightening—here they were, locked up in a strange country, while on the outside these hysterical little girls were spreading stories that could get them killed. I'm not exaggerating—many prisoners have children of their own, and they can be brutal to sex offenders." Silvia has no children; though she was married for eleven years, she found she couldn't conceive and instead became something of a serial adopter. Her little bungalow is abuzz with life from the family she has created by proxy: She took in her single-mom sister and her three children, and after the eldest had her baby, Silvia was an honorary grandmother and the matriarch she'd always dreamed of becoming.

Silvia decided she wasn't going to make Gloria, Sergio, and Mary pay for what her boss had done—she would keep visiting and supplying them for free. Silvia isn't a whiner, but she's a hardworking woman who puts in long hours each day battling infuriating Brazilian bureaucrats and

Brasilia's maddening traffic to support her sister and their four live-in kids, and volunteering pro bono prison visits is an added strain. Her life exhausts her, and worries her . . . and Sergio can tell. "He'll always notice and do something to pick me up," Silvia says. Like the time she was so sick from medication that her sister needed to drive her to the prison: "Sergio said, 'Have your sister take you to a really nice restaurant, someplace pretty and quiet, and order a really good meal. Order a little more than you think you can eat, and imagine I'm with you, telling you stories and picking at your plate.' " It was extremely clever, Silvia says; Sergio could tell she wasn't eating well, so he was trying to create a little fantasy that would lull her into putting away a full belly buster.

She returned Sergio's concern, she says, when he was taken hostage during a prison riot. According to Silvia, a notorious Brazilian gangster named Marcelo Borelli overpowered a guard and took his gun, keys, and cell phone. Borelli began opening cells, freeing prisoners and touching off a violent, prisonwide riot. Sergio remained in his cell, but according to Silvia, Borelli hauled him out and put a gun to his head, figuring that threatening to kill one of the country's most famous prisoners was his best, desperate hope for release. The problem was, Borelli didn't know how to make public his demands, so Sergio suggested he call Silvia. When Silvia answered the phone, she said, she could hear Gloria screaming in the background from her cell in the same wing, "It's true! It's true! Silvia, save Sergio—they're going to kill him!" Silvia ran to her car and sped to the prison.

By the time she got there, the prisoners were in full revolt. "There was nothing I could do then but pray," she says. When riot police finally got the prison back under control, she said, she marched up to the warden and demanded that Borelli be transferred at once. "If you leave that killer in the same building as Sergio and Gloria, you'll be guilty of murder," she claims to have demanded. "They moved Borelli so, yes, you can say I helped save Sergio's life. Borelli would have killed him eventually, just to show people how cruel he is." (While Silvia may have had some influence, Brazilian authorities say Borelli's hostage wasn't Sergio, but the head guard, Marcos Edison do Rego Bandeira. Also, they say, they would have transferred Borelli whether Sergio was at risk or not; it's standard policy in the Brazilian penal system to remove the instigator from the scene of a riot.)

Still, regardless of what actually happened during the Papuda Prison revolt, Silvia certainly wanted Sergio to know how much she cared for him. By then, she says, her feelings for Sergio had speed-shifted from cautious to curious, and then from maternal to full-blown passion. "I really didn't expect it, but after a while, I found myself constantly looking at his hands and I realized what I was thinking—'I want him to touch me,' " she says, flushing a bit beneath her reddish bob. "When you see his hands"—she stops and puts her hand to her mouth to cover a schoolgirl's titter—"you just want him to touch you."

I'd soon find out for myself. Although her relations with Sergio's attorneys are tense at best, Silvia had agreed to help with the plan I had concocted with them: It was still impossible for Sergio to break through the media ban and get his story out to the world . . . but breaking *in* to Papuda, on the other hand, just might be worth a try.

Journalists couldn't get in, but a select few of Sergio's personal friends still could. First, though, they had to be registered with the prison and checked out, a process that could take anywhere from weeks to months. Sergio's attorneys had put me on the list, and Silvia briefed me on how to proceed. Forget subtlety, she said. I should try using ignorance and brashness to my advantage. She didn't need to add that since I was an American, it would play very authentically. So instead of waiting my turn among the mothers and girlfriends waiting at Papuda's gates for their turn to be shown into the visiting room, Silvia said, I should just march to the front of the line and ask to speak with the warden. And request the lawyer-client conference room, Silvia added; if I had to go to the main visiting room, I'd likely be strip-searched and have my notebook confiscated.

From that point on, Silvia warned, I would be on my own. She was eager to do anything that might help turn popular opinion in Sergio's favor and win his freedom, but in the meantime, she was afraid to do anything that might jeopardize her chances of seeing him while he was still behind bars. If she was discovered colluding with me on a lie, she said, she could be banned from the prison herself. At this point, all she had done was tell me how to get an audience with the warden. Whatever story I decided to tell him was my business.

So early the next morning, I made the long drive out to Papuda. I'd decided I'd present myself as an American record producer, an old friend of Sergio's from better days who happened to be in Brazil on business and wanted to see how he was doing. I even had an explanation for the notebook and two pens in my shirt pocket: I wanted to update all Sergio's friends around the world on his condition, I'd tell the warden, so I wanted to take a few notes and jot down a personal message from him. It could work or it could be a disaster—not even Sergio's lawyers were quite sure what the penalty would be if I were caught lying to federal officers. "You might be spending more time with Sergio than you bargained for," Geraldo Magela, one of Sergio's lawyers, said in jest—or so I was hoping.

Papuda is a heart-sinking place. Even at first glance, it's so desolate and bristlingly guarded that escape seems a hopeless idea at best, and a fatal one at worst. You'd have to somehow steal out of a cell and across the floodlit courtyards, then find a way to either scale, cut, or tunnel past one, two, *three* concentric rings of thirty-foot razor wire while avoiding the attack dogs that prowl between them and the constantly scanning tower guards armed with both wide-spraying shotguns and long-range sniper rifles. Once free, you'd have to run—but where? Between you and the nearest place to hide, it's all desolation: Papuda rises from a lunar landscape specially chosen for its single, rarely traveled access road and its surrounding miles of scrub-grassed, empty valley.

I decided to go ahead with the plan. As I'd been coached, I walked past the long line of visitors and headed directly to the entry gate. I speak Portuguese, but this time I dumbed it down to sound as novice as possible while still being intelligible. Luckily, the warden was out; so was his deputy. The third in command, apparently afraid of violating some promise his boss had made, had me buzzed through the steel doors and sent directly to his office. Once there, I explained that I had arranged to see Sergio Andrade in a private room. The officer looked doubtful, but then made an offer: I could meet with Sergio right here, in his office, but he would have to stay and monitor our conversation.

Agreed. And then, minutes later, in walked . . . Sergio?

It couldn't be. Even the photos I'd seen of Sergio couldn't prepare me for the reality. This man was short and shockingly fat; he wasn't prison-pallor puffy, with a few extra pounds from limited yard time, or even self-indulgently overweight from his years of living rich on the outside. The man who was coming through the door, sandwiched by two tall, lean prison guards, couldn't have been much more than five feet tall and looked as overinflated and squishy as a water balloon. He could have been played by Danny DeVito, except with a salt-and-pepper pompadour and an even softer body stuffed into ancient jeans, rotting sneakers, and a lavender sweatshirt. His teeth, bared in flashes as he spoke to the guards, looked jagged and dirty; his jaw was lupine long and stubbly. This couldn't be . . .

"*Eh, Chris!*" the man exclaimed, a look of pleasure flashing to his face as he pretended to be overjoyed at the arrival of a dear friend.

"Sergio!" I responded, breaking out of my stunned reverie and re-membering to play my part. "Good to see you." I opened my arms to hug him, but he raised his hands to show he couldn't: handcuffs. I suddenly re-called what Silvia had said and took a long look at his "magical" hands. They were thin and disproportionately small, shaggy on the backs and knuckles, looking less like the capable hands of a knowing seducer and more like the slender paws of a clever chimp.

We sat knee-to-knee on a pair of straight-backed chairs in the war-den's office. "I still have not figured out exactly what, why, and how all this has happened to me," Sergio began.

x   x   x

In 1962, when he was seven years old, it was obvious that pudgy little Sergio Andrade would never hold his own at sports with other boys in Coatzacoalcas, Mexico. But he didn't care: Sergio had his books and music. Although his tiny hands could barely manage the keys, he had al-ready begun piano lessons, and after school he liked to hole up in his room and scratch out his first attempts at poetry. He was a good student, and so proud of it that decades later he would still boast of winning childhood declamation prizes.

The real star of the Andrades, however, was the first son, Sergio's big brother, Eduardo, whom the family called "Lalo." The two boys were much alike—they were both bookish and intelligent, witty and stubborn—but it seemed that in Lalo all Sergio's qualities were magnified. Sergio was good with words, but Lalo was dramatic and booming; Sergio liked to debate a point, but Lalo would win it. And while Sergio gradually directed his talents inward, devoting more and more of his time to solitary work with his notebooks and sheet music, by the time Lalo was in high school, he was thinking of politics. When he was accepted at the Universidad Nacional Autónoma de México (UNAM), their father decided to uproot the entire family and move them all to Mexico City so he could continue stewarding Lalo's education and career.

Their father, Eduardo Andrade Ahedo, was a short-tempered man whose approach to discipline included humiliation and a touch of the perverse, and Sergio's mother, Doña Justina, was no softer. "His father would whip him, and then his mother would make him get down on his knees, kiss his father's hand, and say, 'I love you, Papa,' " recalls Judith Enriqueta "Ga-Bí" Chávez-Parks, who was one of Sergio's singers and also his girlfriend in the mid-eighties. "Those were the rules of the house. Sergio's mother doted on her boys, but she was completely subservient to her husband."

According to Ga-Bí, Doña Justina used to discipline Sergio as a boy by tying him to a table leg. More serious transgressions brought out the weapons; Ga-Bí says Sergio often complained that his mother would beat him with a stick, her hairbrush, or when she was especially angry, an electric cord. "The blows to the face hurt the most," Ga-Bí recalls him saying.

In later years, Sergio would rarely mention his parents. But while they might have loathed it, both the Andrade boys showed signs at an early age that they'd internalized their father's discipline, and while it was cruel, it was also paying off. Eduardo was excelling at the UNAM law school, while Sergio was gaining the confidence to take his love of books outside of his house and become a top student in secondary school. In 1967, Sergio graduated at the top of his elementary school class, winning several writing and public-speaking awards, and became one of the few students who are accepted each year to begin classical training at Mexico's National Conservatory of Music.

"My dream was to become a concert pianist," Sergio says. At the same time, he was reading voraciously and deciding to pursue a degree in philosophy at UNAM. As if trying to master two of modern culture's most difficult disciplines wasn't challenge enough, Sergio also needed money, and he didn't kid himself about how long it would take to ever earn a living as either an academic or a symphonic musician. So whenever he could find some spare time, he began trying to meld the poetry he'd always written with the music he was learning to master and come up with a few marketable pop tunes.

Much the way Gloria would later, Sergio soon found that one of the most hectic times of his life was also one of the most creative; Sergio was becoming more and more adept at playing with the fresh ideas and turns of phrase he was picking up in his college classes and adapting them to the new rhythms and harmonies he was learning on the piano. If he could use one for the other—either support himself with pop songs while studying the classics or use his reputation as a serious musician to market his lighter tunes—all the better.

He pushed ahead with his two-pronged career plan and soon began succeeding on both fronts. By 1978, Sergio was both the third-place medalist in the Yamaha National Competition for pianists and a new pop music composer and arranger for RCA-Victor records. He tried singing a bit himself, but he really didn't have the voice or stage presence to knock audiences back in their seats. Put him in charge of a raw singer, however, and for such a young manager he was masterful.

It didn't take long for rival labels to notice. When he was twenty-six, CBS Records poached Sergio away from RCA and made him its youngest artistic director ever in Mexico. It was there, in the studios at CBS, that Sergio first ran into the young singer Ga-Bí. "One day I came in wearing a miniskirt, and I noticed it 'disturbed' him a bit," Ga-Bí says. "He couldn't take his eyes off my legs, and made it clear that he liked what he saw." From that opening ogle, their flirting quickly evolved into friendship. "He wasn't considered an attractive man by other people in the studio, but I liked the way he looked," says Ga-Bí, who was much more slender than Sergio and taller than him by a head. She looked, in fact, much like a taller, slightly plainer version of Gloria.

"He seemed extremely pleased when I told him I liked his smile," Ga-Bí recalls in her memoir, *Como Carne de Cañón (Like Cannon Fodder)*. She immediately keyed in on the fact that he was unusually susceptible to attention. "He liked it when I told him to wear such-and-such a shirt and necktie. And back then he used rather common colognes, like Old Spice or Brut, so I gave him a bottle of Aramis." Sergio received the gift with a typical gesture of self-pity: he thanked Ga-Bí with a big hug and told her he rarely received gifts from anyone.

Not long after, Sergio took Ga-Bí home to meet his mother. They dropped in on her one afternoon for lunch, and Sergio was surprised and tickled to see that Doña Justina was honoring Ga-Bí by having not only an elaborate meal already prepared, but a special dessert waiting. But he soon discovered the real reason for his mother's fussing: It wasn't because of Sergio or Ga-Bí, but because Lalo had mentioned he might stop by. Ga-Bí says that when Lalo came through the door with a loud shout—"The heart of the house is home"—Sergio's mother leaped from the table. "From that moment on, Sergio and I ceased to exist for her," Ga-Bí recalls.

Lalo was still in law school back then, but working nights as a sports commentator for Televisa and becoming something of a low-grade national celebrity for his charm and quick-witted between-play banter. "His mother fussed around him so much," Ga-Bí says, "that he had to tell her, 'Mother, stop. Any more, and I'm leaving.'" Even though Ga-Bí knew very well who Lalo was—in fact, her father had often commented that Lalo Andrade was the best damn soccer analyst in the business—Doña Justina began to relate his achievements excitedly to Ga-Bí. "He's so smart, I knew from the time he was six years old that he was going to be something very, very special," Ga-Bí recalls her saying. "This soccer is just the beginning." Meanwhile, Sergio sat there silently while his girlfriend heard what a great man his brother was.

Sergio's diffidence and lack of self-confidence was something he was going to have to conquer. Being mildly pathetic might win him aftershave from women like Ga-Bí who were both tenderhearted and desperate to please, but it wasn't going to get him far in professional entertainment. His job wasn't to coach or advise his singers: it was to command them. If he couldn't radiate an air of authority, he wouldn't last. Luckily, he came up with a solution—he'd work with people he felt comfortable bossing around. He started working almost exclusively with young women.

"In Mexico, your musical director tells you how you have to sing, even to a big star like Luis Miguel," explains Crystal, who was just seventeen when she was sent to Sergio. "I can't say Sergio taught me, in the sense that he gave me lessons. Instead, he directed me in the studio—he told me exactly how I should sing his songs, and they turned out beautifully." At first, however, Crystal's reaction to Sergio was disappointment.

"I *really* wanted Chucho Guerrero as my musical director," she recalls. "Chucho had *the* name at that time and Sergio wasn't well known. Before 1982, he was nobody, and you can ask anyone in the music business." Crystal was only a teenager herself, but she was already being personally groomed for stardom by Televisa's Raúl Velasco. Even though she's been blind from birth, Crystal had started early in show business: at age five she was sent to a school for the blind in Mexico City, and almost immediately she began performing with adults as the group's sole child's voice. In school she was playing the piano before she turned seven, and the guitar and mandolin by nine.

As an eight-year-old, Crystal was cast to co-star in *¿De Que Color Es el Viento? (What Color Is the Wind?)*, a movie about two blind children from different social classes who bond through their disability. The pretty blond blind girl was a big hit, but when the producers began making arrangements for a sequel, Crystal's father forbade her to do any more movies. "He was afraid the movie industry would lead me down the wrong path, and he insisted I go back to my studies." She did, grudgingly, but continued to sing wherever she had a chance. When she turned sixteen, her parents relented and allowed her to enter *Valores Juveniles*, Mexico's national TV youth talent search. There she caught the eye of Raúl Velasco.

Crystal needed professional polish, Velasco realized, but most of all she needed a song. He decided to put her into Sergio Andrade's hands;

Sergio, he knew, could coach Crystal on stage presence and write her some heartbreaking tunes. "When he sang 'Suavemente' to me, I liked it a lot," Crystal says, "It's such a beautiful song, and Sergio had written it so it ended with my name, 'Crystal.' " Sung according to Sergio's explicit instructions, Crystal's version made her an overnight sensation. Sergio, meanwhile, was on a roll: He was named "Best Arranger" at that year's OTI Festival, then returned home to release Lucerito's million-selling album *Juguemos a Cantar* and see Crystal's "Suavemente" hit No. 1 on the charts. By the end of that year, the twenty-seven-year-old savant had won the nickname "Mr. Midas."

"He was extremely demanding," says Crystal. "He would always be in the studio, working long hours with much older musicians. He would really yell at them, but they listened and respected him because he knew what he was doing." Even though she was blind and very young, Crystal wasn't exempt from Sergio's tirades. "When he yelled at me, I thought it was normal, I thought that was his way of working, even if we were just talking about Sinatra." Curiously, she liked the fact that when he screamed at her, he usually did it in front of others. Most people are humiliated to be dressed down in public, but with Sergio, Crystal actually seemed to enjoy the attention. "I tolerated all that because he yelled at me in front of everyone, even my mom," Crystal says. "He did the same to Lucero—he yelled at her very loud."

And the Lucero standard, of course, was the ultimate test: If Sergio treated you the same way he treated Lucero, the gorgeous young TV and singing sensation, that was a sign you had arrived. That was another reason Crystal endured the screaming without complaint: For reasons more personal than professional, she felt herself yearning for Sergio's attention. Even though she had just escaped the overbearing presence of a father who had nearly nipped her performing career in the bud, there was something about the commanding presence of this short, angry, ugly man that attracted her.

"I admired him so much, I fell in love," Crystal says. She felt herself growing increasingly envious, and began wondering just what was going on between Sergio and Lucero. "He would lock himself with her in the studio and stay there for hours rehearsing. Nobody said anything," Crystal recalls, still doubtful years later that those closed-door sessions were as innocent as both Sergio and Lucerito would profess. "I never talked to anyone about what happened inside that recording studio," she adds. Building a wall of secrecy, Crystal would soon discover, was one of Sergio's special talents. Perhaps it was because he never, *ever*, allowed an indiscreet remark to pass his lips, or because he was sharp enough to choose confederates he could trust, but no rumor ever attached itself to Sergio for long.

Crystal would find out firsthand. Shortly after she and Sergio traveled to the OTI Festival together in 1982, they began dating and then sleeping together. But for the first year of their relationship, Sergio insisted that Crystal deny they were involved. "He told me to be discreet because it wasn't good for our careers to let anybody know," she says. "He said we would sell more records if people thought we were single." Crystal had her doubts—and besides, she was in love and proud of her fabulously successful boyfriend. But she obeyed. "Like the old saying goes," she says with a shrug, " 'Trust in God, but adore your lover.' "

They became virtually inseparable. Although she was still a teenager, Crystal was maturing rapidly as a singer and was grateful to Sergio for it. "What I owe him is his talent, his beautiful songs and many things he taught me, that I'll never deny," says Crystal. But at the same time, she was increasingly disturbed by the strange schism in his personality. At first, it was just his severe personal restraint: At the piano Sergio would be sensitive and heartbreakingly passionate; but in private he was guarded and mysterious.

"In three years that we spent together, he never said 'I love you,' although I asked him many times," Crystal notes. "When you love someone you want him to tell you, but he was very rigid."

One day, Crystal finally asked him directly, "Sergio, do you love anyone?"

"How dare you ask me that?" Sergio responded, gravely offended. "You know I do.' "

"But who?" Crystal insisted. "I've never met your father and you've never spoken about him. You don't have anything to do with your mother." In fact, the only person for whom he showed even the slightest fondness was his grandmother, and that was only because he referred to her by the common pet name *Abuelita*. He was proud of Eduardo, but seemed boastful of him as a lawyer rather than affectionate of him as a brother. Otherwise, there seemed to be no one else in his life.

His emotional aloofness really shocked her, however, when she discovered he had a son. "One day, he told me he had an eight-year-old boy that he didn't love," Crystal says. "His name is Sergio Gustavo, and the mother was 'Nora,' Sergio's old teenage sweetheart." Sergio told Crystal that when he found out Nora was pregnant, he gave her permission to do as she pleased, but as for him, he never wanted to see the child. "Nora knew he didn't love her," Crystal says, "but she was very servile to him, and she tried to please him by naming the little boy after him. It didn't matter—Sergio never saw his son."

Crystal knows this story is true because she also heard it from her personal assistant—Nora. Crystal had hired her on Sergio's orders, not knowing that Nora had once been Sergio's wife. Crystal found out when she was performing in Tijuana and had to stop over for a night in Mexico City. "Nora came with me and stayed at our house," Crystal says. "While I was asleep, Nora warned my mother that Sergio wasn't good for me." Crystal's mother was confused—why would Nora think that Mr. Midas, the man who wrote her daughter's No. 1 hit, was a poor manager? At that point, she didn't know a thing about their romance. Sergio was still insisting that Crystal keep their affair secret.

"No, he's a wonderful manager," Nora told her. "But as a boyfriend, he's not right for Crystal. Sooner or later, he'll treat her the way he treated me." That's when Nora gave Crystal's mother her second surprise of the night, the news that her teenage daughter's personal assistant had been impregnated and abandoned by the manager who was now her daughter's secret boyfriend. The next morning this revelation sparked a huge fight between Crystal and her mother, but because she was now of legal age and earning her own money, Crystal decided to remain with Sergio. Her mother moved out and left Crystal on her own.

Years later, Crystal would still resent Nora for sparking that fight with her mother, but her hurt feelings didn't let her grasp what Nora had really done: Although Nora was so devoted to Sergio that she would work as a domestic for his new girlfriend and let him treat her (as Crystal put it) "like his dirty door rug," she still risked his wrath out of concern for Crystal. What's also remarkable about the story is Sergio's ability to control information; despite the hordes of gossip columnists and envious music industry rivals who would have *loved* to hear dirt about Mr. Midas's secret love child, Nora only spoke about it when she began to fear that Crystal was getting herself into serious trouble.

Nora was right.

Once the young blind woman had separated from her mother and became more dependent on Sergio—that's when the punishments began. "If I disagreed with him, if I dared to criticize him, he had different ways of punishing me," Crystal says. "It depended on his mood. When he wasn't that angry, he'd leave me at a park bench. Other times he'd lock me in the car for five hours and tell me not to move. It was a Mustang he had, with automatic windows, so I couldn't even open them to get more air. He was always locking me. I sometimes thought he was born in a dungeon or something, because he was always locking me up somewhere."

If she wasn't playing the piano the way he wanted during studio rehearsals, Crystal adds, Sergio would snap the keyboard cover down on her fingers. By that point—the mid-eighties—a lot of other strange things were going on around his studio. As each week passed, it seemed to Crystal, the studio became more and more chaotic, and the number of girlish voices she could detect chattering and giggling around her had increased since the last time she'd been there.

"Sergio and I weren't living together then, and he was using his house as his studio," she says. "Every day it seemed like there were more girls there. Sonia Ríos, Raquel Ochoa, Mary Boquitas [who back then was still the teenage María Raquenel Portillo] . . . everywhere you went in that house, more girls came out. I didn't want to ask, because he wouldn't like it and I might get punished, but I had to wonder—are all these girls really musicians?"

But finally Crystal had to find out what was going on.

"They come to learn from me," Sergio protested. "I don't ask them to come. They just show up, and if they really want to learn music, I put them to work." None of these young girls were Crystal's rivals, Sergio assured her—not in his heart, and certainly not in regard to her talent. None of them had any special ability, but they were so energetic, and so willing to work, that he was teaching a few of them some instruments and banding them together in a girl group.

Despite her misgivings, Crystal found herself bonding with one of the newest studio girls, a fifteen-year-old from Monterrey who had just been recruited as the youngest member of a girl group Sergio was creating called Boquitas Pintadas. "She was very quiet," Crystal recalls. "She was very tender, very introverted. Often she was depressed. She would cry, and when I asked why, she would say, 'It's nothing.' Sometimes she said it was a song that had made me cry. I didn't believe her but I had to respect her. I didn't suspect what she was living because I wasn't into her life. I always felt like protecting Gloria."

Crystal's brother, who was also blind, would often accompany her to the studio. Sergio was very fond of him, and the two would joke around together. "That's when you would really see Sergio's tender side," Crystal says. Sergio always called her brother "El Ciego" (the blind guy), and whenever Crystal arrived at the studio, Sergio would always call out affectionately, "*Aya*, where's the blind guy?"

But even El Ciego began to sense that something was definitely not right about all the teenybopper bustle he was hearing around Sergio's house.

"These girls smell like trouble," Crystal's brother told Sergio. "Something bad is going to happen if you have all these young girls running around."

"Indeed, they smell like trouble," Sergio replied. "But they also smell like strawberries."

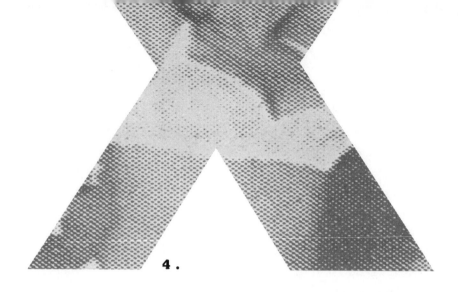

4 .

"Little Lipsticked Mouths"

Sergio drops his manacled hands into his lap and flops back against his hard steel chair. "Yes, I knew there would be trouble," he says. He drops his eyes to the floor and shakes his head. "But I never thought it would be anything like this." He goes silent, then raises his eyes and gazes out through the single small window of the warden's office. It's an iron gray day, and although all he can see is a concrete courtyard, a razor-wire fence, and the sky beyond, for a man who spends twenty-three hours a day in a cell smaller than his former walk-in closet, any view not a wall is a pleasure.

"No," he adds, in a voice so quiet I can barely hear it. "Not even the half of this."

But within a few moments, Sergio is again energized and eagerly hunched forward on the edge of his seat. Until that brief slump, he'd been speaking quickly and urgently, barely pausing for breath from the moment we'd sat down in the warden's office some twenty minutes earlier. He's acting as though our conversation is a matter of life and death—and for him, with extradition looming, it may well be: If convicted of rape, kidnapping, and corruption of a minor in a Mexican court, Sergio faces so many years in prison that he could very well die behind bars.

And that is only if he survives until the trial: Sergio is well aware that a more savage and immediate fate could await him in any Mexican penitentiary. He knows that even in prison, the Mexican code of *machismo* still rules, meaning that men charged with rape and child molestation are targeted for jailhouse justice by their fellow prisoners even before their guilt or innocence has been decided in court. For having dared lay a finger on another man's wife, sister, or daughter, accused sex offenders are often brutalized, sometimes raped, and occasionally beaten to death. Blending in and avoiding attention would be impossible for Sergio; every prisoner will know exactly who he is, as well as be aware of the fame and underworld acclaim that will attach to the convict who takes out one of Mexico's most famous villains.

The irony is, Sergio actually does have some surprising evidence to back up his claim of a conspiracy to destroy him. His challenge will be to survive long enough to present it in court, and that is one reason he is battling extradition, even though he knows his forced departure from Brazil is inevitable, and the delay only means he is serving hard time in a dangerous prison in addition to any future sentence. "I have to stay here as long as I can," he says. "I have to wait until passions cool down and people can listen to me with calm hearts and open minds." He's also desperate to use these final months to win a shade of sympathy to his side: He wants to transform the public image of Sergio Andrade as an evil, lecherous ogre and remind people how many young artists he's helped, how much he's contributed to music and Mexican pop culture, and how much joy his music has brought to so many lives.

So soon he's riding the edge of his hard chair again, shaping the air with his cuffed hands to sculpt his points, rolling and widening his dark eyes as he speaks, pursing his lips and grimacing. Sergio is a wonderfully expressive speaker, with an astonishing memory for detail and a very emotional face, and what has him excited now is the memory of 1983.

"That's the year I became the most successful musical producer, arranger, and conductor in Mexico," Sergio begins. "I was, frankly, dominating the charts. I sometimes had *three* songs in the Top 10 at one time."

That summer Sergio was named "Best Arranger" at the OTI Festival for the second year in a row, and one of his singers, César Costa, won second place with Sergio's latest tune, "Tierno." Herb Alpert and the Tijuana Brass heard Crystal's recording of "Suavemente" and decided to record their own version, bringing Sergio's name to the United States. The song was then picked up by Frank Pourcel, the famed French violinist and movie composer, who released his own take in Europe. Mr. Midas was going international.

Back home in Mexico, Sergio was riding the crest of Crystal's and Lucerito's success. Thanks in part to the popularity of Lucerito's album, Sergio's premier singer had gone from soap opera sweetheart to national idol; when Televisa announced the contest to name a Lucerito look-alike, it touched off a nationwide craze, with tens of thousands of girls clamoring to audition. (It's another bizarre twist in the Trevi saga that the winner, young Gloria de los Ángeles Treviño Ruiz, would grow up to become the ultimate stage antithesis of the always immaculate and professionally virginal Lucerito.)

Besides his knack for training female balladeers, Sergio was also experimenting with rock guitarists like Ricky Luis and more progressive artists like Hernán Visetti, Ciclón, and Grupo Okidoki. They weren't smash performers, and Sergio never expected them to be; he was more interested in adding an art house credibility to his mass-appeal résumé. Sergio had never given up his own dreams of being a star, and he knew the only way for a manager to rise to the level of his singers was through diversity: He had to pop up so often, behind so many different types of performers, that the message would get around that it was Sergio making the stars, not the stars making Sergio. Sergio wanted to be the next Phil Spector, so he had to show that his touch was just as effective as Spector's had been with George Harrison or the Ramones, with the Rolling Stones, Ronettes, or Righteous Brothers.

It certainly seemed he was on his way. Sergio's hits kept coming: the following year, 1984, Crystal popped back into the Top 10 with two new Sergio creations, "Parece" ("It Seems") and "Eso no se hace" ("That Just Isn't Done"), and nearly won the Yamaha International Song Contest in Tokyo. Sergio continued his domination at OTI—the icy blond singer

Yuri won first prize with the Sergio tune, "Tiempos mejores" ("Better Times"), while Sergio notched his third consecutive "Best Arranger" title. Sergio was such a commanding force, he decided to return to singing and release his *own* album. It was nicely received by the critics, but it was more a show of virtuosity than an attempt to crack the charts, because Sergio—as insistent on control as ever—performed every single role, from writing the songs to final remastering of the tapes.

Yet . . . how could he be so lifeless? That's what rock journalist Rubén Aviña wondered when he met Sergio that year. As Aviña would later recall in the as-told-to memoir of Sergio's ex-wife that ignited the Trevi scandal, *Aline: La Gloria por el Infierno,* Sergio was perplexingly cold for such a master of passionate love songs. Rubén got his first glimpse of the boy genius that year at an orphanage, where Sergio had gone to pass out toys. It was already a testament to Sergio's fame that when he turned up with his bags of gifts, so did a crowd of reporters and news photographers. Sergio was certainly kind enough—he came across as "paternal, altruistic and humane," Rubén says—but where was the tenderness you'd expect from a young man playing with a passel of parentless kids?

A few months later, Rubén would get the same impression when he had a chance to interview Sergio in depth. "He talked and talked, but never smiled or looked me in the eyes," Rubén writes. "I sensed there was some sort of invisible, unbreakable barrier he'd erected, as if he wanted to protect himself." Curiously, that didn't put Rubén off—in fact, he found himself drawn to Sergio. "Apart from that, I admired him, and I also began to respect him." That's because he felt he wasn't seeing or suffering any disrespect; he was observing a man completely engrossed in his craft. Sergio was "a little solemn, brilliant, obviously intelligent, speaking with complete mastery of his successes, his achievements and his projects."

The admiration must have been mutual, because a few months after that interview Rubén got a call from Sergio. He needed someone to help out with publicity—would Rubén be interested? There was a crushing amount he wanted to publicize over the next few months, Sergio said: Besides his own album and a new one by Crystal, he was about to launch a special new project that would demand a lot of his time. He had just selected five young girls, and he wanted to spend the next year turning them from cute teens into polished musicians. He'd already picked out their name: They'd be the very image of Lolita-like, kissable lips, so he'd call them Boquitas Pintadas.

Rubén leapt at the chance. "I was very attracted by the idea of working by the side of such a creative genius—'maestro Andrade,' as many called him," Rubén would later write. He took the job and was soon installed in a small office in Sergio's inner sanctum, his rehearsal studio in Mexico City. Right away, things seemed a little strange. For starters, Sergio was either incredibly tightfisted, Rubén soon discovered, or he had a monastically austere approach to work, because his studio had almost no furniture. Rubén, for instance, was given an office that had a sofa, but no table, chair, or desk; he ended up sitting on the floor to type.

Then there were the tantrums. Rubén was fortunate—he somehow avoided being on the receiving end of Sergio's tirades—but he was no stranger to the sight of the short, fat, furious producer screaming scorn and frustration at one of his protégés. "He never shouted at me the way he shouted at everyone else," Rubén notes. "I wasn't afraid of him, and never was," Rubén says—leaving the unstated conclusion that many other people were.

But stranger than either the furies or the furniture-free studio was the mystery of the vanishing girls. It was weird—every day Rubén would show up at Sergio's studio at nine in the morning and work until five or six o'clock, but . . . *where was everybody else?* He knew the Boquitas were somewhere on the premises, but they never seemed to leave whatever room they were in—*ever*. "They were like ghosts in that unfurnished studio," Aviña would say. "I knew the Boquitas Pintadas were around there somewhere, taking music lessons and learning their instruments. But I never saw them. I could sense their presence, because every once in a while I could make out their murmuring voices from a distance, and some snatches of singing."

Even though he'd never managed to actually lay eyes on the Boquitas, Rubén knew who they were. Two were already semiseasoned pros: Pilar Ramírez, the rather dour lead singer and guitarist, was a veteran of

Chiquilladas, the Mexican TV version of *Little Orphan Annie,* while chunky, bubbly Claudia Rosas had been the drummer for Las Vicuñitas, another group Sergio had worked with. The remaining three Boquitas were Sergio discoveries: He'd selected Mónica Rodríguez, a cute blond teenager from his hometown of Coatzacoalcos, to hammer the piano, and María Raquenel Portillo, a tall, fiery-eyed fifteen-year-old, to play bass and add backup vocals. For his final choice, Sergio had found a beautiful, hyperactive young girl from Monterrey to play a neck-slung synthesizer: Gloria de los Ángeles Treviño Ruiz.

Rubén was curious about this last Boquita, because he'd heard she was a real firecracker and a dead ringer for Lucerito. As he set about his job of promoting Sergio's other singers, like Crystal, Rubén would occasionally hear footsteps in the hall and pop out of his office, hoping to run into one of the passing girls. But by the time he got his head out the door, whoever was passing had vanished. "They were closed off in a studio where they had a piano, and there they would spend the entire day, never even leaving—as far as I could tell—to have lunch. I had to assume they were getting there very early in the morning and leaving late at night, after midnight sometimes. They were five little ghosts, those five Boquitas Pintadas."

One afternoon, after Rubén had been working there several weeks, there came a knock at his door. He got up to open it and found a pretty, wild-haired young woman with a spray of freckles across her nose and a portable electronic organ hanging around her neck. "Do you mind if I practice my lessons here?" she asked Rubén. "There's no place else for me to go." Sure, Rubén agreed, and let her in. He took his seat back on the floor and continued tapping out his press releases while Gloria de los Ángeles Treviño Ruiz took a seat on the sofa and began searching out chords on her keyboard.

After a while, she got bored, flopped back on the sofa, and began leafing through a magazine. "Better watch out I don't tell Sergio how you rehearse," Rubén chided her. The teenager laughed, and the two began talking. From that afternoon on, Gloria would use Rubén's office as her regular study nook, dropping by often. Rubén got the feeling Gloria was more interested in talk than privacy for rehearsal; within moments of arriving, she would always launch into some story of her childhood. All Gloria's reminiscences were bittersweet, as Rubén recalls them—each was equal parts pain and joy, always about tragic swings of love and loss. Gloria lit up as she talked about a treasured little dog she'd named Reina (Queen) . . . but then told how Reina was killed by a car. She adored living with her great-grandparents! . . . but she was shifted to the home of a despised aunt . . . then reunited with her parents! . . . who later divorced.

As pinching as those memories may have been, dwelling on them was still Gloria's one sweet escape of the day. Down the hall in the Boquitas rehearsal room, tensions were running high. "It's really tough," Gloria would confide to Rubén. That's when he discovered why, until Gloria appeared at his door, he'd never seen any of the girls during his nine-to-five workday. "We get here at seven in the morning, and don't take a break until four in the afternoon," she said. They'd be back in the room for the second session at seven at night, and from there they'd stay "until death," as she put it. "Sometimes we don't get out of here till four in the morning," she told Rubén. "Then I'll get two hours of sleep, and be dreaming of piano keys the whole time! Usually I don't even have time to eat—I'm always going around starving."

Rubén was astonished by their workload; for a producer who was basically assembling little more than a younger and more musically adept precursor to the Spice Girls, Sergio was extraordinarily demanding. "We had to not only learn how to play, but dominate our instruments," Gloria would later recall in her own book *Gloria, por Gloria Trevi*. "Our music instruction was very thorough—we learned musical theory, notation, harmony, musical history and composition. Sergio gave out the lessons and demanded nothing less than perfection. But we were always learning and learning."

Sergio's relentless tutoring was perplexing, if not a shade cruel: If he'd wanted real musicians, why didn't he hire them in the first place? Instead, he chose his five girls for their teenybop beauty, figuring that's what the public wanted. But then why try to drill-sergeant them into becoming musicians? Why not just back them up with an experienced band and let them hop around, Menudo style, instead of force-feeding them on a decade's worth of technical training in only twelve months? If beauty would be the key to their success (as he'd demonstrated by picking three girls who'd never touched an instrument), who cared whether they were actually strumming their own guitars? No one ever expected a Go-Go to let rip with a guitar solo, yet they sold millions of records.

But the Boquitas' ineptness was exactly the *point*. It was so obvious, from Sergio's viewpoint. *Any* manager could just sit around and hold the coats while his experienced performers were doing their thing, but it would take a Rumpelstiltskin—a true Maestro Andrade—to spin straw into gold. The Boquitas were Sergio's Pygmalion project, his way of creating stars from nothing. There would never be any question about whether these singers could have done just as well without him, *because they weren't even singers!* The Boquitas would be the surest sign to date of his brilliance: he'd pluck five girls off the street and turn them into superstars. Who then could doubt Sergio's brilliance?

The strain, though, was taking its toll. By the time the Boquitas were ready to perform in public, intrigues, resentment, and illicit romance were already invisibly splitting the group. Years later, Gloria would still be mocking her bandmates. Pilar was a closet lesbian, she claims, while Mónica was a face-stuffing convert to some odd cult; Gloria would delight in describing how Mónica would devour creamy pastries, then begin yammering about "some kind of religion or other." It wasn't long, Gloria writes, before the pianist and the lead had clandestinely converted each other. "Mónica made Pilar renounce the Virgin Mary," Gloria says saucily, "and in return Mónica gave herself over to Pilar's 'preferences.' "

An even greater intrigue, meanwhile, was brewing in the guitar section: Sergio had secretly married his fifteen-year-old bass player. No one knew about the marriage—not Gloria and certainly not Crystal, who still thought Sergio was her boyfriend. Sergio had gotten the "blessing and best wishes" of María Raquenel Portillo's parents, as Gloria would later hasten to add in Sergio's defense, but he convinced María to tell absolutely no one else about their secret wedding. "For artistic purposes," he told María—the same thing he'd told Crystal at the beginning of their relationship. Gloria was Maria's best friend by that point, and even she didn't find out until nearly two years later. There was obviously no way María could take Sergio's name while keeping the marriage undercover, so she found another way to commemorate their union: She renamed herself after the group, calling herself Mary Boquitas.

How could none of the other Boquitas, not even Gloria, know what was going on between Sergio and Mary? It seems impossible that they could have missed it; after all, the girls spent all day, every day together in the studio, then ate communal meals together at night. Was Sergio that devilishly discreet? Apparently. More to the point, though, it seemed he'd perfected the model he'd been working on for years: He finally developed a girlfriend who would guarantee him total secrecy. He'd come close with Nora; she was obedient enough to have Sergio's child on her own without complaint and to take orders from his new love, Crystal. But in the end, Nora's discipline cracked and she blabbed to Crystal's mother about Sergio's past. His relationship with Crystal may have contained elements of another experiment: If he couldn't count on a girlfriend to keep quiet about what she saw, he'd have to find one who saw nothing. When even Crystal began asking questions about all the young girls she sensed around the studio, Sergio had to move on again. This time he seemed to have found a girl who was so devoted to him, she wouldn't even breathe a word about her greatest happiness—and greatest heartache—to her greatest friend.

So with homophobia, cult suspicions, and managerial womanizing poised to destroy the group at any moment, the five Boquitas arrived to make their debut on *Siempre en Domingo*. They held themselves together and betrayed no sign that the guitarist was sleeping with the pianist, the bass player was sleeping with the manager, and the manager was sleeping with the country's blind superstar sweetheart. Raúl Velasco came out to greet the girls and was delighted to see Sergio again. "Who could be better than him to direct your artistic careers?" Raúl Velasco told the girls. "You're all very lucky. He's a *genius*."

The girls found their marks on stage, the lights came up, and then, for all the wrong reasons, Rául Velasco turned out to be right. At that moment, all across Mexico and large parts of Latin America, viewers tuned in to see five surprisingly young-looking girls, all dressed modestly in slacks, long-sleeved blouses, and neckerchiefs, launching into a quick, nicely harmonized rock tune. For a girl group, they looked nothing like the hard-bodied, hypermature young bombshells who would follow, nothing like Britney Spears or Christina Aguilera; instead, the Boquitas were adolescently plump, with awkward, overteased hair and delighted smiles. They looked, basically, like extremely talented kids.

"Well, okay," Pilar sang softly, rolling her head back and closing her eyes as she eased into "No puedo olvidarlo" ("I Can't Forget Him"), a new ballad Sergio had recently written for the group. "Today, you want me to trust you enough to confide my hopes," Pilar crooned. "But I don't like you enough to let you see me that way. No wayyyy . . ." Considering the lies they were telling each other backstage. Sergio's tune was an incredibly apt anthem to secrecy.

It was remarkable: Despite the harrowing year they'd been through, and the far-too-adult dramas they were still enduring, the girls had somehow gelled into a nimble, forceful rock group. Pilar's sharp guitar fingering complemented her deep, smoothed-off-shout of a voice, and she traded vocals easily with Mary Boquitas. Claudia lashed out some surprisingly adventurous drumbeats, while Mónica and Gloria stuck to nicely tinkling, metronomic keyboard rhythms.

Gloria took over vocals for one of her own songs. At sixteen, she already had her first two songwriting credits on the Boquitas Pintadas album, and as she stepped to center stage for "Amor cavernicola" ("Underground Love"), Gloria gave the first hint of the growling soprana and grrrl power rebellion she was starting to develop. Love, she sings, is more like a parasite eating away at your insides. Another of Gloria's songs, "Se hace noche" ("Turns to Night"), is also a strangely cynical take on romance for an adolescent. It, too, is dedicated to love—self-love. "Under a thousand stars, I feel like I'm the most beautiful," Gloria writes, describing a normally obedient girl breaking curfew to linger with her boyfriend. "So who cares if they yell at me tomorrow? Bah!" While other sixteen-year-olds might think first love is a thrilling new adventure, Gloria sees it as a war with herself, the ascendant princess, in the center of the battlefield.

Curiously, Sergio's ostensibly more mature perspective on romance matches his youngest protégé's. Another new Sergio tune, called "En el amor todo se vale" ("All's Fair in Love"), couldn't be more coldhearted: "Yes, the other day I lied to you," Pilar and Mary sang in unison.

It was to make you jealous, dear,
to see if a little treachery
could fix things up.

Those gleefully dark lyrics are followed by a shrugging acknowledgment that, well, lying is sometimes just the more appealing option: "I'm guilty of going out with a guy," the Boquitas sing, "to whom I just don't like telling the truth." Perhaps that's why the Boquitas ultimately failed; the intraband bickering didn't help, of course, but maybe the fatal flaw was that the group's core message—that young love is a fraud—just didn't play well with the bubblegum generation. The Boquitas were supposed to be targeting young girls on the verge of their first kisses, but instead of heightening their excitement with guitar-accompanied dreams of romance, they were selling love songs for skeptics. Punk and grunge were built on that kind of nihilistic irony, but coming from five innocent young girls-next-door, it sounded phony and bizarre, sort of like the foul-mouthed Satan talking through the possessed girl in *The Exorcist*.

The problem was, Sergio couldn't keep his master-songwriter hands off his group's tunes. Even though the girls had the majority of the songwriting credits on the album, Sergio's influence on the lyrics is unmistakable. And looking back, it's amazing just how honest Sergio actually was about his feelings—if anyone knew enough to search his lyrics for clues to his behavior. Crystal, however, was getting signs of her own. Shortly after the Boquitas began their first rehearsals, Crystal's mother dropped by the studio to visit. When she walked into a rehearsal room and saw Sergio surrounded by his five new teenage discoveries, she called him on it.

"You want to have sex with these girls, Sergio," she said. "I know you, and I know what's going on here."

"No, no, of course not," Sergio protested. "This is a professional studio." Within a few weeks, he and fifteen-year-old María would be married. Crystal didn't know for sure what was going on, but she was getting unpleasant updates from Nora. Sergio had recruited Nora back from Crystal, saying that with all the new talent he had to train, he needed someone to help keep order in the studio.

Delighted to have Sergio's attention again, Nora threw herself into the job. She continued doting on Crystal, but also began mother-henning the five young Boquitas. She was everywhere, it seemed, for everyone— and only later did Crystal figure out why. "Nora was our world," Crystal says. "Anything we needed, Nora was there to provide it." But gradually, as Crystal twinged to the fact that something was up between Sergio and María, she realized that Nora had to be a part of it, too. "You cannot befriend all the lovers of the man you adore," Crystal says. "She had to be up to something, but I didn't know what."

It was only after the scandal erupted years later and details of Sergio's secret life began leaking out that Crystal understood just what role Nora was playing back in the initial stages. "He just wanted a spy," Crystal says. "She pretended to be our best friend, but she did it because Sergio told her to. Her job was to keep track of everything we said and did, and then tell Sergio. So in order to gain our confidence, she told us some little secrets about Sergio." María was one of the girls under Nora's surveillance; later, after she became Mary Boquitas, she would allegedly replace Nora and step into the role of ex-lover-turned-henchwoman.

This would become Sergio's routine: He'd find a young woman who might not be especially attracted to him, but so hungry for love—and so unsure of her own self-worth—that Sergio could gradually groom her to believe that her worthiness could be measured only by Sergio's satisfaction. If Sergio was happy, then they were not only happy themselves, but *worthy of happiness.* If Sergio was upset, well, they'd earned their punishment, because they didn't deserve to be happy. Still, what would astonish Crystal was how forcefully this indoctrination could penetrate. As she could see with Nora and Mary Boquitas, their devotion to Sergio went far beyond romantic loyalty, far beyond religious faith, and entered the realm of scientific *fact:* They were as convinced of his authority as they were of any law of nature. While a devout Catholic might occasionally break a commandment, Nora and Mary would no more defy Sergio than defy gravity.

By 1986, whispers started to reach her that Sergio was sneaking around with one of his Boquitas. Crystal finally decided to end it with Sergio once and for all. At heart, it wasn't Sergio's cheating that rattled her; it was who he was cheating with. "I had dealt with many other girls he had while he was dating me," she admits, while adding a tantalizing fillip. "I'm not going to say who they were, because they're famous now." A certain amount of running around, she was willing to put up with. She'd been in show business since she was eight years old and had become a realist: With hundreds of eager women desperate to become famous, a powerful male producer is going to slip up every so often. She had learned to overlook it, much as she'd learned to overlook Sergio's tantrums and blooming obesity.

What jolted her, though, was the age of the girls Sergio was now dallying with. "When I heard about this María Raquenel," Crystal says, "I'd had it with him. She was barely fifteen. I said, 'No, thanks.' " As easy as she makes it sound, however, the breakup was excruciatingly difficult for her. For starters, she suddenly didn't have any money, and her sound equipment had vanished. "Sergio handled the money, and never gave me any," she says. "One of my backup singers said, 'This is crazy—how can the number-one-selling artist be broke?' " The backup singer had previously worked with a locally known male vocalist named Juan Gabriel, and she urged Crystal to go to him for advice.

Juan Gabriel was surprised to learn that Crystal and Sergio weren't married. Crystal poured out the whole story to him—about her empty bank account, her missing sound equipment, and Sergio's "punishments" and dalliances. "Don't worry, Crystalisima," Juan Gabriel told her. "I'll get you back together." He promised to have his guys track down her equipment so she could perform again, and in the meantime he would give her all the money she needed. "Five or six thousand dollars isn't much today, but in 1984, it was a lot for him to offer," Crystal says. A few days later, to help boost her spirits, Juan Gabriel invited Crystal to be his guest of honor and sit in the front row for his show that night at El Patio. Televisa was broadcasting the concert, and naturally its cameras kept coming back to celebrity singer Crystal sitting at the foot of the stage.

Early the next morning, Crystal got a call from Sergio. "I want you in my office, right away," he told her. Even though they had broken up, Crystal never thought of refusing. When she arrived, Sergio made her stand in front of his desk while he grilled her about Juan Gabriel. She insisted they were just friends, but Sergio kept at it, hammering away with questions about how they'd met, how often they saw each other, whether Crystal had slept with him, kissed him, hugged him. The interrogation went on so long, Crystal began to get nauseous and faint. Finally, he told her to get out.

When she got home and told her brother what had happened, he was dismayed by Crystal's belief that she was worthless without Sergio. Her obedience was as dangerous and unhealthy as a drug addiction; so much as he would with a chemical-dependent friend, Crystal's brother decided to stage a romantic intervention. He had Juan Gabriel come over, and the two of them talked to Crystal for hours, reminding her over and over how successful she was, how valuable she was to them, how friends and family and fans adored her. "My brother stayed with me the whole time, for days," she recalls. Finally, the message began to penetrate, and Crystal saw, with a new clarity, how emotionally crippled she'd become. "I was shocked that I wasn't even aware that other people cared for me," she says. "I only had eyes for Sergio."

By that summer of 1986, she thought she was finally over him—until Sergio turned up at her door, scared and desperate. He wouldn't tell her what was going on—only that someone was trying to kill him and he needed a place to hide. Crystal had serious misgivings, but hearing the unmistakable fear in his voice, she let him in. Naturally, he took her master bedroom; she moved into one of the smaller guest rooms. Soon the brewing scandal leaked its way into the entertainment press: An article in *TVyNovelas,* the Mexican version of *TV Guide,* hinted at the cause without providing any details. "Rumors are circulating that Sergio seduces, mistreats and exploits young girls," the article says.

And for a man being accused of heinous sexual behavior and professional misconduct, Sergio's response to the charge is strangely noncommittal. "There has been a wave of commentary about me unlike anything I'd ever have imagined," he told the magazine. "They've called me everything from exploiter to child abuser." This was the moment to thunder forth with an angry, outraged denial. Instead, Sergio goes on to say, "I think that these things will eventually collapse from their own weight. If I really am that way, time will tell. If not, likewise."

If I am that way . . . ? After that, Sergio did no more interviews.

Nevertheless, even as Sergio was hiding out in Crystal's house, more of the underage sex allegations were surfacing. Reports were spreading that Sergio had been having sex with the sister half of a brother-sister band, and she'd gotten pregnant. At first, all anyone knew was that just when the group was winning a national audience and being praised by rock critics as "ahead of their time," they suddenly disbanded. Word got out that the girl's father was very serious about exacting revenge, and very calculating: First he was going to sue Sergio, to make sure his daughter would be financially secure; then he was going to kill him.

So that's the reason Sergio had panicked and gone underground, Crystal realized—he knew at least one set of angry parents was after him, and more could follow once the scandal hit the papers. She could tell he was serious: Before the interviews and allegations had even been printed, Sergio had liquidated the studio to prevent it from being seized, then relinquished his client list and disbanded the increasingly bickering Boquitas. Ironically, everything came crashing down just when Mr. Midas was on the verge of seeing another one of his bets prove correct: After one year, the Boquitas had begun getting some nationwide attention, and the song Sergio had written for them, "*No puedo olvidarlo,*" was steadily climbing the Most Requested list.

Sergio's dilemma became the worst six months of Crystal's life. "We were not lovers, but he mistreated me as though we were," she says, her choice of verb indicating just how conditioned she'd become to thinking abuse was a normal part of any love relationship. "There were nights we had sex. Sometimes he came into my room, or I was watching TV and he started," she says, embarrassed by the memory. "By the second night it happened, I realized he was humiliating me, but in my strange thinking back then, I thought, 'I've already done it, so I might as well let him stay.'"

By day Sergio would leave the house and never tell Crystal where he was going. "If he had other girls—which I don't doubt—at least it wasn't in my house or in my face," she says. "It was hard for me, and I'm sure for them, but when he came home he never said to me, 'I was with another girl.' At least he didn't humiliate me that way." She thought constantly about freeing herself—her brother begged her to get rid of Sergio—but she was certain he truly feared for his life. "It's one of the few things he ever told me that I think was really true," Crystal says.

While Crystal tried not to know about Sergio's clandestine affairs, Gloria Trevi would later defend them. Seriously, she asks in her jailhouse memoir, who could blame him? "Women with artistic aspirations or just out for $$$ would offer themselves and throw themselves at him, trying to achieve with their bodies what they couldn't with their talent," she argues. "They all wanted to trap the youngest and most famous producer of the '80s, the boy genius, the starmaker. Journalists, secretaries, women of all ages and status and professions were pursuing him." But, Gloria adds, Sergio did have some self-control. "He didn't sleep with *all* of them," she writes.

One of the girls, Gloria does acknowledge, was a minor with an angry mother, but she remains elusively and tantalizingly vague about the girl's identity: Was it Lucerito or the girl from the brother-sister act? Gloria won't comment, but she has plenty to say about who's to blame in the case. She has plenty of sympathy for the victim—in her eyes, that's Sergio. "They loved each other, and had a true, romantic, consensual relationship," Gloria says. That, to her, is apology enough for a nearly middle-aged man having sex with one of his underaged clients. But even if the parents felt justified in ending it, Gloria goes on, was it fair that they should also try to ruin Sergio? According to Gloria, the girl's parents not only broke up the relationship and threatened to have Sergio killed, but they also went to Televisa and demanded that he be blacklisted.

What's so fascinating about Gloria's analysis of Sergio's affair is its eerie ring of adolescent logic. At the time she wrote her memoir, Gloria may have looked like a teenager, but she was actually a middle-aged woman, a self-made millionaire, and a mother. She had been in enough adult relationships, both personal and professional, to know the difference between a romantic partnership between mature and experienced adults, and the seduction of a middle-school girl by her manager. Gloria should have known the risks this posed to the girl—in fact, by her own admission, she had *lived* those risks: In interviews, she talked over and over about the sex-hungry record executives who tried to lure her to hotels while she was pitching her first solo album. Yet when she defends Sergio, she sounds exactly like a teenager rationalizing a crush on her father's best friend. Gloria poses the question as an adolescent might: What's wrong with a girl dating an older man, as long as they're in love? But the real question, as she should have known, is, What's wrong with an older man using his power and position to date a young girl? A teenager wouldn't have the experience to know the difference between attraction and manipulation, but Gloria—at age thirty-three—certainly should have.

So was Gloria lying? Probably not. As strange as her logic sounds, it's not only angry enough to be sincere, but consistent with the same rationale she would fall back on, again and again, when Sergio was accused of taking advantage of his teenage charges. Gloria truly seemed to believe that Sergio was justified in sneaking into a sexual relationship with a girl one-third his age, and convincing the girl to lie to her family and friends about it. It's as if Gloria's worldview and judgment hadn't developed since the time she was a teenager—since the time, in fact, that she'd first met Sergio.

But by 1988, after a year or so had passed, the storm with the girl's parents seemed to be subsiding. Quietly, Sergio had been feeling out the possibility of his return to show business, and he'd enlisted a very influential ally with Televisa: his brother, Eduardo. Eduardo had put himself through law school as a popular Televisa soccer announcer, then gone on to become one of the network's corporate attorneys before springing into politics. Lalo began beaming that killer smile of his, and with that all-charm-but-deadly-serious manner of his, he was able to flex a little muscle: Word got around that anyone who hurt his little brother would be dealt with. Sergio began feeling more confident. He was ready to come out of hiding, start over again. And the timing couldn't have been better—by the end of 1988, Gloria really needed his help.

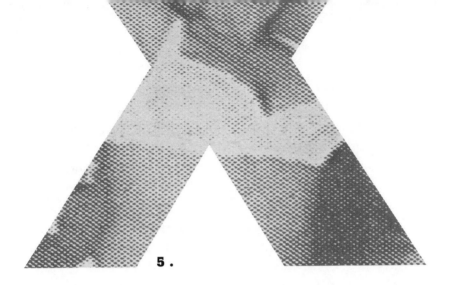

5

What Am I Doing Here?

*O*kay, dear, your 'artsy little adventure' is over," Gloria's mother told her when the Boquitas broke up in 1986.

It was time to face reality. Gloria's chance of a lifetime had come, and she'd gone nowhere. After being trained, produced, and promoted for nearly two years by one of the hottest young musical talents in the country, Gloria was now further from the top than when she started. At least when she arrived in Mexico City two years before, she'd been a promising young performer with Televisa's powerhouse backing. Now she was just another cute girl from the provinces who'd tried, and failed, to captivate the country with nothing more than a pretty face and giggly natural charm.

After all, Gloria hadn't even been the most remarkable performer in a rather unremarkable group; on most of the Boquitas' songs, Gloria's voice was barely noticeable, a faint adolescent echo chiming in on the chorus. No one was hungrier than Gloria's mother to see her make it big, but as a former dancer, Gloria Ruiz also knew just what kind of danger an ambitious teenager could be lured into while nibbling desperately at the fringes of Mexican show business. Gloria Ruiz wasn't about to let her daughter go scrounging around on her own without professional sponsorship, or at least the minimal supervision of a TV training academy. She ordered Gloria to catch a bus home to Monterrey.

"No," Gloria told her. "I'm not coming home. I want another chance."

"Don't you understand?" her mother said. "You don't *get* another chance." Did Gloria believe her mother had really *wanted* to end up giving dance classes for a few pesos a night to factory workers' kids? But she'd taken her best shot, and when she couldn't become a wealthy dancer, she set out to become the next best thing: a wealthy wife. It took a few years, but she'd finally done it—she finally married a well-to-do physician with homes in both Mexico and the United States. Now it was Gloria's turn—and quick, before her teenage beauty began to fade or, God forbid, she followed in her mother's original footsteps and found herself pregnant and married at an early age.

"No," Gloria repeated. "I'm still young. I can do it."

"Well, not with my money," her mother stormed. "You're on your own."

This was a consequence Gloria would immediately regret, but later conceal: Until that climactic argument with her mother, Gloria's Televisa scholarship and her Boquita preparations under Sergio had been subsidized by a cash allowance from home. As a star, she would reinvent her past and depict herself as a scrappy street kid who climbed to the top on nothing but talent, pluck, and hustle, but the truth is, that scrappy street kid had her rent and meals paid for during her first two years in Mexico City by her mom.

But now, with Sergio's studio closed and her parents cutting her off, Gloria really was on her own. She was desperate for money; much like Crystal, Gloria had spent a year recording and touring for Sergio and somehow ended up with nothing to show for it. She was living in a boardinghouse for students, but was soon evicted when she couldn't pay the next month's rent. She found another, cheaper place that would let her pay by the week, and then . . .

And then what? For the next three years, Gloria would virtually vanish. As far as human contact and documentable evidence are concerned, she was invisible. It would be the most critical period of her life, the time she made her astounding transformation from B-grade backup singer into one of Latin America's greatest pop stars, but no one saw it happen. No one, that is, except two people: Sergio Andrade and Mary Boquitas. To the rest of the world, Gloria had become a ghost.

The only account of those missing years came from Gloria herself. In the thousands of interviews she gave as a star, she looked back and described how the struggle to survive during her "hungry years" opened her eyes to the drama and poetry of the world around her and taught her lessons about sex, injustice, and *machismo* that would stir her outrage and come erupting out of her as music. In article after article, Gloria gave a standard account of her post-Boquita years. This would become her myth, and nearly every one of the details in these accounts would end up in her songs.

"She said she abandoned her conservative, middle-class life at the age of 14, when she left Monterrey for Mexico City," a typical recounting of the Gloria saga in the *Los Angeles Times* began.

> *Friendless and penniless, Trevi survived by selling gum on street corners; once she taught aerobics classes for 12 hours straight.*
>
> *"For the first time I dealt with real life and people's problems,"*
> *she says. "I met people who were in love and having problems with virginity—all these male-invented values. All these things were in my heart and mind, and I became so angry I wanted to say something.*
>
> *"But it wasn't only anger. Young people are not only rebels. They have a special heart. My songs deal with problems that affect everyone but I treat them with laughter and irony. Underneath, there's knowledge of a solution. I wanted to transmit my dreams to everyone."*
>
> *. . . For the next three years, a jealous lover kept her quiet in the kitchen, where he thought good Latin women belonged. "I was in love once," she says, laughing. "It was terrible."*

Even as far afield as Canada, Gloria's uncontested version of her lost years was accepted as fact:

"Shortly after she sang with a group called Boquitas Pintadas, her mother cut her off," the *Toronto Star* reported in 1993.

> *The 16-year-old Trevi lied her way into a job teaching aerobics 12 hours a day, met a man twice her age, and moved in with him for three years.*
>
> *He threw her out when she refused to marry him, and she found herself "without work, without family, without friends, because for him I had broken off with everybody. . . . I was in the street with one change of clothes."*
>
> *She sang for money in the subway and started knocking, unsuccessfully, on record company doors. Finally she auditioned for Sergio Andrade. . . .*

Pressed by reporters for details, Gloria would comply with fascinating tales of her life on the streets. She'd tell vivid stories of her wild adventures as a homeless girl and her strange, semisadistic romance with this mysterious older man. "During my hungry years, I ate tacos stuffed with pig eyes, or the tongue or the throat," she told *Más* magazine. "My God, I was so famished they tasted delicious!" She begged at bus stops, she said, and tried to get hired as a domestic servant, and sang for pesos on street corners. Her mother tried to tempt her home by offering her a new car, but Gloria said she refused, even though she was so desperately broke by then that she'd had to sell all the clothes she owned except the ones she was wearing.

"I had to scrub out my bra and panties at night, so I'd have something clean to wear in the morning," she said. "I was a true vagrant." She said she preferred begging around Colonia Polanco, the ritzy Mexico City neighborhood thick with banks, art galleries, foreign embassies, and the kind of super-luxurious hotels that *The Economist* lists as "decadent" in its guide for business travelers. Gloria used to zero in on elderly ladies, telling them she had "a terrible problem" and then contorting her pretty, deceptively preadolescent-looking face into a mask of anguish. It worked beautifully. "Usually, they gave me something," she recalled. Bit by bit, she'd gather enough coins for a night in a flophouse.

She generally avoided wealthy-looking men, however, because they either assumed she was a streetwalker or were eager to convert her into one. An old man once offered her 100,000 pesos to have sex with him, she claimed, but she "banged him in the face and left him whimpering on the ground." She then took off running. "Prostituting myself would have been very easy," she said, "but no. That won't go for me. If I love you, I give myself to you completely. But if I don't, you don't even get to touch my hand."

Often in these stories her colorful details would collide: In some versions, she survived on pig eyes before meeting her boyfriend, in other versions the pig eyes came later. She'd say she walked out on her boyfriend when he tried to stifle her dreams of becoming a singer, and then later say that he was the one who'd done the door slamming when she refused to marry him. And it was never clear how many boyfriends she was talking about; sometimes she'd say she'd only had one boyfriend her entire life, then it would be two, and then, in keeping with her public image of a sexually voracious vampire, she'd suggest her conquests were countless. "One day I told my father I wanted to be an artist," she told the reporter for the *Toronto Star*, "and he said, 'Not my little girl—an artist has to sleep with everyone.' And I said, 'Yes, papa—that's why I want to do it!'"

She never eased the confusion by mentioning names or dates. Everything in her post-Boquita life, the way Gloria told it, occurred in a timeless, faceless, factless swirl, a fairy-tale adventure peopled by characters who were only identified by a single name or freaky feature, like the seven dwarfs. But in every story she told, the one constant is the shadowy love of her life, the man she lost just before she rocketed to stardom.

So who was this mysterious brute who'd penned up Mexico's future sweetheart and then threw her out in the cold? Strangely, he remains anonymous to this day. According to Gloria's account, she became famous just months after separating from him—so why didn't he ever come forward to try to share her spotlight, or win her back, or set the record straight about his own behavior? After he and Gloria had spent three years together, they must have had dozens of mutual friends and known many more people in common, so wouldn't he speak up to clear his name? If not for dignity, then at least for vanity—after all, who wouldn't want to be known as the man who'd rejected the most desirable woman in the country?

And yet ... nothing. Gloria never named the man who broke her heart, or even hinted at his identity. The most detailed account of this strange romance was gathered, once again, by Rubén Aviña, who gleaned a rare insight into Gloria's past because, basically, he was the only one paying attention to her in those early years. Several years after returning to journalism when the Boquitas folded and Sergio's studio was shuttered, Rubén reunited with Gloria. She had released her first album and was starting her first major publicity tour. As usual, he says, she held Rubén spellbound with tales of her past; this time she updated him on how she had survived since the last time he'd seen her, during her Boquitas days.

"I had just turned seventeen when they threw me out of my boarding-house because I couldn't pay the monthly bill," Rubén recalls Gloria telling him as they chatted together in Sergio's studio. "I went to another one, and when they threw me out of there, I moved to another. . . . I didn't have anything left to sell, and I was looking everywhere for a job, as a housemaid, or waitress—anything." She was at the end of her rope, she told Rubén: "I was starving to death!"

That's when Gloria finally got lucky. She saw an ad in the paper for an aerobics instructor, she said, and even though she wasn't trained, she figured she could fake it by running together a few moves she'd learned in her mother's dance classes. She got a tryout in front of the students, and wowed them so much that she was hired on the spot. It was better than busing tables or scrubbing floors, Gloria would discover, but not much easier: The gym owner forced her to keep hopping and kicking in the front of the class for up to twelve exhausting hours a day. Still, as she later pointed out in other interviews, the job had its subtle residual benefits for her future ambitions: She was being paid to practice dance moves, rehearse song lyrics in her head, and hone her skills as a performer.

A handsome older man joined the class a few days after she'd started, Gloria told Rubén, and she finally revealed his name—at least, his first name: Alejandro. "I was still only seventeen, and he was thirty-two," Gloria said. "He was a doctor, specializing in gynecology." One night, Gloria was leaving the gym during a downpour. Alejandro offered her a ride back to her boardinghouse. They began dating, and Gloria soon fell in love—hard. "I was crazy for him," she said. "And this love kept growing by the day. He just swept me up until I agreed to move in with him."

At first, Gloria said, her gallant gynecologist was "respectful of her independence." But bit by bit, he grew jealous and possessive. To avoid fights, Gloria began surrendering more and more control of her life— even to the point of giving up contact with her family. She'd already begun minimizing her calls home, afraid that her mother would start asking sticky questions and fly off the handle once she learned her daughter was living with a man nearly twice her age. But then Alejandro demanded that she stop speaking with her parents altogether. "He thought they were putting ideas in my head," Gloria told Rubén. "That's how dominant he was," Gloria said—but she obeyed. "After all, I was wild about him!"

Alejandro wasn't satisfied with estranging Gloria from her parents; he also cut her off from her brothers, her few friends, and finally, her aerobics students—he made her quit her job and remain alone in his house. "I'd spend all day shut up inside there, and since I had nothing to do, I'd paint little monkeys on the wall, to kill time and to calm myself down a little," Gloria told Rubén, hinting at the strain of being sequestered for weeks at a time. "But as soon as he came home at night, I forgot everything and was once again the happiest and most head-over-heels woman in the world!"

Her seclusion, however, soon turned into incarceration. Gloria's willing obedience turned into intimidated subservience when, as she saw it, she made a strategic error in the middle of yet another ugly fight with Alejandro. She'd suspected he'd been seeing other women while she was trapped at home, and one day, she threw it in his face. Instead of offering a cool denial or heated outburst, Alejandro astonished Gloria by crying. "I felt so awful," she said, "that I ended up pleading with *him* to forgive *me*. I told him it was all my fault. . . ."

Alejandro seized on the admission. It *was* her fault, he agreed, and from that moment on he turned her surrender against her whenever they had an argument. He'd remind her of how wrong she'd been before, how she had even *admitted* it, and how unfair the whole thing had been to him. It was terrible how she behaved; she'd even said so herself. "And if I wanted to be pardoned this time, I would have to accept his punishments," Gloria told Rubén. She wasn't talking about a cut in her allowance or extra chores around the house: She meant real physical torture. "His punishments were quite cruel," Gloria told Rubén.

Alejandro's standard method of tormenting her, Gloria said, was to shove her into the bathroom, lock the door, and leave her there—not till she apologized, but for days at a time. "Entire days locked in the bathroom!" Gloria said. Once, she added, he left her there for a week. "My God!" she exclaimed, shocked by her own memory. "I'd spend the time crying, sleeping on the floor like a dog. Alejandro brought me food, then locked me in again, like I was in a cell." When he finally freed her, Alejandro would bathe her in affection, taking Gloria out for a fine meal and telling her, over and over, how much he adored her.

"He'd say I was the most important person in his life," Gloria recounted. "Many times, I made up my mind to walk out on him, because as deeply in love as I was, at the same time I was really afraid of him." But whenever she told Alejandro that she was leaving, he would take her by the arms and beg her to stay. "He'd say, 'Before you leave, look me in the eyes and tell me you don't love me,' " Gloria said. "And I couldn't do it. I couldn't escape that vicious cycle."

Rubén was listening in disbelief—Gloria Trevi, the church-defying, man-crushing hellcat, the rock queen of rebellion, had not only made her name by scandalizing the archbishop, but had also forced the toughest man in Mexican entertainment, The Tiger of Televisa, to back down. Yet this same woman had allowed herself to be *caged like a kitten inside a bathroom?* The scene was too bizarre to imagine. Gloria's image was based on her fiery feminism; she rarely ended a show without stripping some man to his underwear on stage and smacking him with his own belt, but here she was, admitting that only two years before, she had been so cowed by a boyfriend that she'd taken food from his hand, then obediently curled up on the cold tile floor and wept herself to sleep under the toilet.

Although he's apparently unaware of it, Rubén's recollection of Gloria's story mirrors the classic formula for brainwashing. All the key elements of coercive persuasion are present: isolation, debilitation, degradation, discipline, and fear. Much like a new cult member, Gloria was kept away from family and friends who could bolster her self-esteem, then humiliated to make her feel worthless. Gradually, her entire self-image would become dependent on her dominator. Contributing to mind control, as Pavlov first discovered in his groundbreaking animal experiments, are physical exhaustion and denial of food—and until Alejandro shut her in for good, Gloria was exercising from dawn till dark in her aerobics classes and largely relying on Alejandro for her meals. While locked in the bathroom, she only ate when Alejandro fed her.

Finally, Gloria told Rubén, after three years, she was able to break free of Alejandro, but only because he tired of her. "I'd tried many times to leave him, but every time I tried, he cried and begged me to stay. Then one day, he walked out. He said he was sick of me. He told me to hit the road."

By this point, Rubén was finding Gloria's story very difficult to swallow. The gaps of logic and circumstance were simply too much to believe. How could any young woman survive that kind of treatment without ending up in a hospital? And if this mysterious doctor truly had brutalized her when she was too young and inexperienced to do anything about it, why wasn't she roaring after him for revenge now? What was stopping her from using the tremendous media power at her disposal to make sure he never hurt another young woman again? After all, if Gloria was holding herself up as a defender and liberator of young Mexican women, why didn't she start with the one oppressor she knew firsthand?

But for all the problems Rubén had with Gloria's story, there was something oddly familiar about it that made him believe that beneath her layers of fabrication, Gloria was hiding a painful kernel of truth. The punishments . . . the possessiveness . . . the rages . . . the abrupt rejection of a young woman who depended on him—wasn't that exactly the kind of behavior that Sergio was becoming notorious for? Rubén had heard all the rumors, all the reasons people were saying Sergio once had gone underground. In fact, Rubén had actually witnessed some of the things people were whispering about, like Sergio's vein-throbbing tantrums and obsessive insistence on control. No one really knew what happened with the young girl whose parents Sergio had enraged, but the rumors sounded much like Gloria's tale of her life with "Alejandro."

And another thing—was it only by chance that "Alejandro" was so much like those fantasy figures from Gloria's youth, the generous physician who'd showered Gloria with gifts while courting her mother, the gentle M.D. who became her stepfather? The coincidences were too much to swallow.

Rubén asked her point-blank if "Alejandro" was not, in fact, Sergio, and Gloria denied it: She insisted her abusive ex-boyfriend actually was the vaporous "Dr. Alejandro"—a man who would never be heard of again—and not her manager. However, there was one interesting fact that she decided to keep to herself: the slave-driving gym teacher she would mention in dozens of interviews but never name, the tyrant who forced her to dance herself to exhaustion teaching twelve consecutive hours of aerobics classes, was none other than Sergio Andrade.

For more than a decade, she kept that part quiet. Only when she published her own book from behind bars in 2002 did Gloria offhandedly reveal that it was actually Sergio she'd been complaining about when she talked of the brutally hard jobs she'd had to take to survive before becoming a star. After Sergio had reemerged from his six-month exile in Crystal's house, Gloria would later reveal, he'd created his first star factory and put two of his former Boquitas—Mary and Gloria—to work.

"Sergio Andrade had opened an art school where he offered classes in singing, dancing, acting, music and aerobics," Gloria would say years later. "It turned into an academy with a tremendous number of students—I'd say there were more than 500 at a time in different classes—and I came to ask Sergio for a job. He had me doing a little of everything, even handing out badminton birdies, while I was being trained as an aerobics instructor."

Once again, Sergio had managed to surround himself with legions of fame-hungry teenagers who idolized him, and even Gloria would have to admit that Sergio's affairs had again become dangerously numerous and complex. "There didn't seem to be any cure for Sergio," she says with a shrug. "He was intelligent, sensitive, talented, hardworking, doesn't smoke, not obsessed with sports, but . . . he had one weakness: women." She then adds, "One woman can be a man's damnation, but many, his destruction."

By that reasoning, Sergio was back on the highway to hell. He was still secretly married to Mary Boquitas, though their relationship had twisted into a confused tension between domination and rejection. On the one hand, Sergio believed himself separated from Mary and often spoke of divorce; he treated her as a friend and was open about his new passion for Sonia Ríos, another teenager who had also turned up at his studio, like Gloria and Mary, with a hint of talent and an eye for fame. On the other hand, Gloria notes, Sergio was "excessively jealous" and reluctant to let Mary go. This archly selfish desire to possess but not be possessed wasn't Sergio's fault, explains Gloria, who goes on to offer a novel defense: Sergio had been victimized by too much attention and easy sex.

"His experiences with women had brought him to the conclusion that if not all, then at least 90 percent were unfaithful piranhas, since all kinds—married, single, of any age and any social level—threw themselves at him," Gloria writes. "And I believe he was afraid that his partner would do, with another man, what other women had done with him." Although Gloria intends this apology in support of Sergio, it's actually an unwitting condemnation: In essence, she's confirming that Sergio really does distrust women and feels a need to punish and control them.

Mary, nevertheless, was still desperate to rekindle their romance, and was spending many long hours asking for Gloria's advice. Those conversations made Gloria acutely uncomfortable, because she realized that despite Sergio's physical shortcomings, frightening tantrums, and relentless womanizing, she was falling in love with him herself.

"When did it start?" she wrote later. "I don't know . . . our relationship was, and had been for several years by then, strictly work-related and a little stormy. I was a rebel by nature and impulsive; he was methodical and demanding. That's why, all during the Boquitas Pintadas period, I was often at the end of my rope with him and was seriously tempted a number of times to leave and never come back. What kept me there, though, was my desire to become an artist, to triumph, to become famous. I know I irritated him, but he put up with it because he could see the artist in me. We mutually tolerated each other, and I actually admired him as a composer and producer."

Her appraisal of Sergio is surprisingly frank, and not especially flattering to either of them: He wasn't the best-looking guy in the world, Gloria admits, "but he was a leader, a boss, and that is very attractive to us women—not to mention the fact that he was famous and wealthy, a musician and poet, and not the least of which, an excellent lover." She was so desperately in love with him, Gloria says, that she had to quit working at the studio and put some distance between them. She didn't want to betray Mary, her best friend, and besides, Sergio was prickling her with incessant stories of past and present girlfriends. He didn't seem to realize the intensity of her feelings and kept sharing his carnal cowboy tales with her.

"There were a lot of stories he told me, a lot that he held back, and a lot that I discovered without wanting to, either because people told me or they happened right before my eyes," Gloria relates. "So I had to get my thoughts and feelings toward Sergio in order, and figure out my future." Sergio didn't discourage her; in fact, he urged her to head back home to Monterrey and move back in with her family. The suggestion infuriated Gloria: Sergio, she felt, wasn't treating her like a colleague and an adult, but more like a schoolgirl who'd begun to annoy him and whom he'd be happy to see scamper back to the provinces. She left Sergio's studio in a rage, vowing never to return until she was as powerful and famous as he was.

But the sticky question remains—had Gloria actually begun a secret affair with her best friend's husband? Although she claims to have taken herself outside the reach of temptation before acting on it, discordant notes and contradictions once again weaken her story. In her entire 260-page autobiography, for instance, there is only one sentence devoted to her still phantasmic boyfriend: "At 18, I broke up with my boyfriend because he wanted to get married and I wanted to be an artist." That's it. No name, no mention of how they met, what he was like, why she loved him or how he reacted to her leaving. And according to Gloria's own chronology, her attachments to Sergio and this mystery man overlap perfectly: She was with this boyfriend at the same time that she was falling in love with Sergio, and she happened to break up with him *just* when she was storming out of Sergio's studio. If she's really referring to someone else, wouldn't she mention the fact that she was simultaneously losing the *two* most important men in her life rather than giving her boyfriend only a passing mention in an unrelated passage?

But why lie about it? At first, her elusiveness on this point seems peculiar—after all, it wouldn't come as any surprise that Sergio might have begun yet another sexual relationship with yet another teenage protégé, and it's doubtful Mary would have been shocked after watching Sergio's circle of steady lovers expand to more than a dozen women. So why would Gloria continue shading the truth? Most likely, it was to protect Sergio: If Sergio truly was the "Alejandro" she'd told Rubén Aviña such shocking stories about, masking their relationship would allow Gloria to indulge in one of her great loves—capturing an audience with eye-bulging stories—without betraying the man she adored.

And besides, Sergio didn't need to have any more sexual hijinks attached to that moment in his life, because once again he'd gotten himself into a jam and had to flee. Shortly after Gloria departed, Sergio shuttered his music school and disappeared. From sometime in late 1986 until he reemerged in 1988, Sergio was an invisible man.

"All the problems he was having had left him disenchanted with the artistic medium," Gloria says, though she doesn't specify what those "problems" were or how they could be solved by shutting down a booming music academy. "He was feeling used, and he didn't want to know anything about producing records or representing artists."

Sergio, strangely, offers a completely different explanation for this second sudden disappearance: In a letter he sent me from prison in March 2003, he writes that the death of the person he loved most, his grandmother, the devoutly named Encarnación del Divino Verbo ("Incarnation of the Divine Word"), had dealt him "a profound psychological crisis," leading him to "abandon music and the artistic medium."

What was he doing? "Studying and traveling," Sergio writes in his letter. "Writing poems and stories." But why, then, would he cut off contact with Gloria and Mary? Gloria may say that she left Sergio's school to sort out her feelings in private, but in a tightly knit entertainment community like Mexico City's, Sergio could have tracked her down in a matter of days—if he'd wanted to. The truth, however, may be that he decided to disappear not only to escape trouble, but to escape the girls—all the girls, including Gloria and Mary. Sergio's pattern over the previous few years of dalliances and disappearances was that of a person with a war raging within him: He would immerse himself in a clatter of young girls, get too close to one, or several, go on the run, get scared straight and confine himself to a self-imposed prison of isolation where he'd have no contact with young girls . . . but then, after the trouble abated in a year or so, he'd throw himself back into his previous life with more abandon than ever.

And while Sergio was making his most recent personal penance, Gloria was handling his exile in her own way. In addition to scrounging for handouts in Colonia Polanco, she had begun a little business preparing pre-made quesadillas, the cheese and tortilla snacks, which she cleverly dubbed *Quesabrosas!* (a punning reference to cheese—*queso*—embedded in the phrase "How tasty!"). She'd noticed that even college students were earning pocket money as street performers, singing outside shopping centers, so she decided to give it a try herself. Her chief preoccupation wasn't survival, however, but avoiding anyone who might know her parents. "I only did it for two or three months," she says.

She still had enough spare time to polish the songs she'd been writing for the previous two years and compose some new ones, and within six months she felt she was ready to record. "I was no longer a little girl with dreams," she says. "I was now a woman with the hunger to succeed, and Sergio always said that was the key to success: talent and hunger." It was time to track him down.

When Sergio resurfaced in 1988, it was in the conveniently detached and enclosed space of a radio booth, a place where he could exercise his taste for talk and his expertise in pop music, while secluding himself from any teenyboppers—or the parents of any teenyboppers with lingering grudges. Sergio had taken a job as a deejay, hosting a late-night program called *My Personal Collection* on the popular Mexican radio station XEW, where he handpicked his favorite music of the moment from around the world and gave listeners his own rambling minilectures in composition, arrangement, and vocal styles.

One evening that same year, Gloria showed up at the station and talked her way into Sergio's booth. She'd gotten much thinner since Sergio had seen her last, and was looking a little ragged and scruffy. Gloria was carrying something that looked like a schoolkid's notebook, some kind of a battered, stained portfolio scrawled all over with adolescent-looking graffiti, cartoonish drawings of round-eyed girls and soaring birds and rainbows. Gloria couldn't wait to get it open. Before she and Sergio had even caught up, she was hauling out sheets of paper covered with her childlike, looping script. Could she sing him a few of her songs? she asked. If he liked them, would he help her cut a record?

Sergio was doubtful; he wasn't at all eager to get back into the business just yet. Still, she'd obviously been working furiously to get so many songs together, so he'd take a look, and maybe sit her down with a piano and have a listen. So what did she have? Gloria shoved the entire portfolio at him, and Sergio began leafing through her song sheets, mouthing the words for his inner ear as he imagined a melody and accompanying backbeat.

He began to smile. This was impressive, and rather surprising; despite the nice work Gloria had done on her two songs for the Boquitas Pintadas album, she was still just a teenager who hadn't finished high school and a relatively novice songwriter. Yet the lyrics she showed him weren't just tight and nicely rhymed—many were unexpectedly sophisticated and deftly phrased. And they expressed something that Sergio never could. For all his flair for romance and his ability to twinge his listeners' sentiments, he couldn't put himself into the mind of one of pop music's most devoted audiences: adolescent girls. In that regard, he learned as he scanned the words to "¿Qué hago aquí?" ("What Am I Doing Here?"), Gloria clearly had him beat.

The song began with the gripping setup:

What am I doing here?
Stuck here in the house,
where I can't stop crying. . . .

It then builds to that jarring line that compares her parents' wedding photo to bodies lying in state.

A snippet from another song, "¿Que voy hacer sin él?" ("What Will I Do Without Him?"), caught Sergio's eye:

I know my way of being,
isn't exactly what he wants. . . .
And I know very well he'll never want me. . . .
What will I do without him?

Years later, Sergio would say, "The instant Gloria sang those songs for me, I knew if I could make her record, she'd be a sensation. She had it all—looks, presence, a one-of-a-kind voice, and a brilliant head for music." Gloria, of course, remembers it differently; she says Sergio doubted her ability to make it big at once, and floated the idea of selling her songs to a more experienced singer and using the proceeds as development money. They both agree, however, that Sergio didn't sugarcoat the chance Gloria had with her songs.

"These are very good," Sergio told her, "but you have to understand, the music business is in crisis right now. The record companies aren't spending right now, and if they did, it wouldn't be for another female vocalist." The Latin market was way overstocked with female vocalists, Sergio told her, nearly all of them warbling out interchangeable, melancholic ballads of love-gone-right and love-gone-wrong. If she were to do this, he warned her, Gloria would have to be absolutely ferocious about grabbing attention, and be ready to perform anywhere, anytime, for any audience. Otherwise, she didn't have a prayer of even getting her album distributed.

"Okay!" Gloria responded eagerly. "Whatever it takes."

"All right," Sergio said. "So—who do you know who has money?"

Money? Gloria had spent the last few months begging for flophouse rent. How much cash did Sergio think she could come up with from the old ladies in Colonia Polanco? They were going to have to finance this on their own, Sergio was explaining; the record companies at that time were so tightly budgeted and risk adverse, their only hope of making the kind of groundbreaking album Sergio had in mind was to do it independently. They'd have a much better chance of landing a production deal if they showed up with a recording in hand, Sergio told her, and besides, they'd retain much more control of the product.

"I really don't think my father likes the idea of me singing," Gloria answered despondently. "And my mother and I aren't talking to each other."

"What's this?" Sergio asked. "Since when?" He'd gotten to know Gloria's mother during the Boquitas Pintadas days, and remembered her as not only a crackling, fun-loving gal, but also as a showbiz-dazzled mom who was committed enough to Gloria's fantasies to bankroll her first two years in Mexico City, the way other parents pay for private school.

She and her mother hadn't spoken in months, Gloria said, or seen each other for much longer. Ever since she'd defied her mother's order to come home three years earlier, they'd been alternating between heated battles and Cold War silences. There was no way, she said, that her mother would forgive all that and suddenly drain her savings to pay for her un-grateful, runaway daughter to record a bunch of songs she'd scrawled on notebook paper between bouts of sidewalk begging and quesadilla vending.

But Sergio knew otherwise. He understood Gloria's mother better than Gloria did and urged her to give it a try. With no alternative, Gloria relented, and soon she and Sergio were on their way to Monterrey. And just as Sergio had predicted, Gloria's mother was thrilled with the idea. She didn't ask what Gloria had been up to for the past three years. That was all the irrelevant past; the present was exactly what she'd always dreamed of, exactly what she'd always wanted, but doubted Gloria could achieve by knocking around on her own in the Big Monster. But she'd been proven wrong: Here was Mr. Midas, sipping coffee in her own living room, and promising to make her daughter a star.

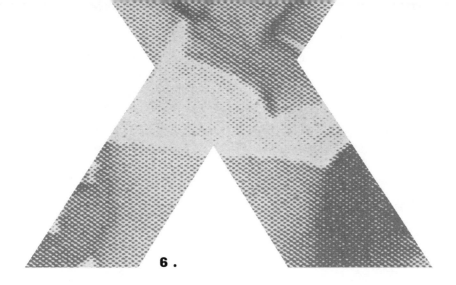

6

"Most Virgin of the Virgins"

When she returned to Mexico City one week later with *¿Qué Hago Aqui?* recorded on a raw demo tape, Gloria was still thrilled by her mother's words at the end of their studio sessions. "You were fantastic!" Gloria Ruiz had said. "I never knew you could sing like that. It's going to be a hit—I know it!"

The sessions had gone amazingly well. Even though Sergio was notoriously hard to please and Gloria was still a raw singer trying to master untested material, she nailed her songs in just a few takes. Sergio even threw an extra challenge at her; because he wanted something on the album that listeners would recognize, he made her include a variation on one of the most covered tunes in rock history—the Rolling Stones' classic "(I Can't Get No) Satisfaction." It meant that in her first week as a soloist, Gloria would be taking on not only "The World's Greatest Rock Band," but also soul legends like Aretha Franklin and Otis Redding. (Interestingly, "Satisfaction" would turn up years later in the early repertoire of another teen bombshell aiming to storm right to the top, Britney Spears.)

But rather than aiming for easy audience reaction by vamping the tune (as Britney would later) into a teasing invitation for sex, Gloria made her "Satisfecha" ("Satisfied") an anthem for angry young feminism. The opening lines suggest the image of a young loner coming to grips with her problems:

Everybody says
I'm out of control.
and not just with food. . . .

But the promise of self-improvement twists into a sinister little smirk, as the singer vows to follow her whims and suggests that if she changes in any way, it will be to become more rebellious:

And I'm not going to change,
Not until I feel like it.

In other words, forget about teen heartache and anorexia. As Gloria growled out her new words to the old rock chestnut, she was announcing the arrival of a different kind of pop performer and a different kind of teen love song: a *self*-love song. It was a clever strategy: Instead of going the usual route of packaging herself as the perfect teen dream, Gloria was flaunting her flaws. She wouldn't try to imitate Madonna's haughtily unshaven armpits, however, or Chrissy Hynde's leather chick toughness—Gloria had hit on the revelation that in an entertainment world of bigger-than-life images, acting like Everywoman had become a radical stance. The really crazy girls, Gloria was saying, were the ones torturing their hair with peroxide and starving themselves to impossible thinness. Gloria's niche in the crowded female soloist spectrum was going to be her attention to inattention: She wasn't going to act girlish or slather on the makeup, and if anyone expected her to be an eye-batting baby doll—well, they'd better try Lucerito.

To an undeniable extent, of course, it was an act—Gloria knew she was a rare beauty with a to-die-for figure she herself would say was "designed by God when he was feeling naughty." But right from the start,

Gloria understood that the more she encouraged girls to relax and be themselves—the more she portrayed herself as one of them, not one of Them—the more Mexico's teenagers would reward her with fan appreciation and record sales. That's why, when the music press reacted to her tremendous popularity and rapid rise through the charts by nicknaming her "The Mexican Madonna," Gloria would reject the compliment and insist, over and over, that her biggest influence was Janis Joplin—the heavyset hippie who, thirty years after her death, still remains rock's least glamorous female singer.

All during these studio sessions, Gloria Ruiz had stared at her daughter in amazement. Where had all her brash stage presence come from? Gloria Ruiz never doubted her daughter had a pretty face and a certain exuberant charm (that is, ever since she'd outgrown her awful Squaw Treviño phase), but as a former performer herself, Gloria Ruiz knew that her daughter had somehow acquired something exceptional and unteachable, at least by conventional means. The change since Gloria's Boquitas days was amazing; from a forgettable face hiding behind four already forgotten musicians, Gloria had turned into a voracious spotlight grabber.

What her mother didn't know, of course, was that Gloria's new boldness was at least partly attributable to her bouts of street begging, which had forced Gloria to shuck all reticence and self-consciousness and put on a show. When she was working the dog-walking dowagers of Colonia Polanco, Gloria had to either demand attention and manipulate her audience or go hungry. Before her mother's eyes, the sweet-faced, cute-as-Chispita-look-alike named Gloria Treviño was turning into "Gloria Trevi," a love-scarred siren who made "rock" seem as much a description of her heart as her music.

Another secret influence on Gloria's brassy new showmanship, and one that privately contradicted her tough-chick pose of intouchable independence, was her closeted passion for Sergio. With so many young girls clamoring around Sergio in the studio, Gloria knew that only the ones who screamed for his attention would get it. Her personal life, consequently, was turning into the perfect daily training ground for the broader world of show business. She'd learned from her mother long ago that in Mexico a woman often had to ignore risks and be as aggressive as any man to get what she wanted; otherwise her mother would still be rushing home from twelve hours of dance classes to make dinner for an angry, suspicious husband. That same sense of desperation is evident in Gloria's approach to singing. She didn't want to become another Mary Boquitas, either as a singer or a lover. "When it came time to record my voice," Gloria would recall later, "I was throwing off sparks, I gave it everything I had . . . I knew this was my last great chance."

The trio—Sergio, Gloria, and Gloria Ruiz—had a fantastic week. They spent their nights in the studio (when rates were cheaper), and by day Gloria and her mother scoured second-hand stores and consignment shops for Gloria's new wardrobe. They would bring their purchases for inspection to Sergio, who was following his all-nighters with long days in the mixing room, checking arrangements and overdubs. Sergio would okay the clothes or send them back; according to Gloria, he had a clear image in his mind of just how she should look when she made her next attempt. She needed to erupt onto the stage, since she was running the risk of being dismissed as a has-been staging a comeback. Gloria would have to overwhelm critics and listeners alike into forgetting she'd already failed as a Boquita.

That's why Sergio didn't want Gloria wearing anything that smacked too much of rock's typical black uniform or, on the other extreme, anything too neat and tailored, like the Boquitas' outfits. "Colors, Gloria!" Sergio would instruct. "Happiness, youth!" Sergio was thinking ahead to the demands of the TV market, where the rule is the brighter, the better. Sergio already had a backup scheme in mind if Gloria's album didn't get enough air time from the radio stations: With her sparkly, made-for-Magnavox outfits, he had a fighting chance of making her at least a temporary TV attraction if her songs didn't take hold right away. If she looked good on television, the radio stations would necessarily have to fall in line and play her songs.

After their exhausting week, the trio split up. Gloria's mother headed back to Monterrey and Sergio returned to Mexico City, where he was eager to start shopping the album around to record companies. This time Gloria Ruiz didn't object when her daughter insisted on returning to Mexico City as well. Their relationship had changed dramatically after

Gloria had walked back in the door with Mr. Midas at her side. At that moment, Gloria showed she could deliver on her mother's lifelong dream of fame. It was even better than her mother had imagined: This time Gloria wasn't striking out on her own as one-fifth of a girl group, but she was bringing the star maker right into her mother's home and giving her mother a chance to share in the glory.

Perhaps that's why even though Gloria Ruiz had been so distant from Gloria during her early struggles, she would later be by her side when the demands were much greater: Throughout all the scandals that would erupt, Gloria's mother would never publicly doubt her daughter or dodge the notoriety. Actually, she seemed to thrive on it: The louder the cries became to bring Gloria to justice, the more her mother's face appeared in the papers. Her platinum hair was always beautifully styled, and instead of looking drawn or haggard, she seemed to grow curiously younger with each succeeding crisis. By the time Gloria was turning up on national "Most Wanted" posters, her mother was looking as glamorous as her sex-symbol daughter.

X   X   X

Once back in Mexico City, Gloria faced an immediate problem. Even though Sergio and her mother convinced her she had a hit record on tape, Gloria didn't have two pesos in her pocket. "I didn't have anywhere to live, or a job, or any kind of financial setup, nothing," Gloria says. "And proud as always, I didn't want to bug my mother for little things." After all, her mom had just drained her savings to pay for Gloria's studio time—how could Gloria then nickel-and-dime her for an allowance? "I'd do it on my own," Gloria decided.

Sergio helped out—a little. Throughout his entire career, just how much money Sergio had would always be a mystery; he always cried poor, yet seemed to live quite well. So when he gave his singers stingy assistance, no one could be certain if he was rich and miserly or strapped for cash and generous. Later, when he was behind bars in a Brazilian prison, he would cadge soda money from his cash-strapped new fiancée, Silvia Beeg, yet somehow come up with the money to pay two teams of crack defense attorneys in two different countries. At the start of Gloria's new career, Sergio told her he couldn't afford to pay for studio time, yet he owned several homes and cruised around Mexico City in a new Mustang convertible. And when Gloria needed something to live on while Sergio negotiated her record deal, he didn't give her a stipend or an advance on projected sales—instead, he made his future star work as the gopher for his radio show. At night he let her sleep on the sofa in his studio at 108 Adolfo Prieto Street in the Colonia de Valle neighborhood.

Sergio remained as strict with his discipline as he was with his cash. Shortly after Gloria had begun her gopher duties, Sergio was chatting with an executive at the radio station and mentioned he'd taped a segment the day before at four o'clock. Gloria corrected him. "No, Sergio," she interjected, "it was two o'clock." Sergio waited till the executive left, then he erupted, calling Gloria "stupid" and "indiscreet." She might be a star on the rise, but she still had to obey Sergio's special rules. Amazingly, Gloria didn't object to the scolding. "One always spoke to Sergio with extreme courtesy," Gloria would later say. "Sergio drew the line and demanded respect, so even though we shared friendship and confidences, our relationship was that of a boss and his subordinate."

They were nothing of the sort, of course. Gloria was no longer Sergio's subordinate, but his equal collaborator on a joint project. She might have been low on funds, but if anything, *Gloria* was actually the boss at this juncture, not Sergio. She was an emerging talent who had supplied not only the vocals and original material for Sergio's latest album, but the financing as well. Sergio, technically, was just a night-shift deejay moonlighting as her agent and recording engineer. In fact, he had Gloria to thank for getting him back into producing at all. There was no reason Gloria couldn't have fired him and taken her album to another agent—no reason, that is, except one: Sergio had so thoroughly convinced Gloria of his dominant role in their relationship that years later, even after she'd become an established star and a national symbol of feminism, Gloria would *still* defend Sergio's right to humble her. "*Everyone* in the office addressed Sergio that way," Gloria recalled. Even Mary Boquitas, Sergio's teen wife, had to address her husband as *"Señor."* "At work," Gloria says, "Sergio treated Mary just like everyone else."

Actually, a little worse. The other employees earned at least enough to afford a place to live, but Mary, like Gloria, was bunking on a sofa in the studio. After Sergio had unofficially divorced her, Mary had been too ashamed to return home; while her parents had given their consent to the engagement, they had no idea she and Sergio planned to wed right away, assuming the couple would at least wait until Mary was a few years older. When they found out Mary had gone ahead with the wedding, they were furious; they warned their thirteen-year-old daughter that she was making a horrible mistake. After the marriage broke up within a year, Mary didn't want to face them. Instead, she hung around Mexico City during Sergio's exile and returned enthusiastically when, in late 1988, he decided to manage Gloria and reopen his "star school." Mary became sort of the school's live-in housemistress, and there was plenty for her to do: Despite the taint of scandal clinging to Sergio, more girls were signing up all the time.

Sergio, for his part, didn't seem in any hurry to formalize his separation from Mary, so Mary may have nursed the hope that if she hung around long enough and made him happy, Sergio's eye might turn her way again. That all changed, however, when skinny, thirteen-year-old Érika Aline Hernandez—better known as "Aline"—came through the door on a Saturday morning in June 1989. There are two very different versions of what happened next, but both end the same way—with Aline plunging into Sergio's most intimate inner circle and then fleeing in the dead of night to ignite the scandal that would set Mexico's most glamorous star, and its most successful star maker, on the run.

For all the furor it would unleash, Aline's arrival at 108 Adolfo Prieto Street was completely forgettable, Gloria says—yet she remembers every detail. "For me, it was a day like any other, and she was just another hopeful who'd turned up to audition for Sergio," Gloria sniffs in her jailhouse memoir. If she noticed Aline at all, she says, it was as one more starry-eyed schoolkid crowding around Sergio in the already jammed studio. But it wouldn't take long, Gloria claims, before Aline would set herself apart as a cold-eyed gold digger, a preternaturally savvy young girl determined to land either a fat record deal or the fat record producer—preferably both.

The only reason she didn't spot Aline's intentions sooner, Gloria says, is because she was so absorbed in preparing for her record launch. "All this was going on outside my rehearsal room, where I spent the days practicing 'play-backs,' live singing and dancing, working out to get myself into condition to perform, and to improve my body," Gloria says. Then one day, out of the blue, this skinny girl entered Gloria's rehearsal room and began talking. Although Gloria claims not to remember much about Aline's arrival, she can somehow recall with uncanny precision everything about that first meeting, including Aline's behavior, the shade and cut of her clothes, and her taste in undergarments.

"She was very extroverted, dressed in a pink outfit that consisted of a 'bellybutton' shirt and a mini-skirt," Gloria says. "The blouse left her stomach uncovered and her back naked, and it was evident she wasn't wearing a bra. She was taller than I, wearing a lot of makeup, and I was surprised when she told me her age—to tell you the truth, I didn't believe her, because she seemed a lot older." In other words, the woman who would earn millions of dollars by stripping off her panties onstage and throwing them into the audience, and who not only posed naked for calendars, but recruited teenage girls to pose alongside her in their panties and bikinis, was aghast at the appearance of a belly button.

Aline's mother was just as bad, Gloria says. "To dress that way in Mexico City was to risk losing people's respect, even when accompanied by her mother," Gloria wrote in her autobiography. Aline's mother, Jocelyn, was a thirty-four-year-old radio announcer who worked at the same radio station as Sergio and accompanied her daughter to the audition. "The *señora* herself was in a mini-skirt, and acted like a hip teenager, just like her daughter, and she was obviously older than she said." According to Gloria, it was this tarted-up mom who steered Aline toward Sergio, but Aline didn't need much pushing: Within a few days, Gloria says, the skinny schoolgirl was "circling Sergio like a shark."

Aline was constantly badgering her for inside information about Sergio, Gloria says, and when she wasn't asking questions, she was "shocking" Gloria with her sex stories and raging teen libido. "She told me that she drank alcohol, and smoked, and had experienced adventures and wild times that I'd never tried," Gloria says, claiming remarkable innocence for a nineteen-year-old woman who'd already toured with a rock band, spent a year backstage at a TV network, begged for flophouse money on the streets of Mexico City, and lived with a semi-sadomasochistic boyfriend. "This type of confession always surprised me, probably because from the time I was 13 until I was 18, I didn't regard as normal the things that many girls consider normal: a fling, an adventure, an experience. For me, making love is exactly that, to do it with love, and I was always astonished when someone managed to regard it so lightly, with so little magic."

Gloria ratchets her shocked moralism even higher when she describes her reaction to Aline's tale of her first fumbling encounter with sex. When she heard Aline's alleged account of a late-night tussle with a handsome neighbor, Gloria professes to be shocked. "My eyes were as big as plates!" Gloria says. According to Gloria, Aline showed up at the studio one morning with shining eyes and a beaming smile and pulled Gloria aside for a talk. "I'm not sure if I'm a virgin anymore," Gloria claims Aline said.

"What? When? With whom?" Gloria recalls stammering.

Aline, she says, told her that a "super-hot" boy lived in the house next to the one her family had just moved into. "I took one look at him and I started drooling," Gloria quotes Aline. That same night, Gloria continues, the hottie next door invited Aline and some of her girlfriends over to watch some porn movies. ("I don't like them," Gloria adds in an aside, "and I can't imagine how she could watch those types of movies in the company of other young men, let alone boys she just met.") When Aline went for a drink of water, Gloria says, her young neighbor followed her into the kitchen and began kissing her and removing her clothes. The two fell into a side room and onto a sofa, but before the boy could fully penetrate, they heard their friends approaching. The two hastily zipped and buttoned up. So what Aline had wanted to know, Gloria said, was this: Was she still a virgin?

"And me like an idiot, with my mouth hanging open," Gloria claims was her first response. Her second, she says, was to satirize Aline in a song, "Virgen de las Vírgenes" ("Virgin of Virgins"), which would become a hit on her second album, *Tu Ángel de la Guarda (Your Guardian Angel)*. If Gloria is telling the truth, then her song was a devilishly clever act of humiliation, because Aline was one of her backup singers on the album. The object of Gloria's scorn would have been crooning along with the lyrics composed to mock her. Gloria begins the song describing a girl who's had sex with "as many as ten," but tells each guy that he's the first. Why, it's a miracle to rival the Immaculate Conception, Gloria sings in mock amazement:

She's the most, most, most, most

Virgin of the virgins

But beneath her scorn and leather-tough facade, Gloria was suffering. The more Sergio favored Aline, she would later admit in her prison memoir, the more hurt and rejected Gloria felt. It was a pain she couldn't relieve by talking, because who could she discuss it with? Her mother? Impossible—Gloria had always denied that Sergio was anything more than a mentor. Mary? Even worse—Mary felt the same way toward Gloria as Gloria now felt toward Aline. Her relationship with Sergio had left Gloria in almost perfect isolation, without any friend or confidant besides Mary. Gloria would later absolve Sergio of any blame for her hurt feelings and desperation, claiming that they were not having sex at the time and that Sergio had no idea of her true pain and devotion. It was her own fault, Gloria would declare in her memoir, for trying to turn herself into a platonic vassal like Mary, and for failing.

But according to Aline, what had changed for Gloria wasn't the sex, but her status: Sergio was still sleeping with Gloria and Mary whenever he wanted, but now Gloria was just another toy and not Sergio's main interest. Gloria was Sergio's fallback for those nights when Aline had to hurry home to her mother's house, and the demotion was devastating.

One night not long after Sergio had begun spending long hours with Aline in his office, Gloria found herself alone in the studio. She began searching the cabinets for pill bottles, gathering a collection of sedatives and sleeping pills. Weeping, she dumped the pills out into a pile and began swallowing them by the fistful. "No man has ever loved me," she recalls thinking. She felt "deformed," and as she sank into a stupor, she thought about "the treachery of my few friends, the disaster I'd made of a love life, the horrible feeling that I didn't matter to anybody."

Suddenly she felt someone shaking her and shoving fingers down her throat to make her vomit. Sergio had come back to the studio after dropping off Aline and found Gloria unconscious on the floor. He splashed her with cold water and forced her to drink milk, which he knew she detested, so she'd vomit it back up. He hauled her to her feet and made her walk, following every step of street wisdom for how to keep an overdose victim alive except, apparently, for the one step that would have brought him unwanted attention: In Gloria's account she never says Sergio drove her to the hospital or called a doctor.

Nevertheless, Gloria reveres Sergio for saving her and blames herself, not him, for what happened. From that night on, she says, he ordered Mary to never leave her side. "Forgive me, Sergio," is how she concludes the story of her suicide attempt in her memoir. "Forgive me." Any blame she might have given Sergio for keeping her heartsick, friendless, and penniless is gone by the time, a few weeks later, she writes the title track of *Tu Ángel de la Guarda,* one of her most disturbing and, perhaps, unconsciously revealing songs. In it, Gloria describes a girl who is tormented by an uncaring boyfriend, and decides to end their relationship with "seventy pills." But instead of following the cliched routes of either "girl-tragically-gone," or "love-tragically-wronged," Gloria adds her own unexpected twist: the dead girl proves how worthy she is of love by being more compassionate in death than her boyfriend is in life.

In a final act of self-recrimination, the dead girl decides that her boyfriend deserves soothing more than she does:

> *You feel you're to blame*
> *for rejecting me*
> *and when you cry*
> *I want to console you*

Gloria occasionally referred to that night in interviews, but always in the vaguest of terms and only to make the point that she'd had it tough before making it big. Reviewing the canon of Gloria's press clippings, this is one of the few stories she doesn't embellish with melodramatic and sometimes questionable detail. "For a long time, I felt very alone," she told *TVyNovelas* in 1991, about a year after she'd rocketed to stardom. "Before my career was launched, I had suicidal thoughts, and there were times when I seriously thought of killing myself. I'm over that now. I don't feel so alone anymore." And that's all. She never hints that Sergio was involved. (In fact, she denies ever dating Sergio in that same interview; under the subhead "I'm not dating Sergio Andrade," Gloria declares, "*Híjole,* they never leave the poor man in peace! I love him like a brother, but there is nothing more than that between us.")

She never mentions Aline's role in her near-fatal despondency, either. Before the scandal erupted, in fact, Gloria never really mentioned Aline at all. It was only after Aline revealed the secrets of Sergio's studio that Gloria suddenly began lashing out at her as a jealous failure and a husband-hungry slut. Aline, curiously, never responds in kind, no matter how vicious the attack. As much as Gloria contributed to her suffering, she seems certain that Gloria was suffering, too. The title of Aline's book, Aline: *La Gloria por el Infierno,* says it all: "Going through hell for glory" also means "Gloria's trip through hell."

But that doesn't mean she doesn't hold Gloria accountable. Long after she'd fled Sergio, Aline interrupts a question about Gloria with a question of her own.

"Did Gloria mention the spankings?" Aline asks bluntly.

"No," I answer.

"I didn't think so," Aline says. "I don't think she'll ever talk about it—to anyone."

By the time I met her, in the spring of 2003, Aline had become the twenty-seven-year-old host of a TV Azteca variety show. She had long blond hair, a runway model's figure, and a gleaming smile—a smile that disappeared as soon as I mentioned Gloria and asked what had gone on behind the closed doors of 108 Adolfo Prieto Street.

We are speaking on one of the TV Azteca back lots, where Aline has just finished taping a show. Moments earlier, I'd watched on one of the monitors as she sang and danced with careening glee, flinging her arms around castmates for hugs and laughing so giddily that she seemed, sincerely, to be having the absolute time of her life. Her unrestrained joy was actually her principal virtue as a performer; she wasn't a powerful singer, or an especially polished dancer, or, frankly, a remarkably attractive woman by TV standards. What she contributed to the program was infectious jubilation; Aline *loved* being on camera—so much that she seemed more like a surprised fan plucked from the audience and brought onstage than a seasoned pro. Even off camera, Aline was bouncy and keyed up, preferring to stand while she talked rather than take a seat on a shady bench. During our introductory chitchat, her hands are constantly in motion, fidgeting with her necklace and smoothing the hair back from her face. Occasionally she breaks into an unconscious, hip-swinging little dance, as hyperactive as a schoolkid in springtime.

But when the subject turns to Sergio and Gloria, the fidgeting and hair fussing stops. Aline drops her eyes to the ground and falls silent. When she resumes talking, she doesn't sound angry or even bitter; she sounds determined. "I trusted Gloria," Aline begins, speaking slowly and keeping her eyes fixed on the black asphalt, as if scenes from her past are flashing across the tarmac. "I thought she was my friend. She was big back then, as big as Shakira, and here she was, a superstar—the biggest star in the country!—spending time with *me*, a little nothing, a goofy little thirteen-year old."

Aline knows her story is hard for most people to believe, and that's one reason it took so long for her to tell it. It was three years from the day she left Sergio before she told Patricia Chapoy, her new boss at TV Azteca, what happened to her in Sergio's studio, and another year before she went public with her story in a memoir written for her by Sergio's former publicist, Rubén Aviña. But even after the publication of *Aline: La Gloria por el Infierno* in 1998, it was still easy for Gloria Trevi to appear on television and make Aline look like a liar. Not only because of the bizarre and sordid claims Aline was making about the private life of a beloved superstar, but also because even in her own book Aline's behavior seems suspiciously illogical.

Aline understands that. It took years of therapy before she could make much sense of it herself. Many trauma victims, she came to learn, contend with the same problem; to outsiders, the inability to flee a destructive relationship seems incomprehensible. Whenever she tells her story, people look at her in amazement. They want to know, for instance, if Sergio really began whipping, starving, and humiliating her at age thirteen, why on earth did she marry him at age fifteen? And once Gloria revealed her true role in Sergio's schemes, as Aline contends, why did Aline continue to trust her? And finally: Aline's mother even went so far as to lock Aline inside the house and hide the keys to keep her away from this "monster"—so why did Aline plot so hard to escape and return to a man who had forced her into sex with women and kept her a naked prisoner in his hotel bathroom?

"Fear," Aline answers. It's her answer for every one of those questions. "Every day I wanted to leave," she says, "but I was afraid, and I didn't have the courage to do it." All the girls in Sergio's studio reacted the same way, Aline says. "There were only girls and no men," she explains. "Very few men ever came into the studio, and when they did, we were forbidden to talk to them. Not even to say 'Good morning.' If anyone came close to me, I had to step away and conceal myself. We obeyed him because we were afraid."

But Aline's explanation seems illogical. If she was really so afraid of Sergio, wasn't that all the more reason to run away from him? Once Aline was out of Sergio's grasp and back in the protection of her family, there was no way Sergio could harm her. Sergio wasn't going to *kill* her, was he? So in the end, how scary could he really be? And that, essentially, is the key to the Aline mystery, and the hardest thing to grasp about her mentality: Why didn't she react to fear by avoiding the thing that made her afraid? It's the most difficult thing for her to explain, because it's the most difficult thing for her, personally, to confront. Perhaps it wasn't fear of Sergio so much as the fears Sergio was able to awaken within her. Sergio was probably able to read Aline and locate her anxieties, her own sense of her inadequacies. Sergio understood how much Aline longed to be loved, and he played on her fears that she never would be if he left her.

Aline might have been afraid of Sergio, but on a deep-seated emotional level, she was possibly more afraid of a life without him.

She wasn't conscious of it at the time, but at thirteen years old, Aline was struggling with the memory of her father's freak death and her fear of being alone. She was not only afraid of being abandoned, but at heart she also seemed to fear that she'd never be loved because she's unlovable. That's why once Sergio became a force in her life, she became dependent on the sensation of being surrounded by attention. His attention might have been oppressive, it might have been cruel and demeaning—but at least it was reassuringly constant. Sergio both inflamed and comforted the worst kinds of fears in Aline—the ones she could never run away from because they came from within.

"Were you attracted to him in the beginning?" I ask.

"Not at all," she says. "He was thirty-three, fat, and ugly, and I was thirteen. When I first met him, I though he was rude and unbearable, and pretentious. Attraction for him? Never."

"So how did your perception of him change?"

"It changed because he knew how to handle me. Sometimes he would talk to me as if he were a little boy, and I would think, 'Oh, poor man,' and feel sorry for him. Other times, he would sing me his compositions and tell me jokes. I started to like him. I thought he was intelligent, fun, interesting, talented, sensitive. He understands people very well—he knows exactly how to make each person like him as well as he knows how to make each person afraid of him. With a song he could make you fond of him, and with a scream he could frighten you."

"How about the other girls—did they react the same way?"

"As time went by, I grew and matured a little more. I think I was one of the rebels of the group. When he was hitting me, I always said, 'Why, Sergio? Why are you doing this?' The others just curled up and said nothing."

"How many others were there?"

"When I finally ran away, there were six of us living with him. There was Marlene, one of the girls I helped recruit, and Gaby, Katia, Sonia, and Andrea. Plus Mary, Gloria, and Sergio. Six of us, in three bedrooms."

"You helped recruit other girls?" I ask.

Aline swallows hard and looks away. For the first time, tears spring to her eyes. She remains silent for a long time. She watches the young actors hurrying past us on the sunny Azteca lot, laughing and chatting as they head for coffee in the outdoor cantina. When Aline answers, her voice is almost inaudible, either choked with emotion or deliberately lowered so her friends and colleagues won't hear what she's saying. Her whisper sounds like a combination of grief, remorse, and shame.

"Yes," Aline whispers. "Yes, I did the same thing that Gloria did to me. I think . . . I think I so badly wanted to be like her that I didn't realize what that meant. I trusted her, because I really thought we were friends."

Aline pauses. "But when I look back," she concludes, "I don't think Gloria ever really liked me at all. If she cared about anyone except Sergio, she would have saved me."

When Aline and Gloria first met, they were alike enough to be sisters. Both were slender brunettes with long hair and fine, almost European features. They had remarkably similar backgrounds. They'd both been raised by tough single mothers who yearned for stardom, and both girls started performing shortly after losing their fathers: Gloria began vamping around her neighborhood in miniskirts and thick makeup soon after her parents' divorce, and within three years she was vying to become the next national soap opera starlet. Aline, meanwhile, began dreaming obsessively of pop stars right after her father was killed in a car crash when she was six years old.

But the most important detail they shared was timing: Aline and Gloria were both drawn into show business at age thirteen, that dangerous, identity-shifting year when girls are torn between safety and sexuality and their egos are at their most fragile. Erik Erikson, the great developmental psychologist, believed it was precisely at that age—at the transition from child to teen—when judgment is most uncertain and insecurity is most acute. "Identity Versus Role Confusion" was Erikson's name for the stage, since it's the moment when rapid body growth and maturing genitals leave the thirteen-year-old wondering who she's supposed to be. Aline, for instance, had just begun wearing a bra at thirteen, which she would stuff to look older or forget to put on when she was feeling younger.

Perhaps not surprisingly, many of the girls who came under Sergio's influence were recruited at exactly that age. Was it pure sexual attraction on his part or strategy? To put it another way, was Sergio involuntarily drawn toward girls who were not yet women, or did he deliberately choose thirteen-year-olds because he knew they were more likely to revere, obey, and never betray him? Was he astute enough to understand that thirteen is exactly the age when a girl's ego and identity are plastic enough to be captured and shaped? In any case, whether it was by design or desire, Sergio had centered his attention on the kinds of girls who would be least likely to resist and most likely to blame themselves for anything he did. In addition, a fair portion of thirteen-year-olds also come preprogrammed for silence: Since they're at the age of challenging their parents, they are less likely to reveal what they're doing—or what's being done to them.

"The growing and developing youths, faced with this physiological revolution within them, and with tangible adult tasks ahead of them are now primarily concerned with what they appear to be in the eyes of others as compared with what they feel they are," Erikson explains in his landmark text *Childhood and Society*. "In their search for a new sense of continuity and sameness, adolescents have to refight many of the battles of earlier years, even though to do so they must artificially appoint perfectly well-meaning people to play the roles of adversaries; and they are ever ready to install lasting idols and ideals as guardians of a final identity."

It's precisely because that year is so volatile that prizewinning director Catherine Hardwicke chose to focus on it in her film *Thirteen*. "You know, okay, you used to have fun running around in overalls and pigtails, and suddenly you go to school and boys are making fun of you if you're not a hottie, and if you don't have a good ass or whatever," Hardwicke explained in one interview. "And so *bing*, the light bulb goes off, if you're a girl, you suddenly gotta change things. And it's confusing. So she started getting really angry with her mom, really angry at her dad, angry at her brother, hating everybody, hating herself, and she was just kinda like obsessed with living up to the beauty thing."

And the closer the bond has been between mother and daughter, the more it's in jeopardy, adds Nikki Reed, Hardwicke's cowriter and a thirteen-year-old herself when she helped write the screenplay. "You can be so close to your mother, you have to break away," she explains. "You can't stand to be in the same room." The drama *Thirteen* portrays is exactly the scenario Erik Erikson described and the one Aline lived through: Because she doesn't trust her own judgment, a thirteen-year-old girl often puts too much trust in others. Having no sure concept of her own identity, she can allow others to shape it for her.

Aline had such a fragile identity, in fact, that she even invented a celebrity bloodline for herself, turning her father's death into a tragedy of mythological proportions. It wasn't just the loss of someone she loved— the way Aline recalls it, her father had been the focus of a swirl of supernatural forces that had first threatened his life, then taken it. In Aline's eyes, Heriberto Hernández had died like a tragic hero, and the fact that he joined the family as a villain only added to his posthumous dazzle. His wasn't a normal death, in other words, so he couldn't have been a normal man; Aline, therefore, couldn't be a normal girl.

Aline's parents had met when Heriberto was twenty-two and her mother—Jocelyn "Jossie" Ponce de León—was only twelve. Jossie's father forbade his preteen daughter from having anything to do with this electric company worker, so Jossie and Berti began dating on the sly— and kept it on the sly for nearly seven years. Even after they secretly married in a civil ceremony when Jossie was eighteen, the couple didn't tell Jossie's parents. After the ceremony, Jossie went home and continued sleeping in her childhood bedroom. Heriberto didn't formally request Jossie's hand until she was nineteen, but because Jossie's father had always suspected they were running around behind his back, he refused to attend the church wedding.

Aline was born nine months later. Shortly after her sixth birthday, her father was killed in a car crash just a few blocks from their house. Aline was not only grief-stricken by the news, but terrified: Her superstitious mother kept talking about how Heriberto's death was forecast by "dark omens" and preordained by "dark forces," like a black butterfly which once flew in the house. But for Jossie, reality had suddenly become more ominous than her superstitions. Now a thirty-year-old widow with two young girls to support, she had to find a way to start over. She got lucky, though; even though she'd dropped out of college as a pregnant freshman, she managed to talk her way into an audition as a radio announcer and landed a job at XEW—the same station, coincidentally, where Sergio would arrive in a few years when he also needed to build a new life. Within a few years, she began dating, and by the time Aline turned fifteen, Jossie had remarried a much younger man who would be more of a friend to Aline than a surrogate father.

Aline, meanwhile, was developing a love interest of her own. After a friend had lent her the *Thriller* tape, Aline developed a crush on Michael Jackson that bordered on obsession. She got a life-size poster of him, which "made me feel like I had him all to myself," and even put Michael Jackson posters on her ceiling; since she slept with a light on, Aline could look at him when she woke up from nightmares and feel that "someone was with me." She stopped calling out for her father after nightmares, and instead awoke to look into Michael Jackson's warm eyes. After school, Aline would put *Thriller* on the tape player and pretend she was dancing with her idol. It was during those long afternoons, alone with lyrics she couldn't understand, that Aline wrote poems of her own. She can't remember the words to those early verses, she says, just that they were about Heriberto. It was at that moment, when her feelings for Michael Jackson and her dead father had become intertwined, that Aline began to feel what she would call "my artistic anxieties."

She began organizing dance contests and singing at family gatherings. Jossie was excited by her daughter's interest in performing, and even tried to get eleven-year-old Aline on television: She began drilling Aline and her cousin as a duet, and entered them in an on-air talent contest with none other than Raúl Velasco. But gambling on their natural ability wasn't good enough for Jossie; unlike the other mothers whose kids who amateurishly warbled their way through some popular tune, Jossie hired a professional songwriter to compose an original work for the girls. She designed and sewed special outfits, then took glamour shots of Aline and her cousin to submit along with the contest application. Unfortunately, Televisa never called, and Aline took the letdown unusually hard for a girl not yet in her teens. "After all my dreams, reality seemed very ugly," she says. "Being a performer seemed almost impossible, something very distant and impossible to reach."

She got over her disappointment, not to mention her Michael Jackson fascination, with a new attraction to Menudo, the Latin boy band with the pastel clothes, floppy bangs, and *Flashdance*-style headbands. Already Aline was showing a little daring: Unlike millions of other girls, she wasn't infatuated with Menudo's handsome lead man, Robi Rosa, or the devilishly cute fifteen-year-old, Ricky Martin—she was crazy about Sergio Blass, the Menudo bad boy in black leather with long biker hair. Once, her mother walked in to Aline's room and found the twelve-year-old kissing the Sergio Blass poster on her wall.

A few months later, in the autumn of 1989, Aline's mother came home from the radio station with thrilling news: XEW was cosponsoring a Menudo fan club contest, and the winners would be flown to Puerto Rico for a special concert with the boys. It basically would be a junior beauty pageant minus the swimsuit competition. The teenage contestants would have to parade onstage in skirts and heels, then answer a battery of Menudo trivia questions. Aline rushed down to the station to sign up, but when she got there, she discovered that entrants had to be at least thirteen years old. Aline explained that she'd be old enough in just a month, but when the contest official refused to bend the requirement, Aline dropped to her knees and began to beg hysterically. "Please, please, I'll die if you don't let me enter," Aline pleaded, her hands clasped beseechingly. "I'll die of pain and disappointment . . ."

The contest official looked Aline over and had to think a minute. This girl was acting a little nutty, but that was also the kind of manic adoration that would play beautifully on TV. She was also tall enough to convince anyone who didn't know that she was at least fifteen. "OK," the official warned. "But no one can know you're only twelve."

"They won't," Aline promised, still on her knees. "I swear."

"You're in," the official said.

Over the course of several weeks, Aline survived several elimination rounds that narrowed the field from thousands down to one hundred, and then to a final eight. All that was left was the Mexican championship, and if she won that, it was on to the international bout in Puerto Rico. "But on the day of the final, a big scandal erupted when the other contestants found out that my mother would be hostess of the event," Aline later recounted with an air of wounded innocence. Behind the scenes, it turned out, Jocelyn had been working hard to ingratiate herself with the contest administrators—so hard, in fact, that they'd even accepted Jocelyn's offer to volunteer as mistress of ceremonies for the final round.

"That's when the rumors and jealousy started," Aline recalls plaintively. "They thought that for no other reason I would win because my mother had leverage with the organizers, and also because she worked for XEW." As if *anyone* should expect funny business from Team Aline, which included a daughter who'd broken the rules to get in and a mother who had out-stage-mommed the best in the business by actually taking control of the stage. No wonder, then, that Aline would say, "I just knew I was going to win."

She didn't. Aline was stunned to hear her name called for third place. That meant the only chance she had now of kissing the poster boy instead of the poster would be if two other girls dropped out, and no amount of begging on Aline's part, or finagling on her mother's, could pull that off. Still, even though Aline was once again disappointed, she remained undeterred. She'd made friends during the pageant with two sisters who were just as star-dazzled as she, and the three teenyboppers soon rebounded from the pageant by running around Mexico City to get autographs from singers making live appearances.

One afternoon, Aline says, they went down to a radio station to see Pablito Ruiz. The street outside the station was crowded with adoring young girls, all waiting for Pablito to appear. As Aline and her two pals began elbowing into the scrum, Aline noticed a sleek white sedan parked a few yards away, as if stationed there for a reason. One of the sedan's doors opened, Aline says, and she watched as a beautiful young woman with a thick mane of long dark hair got out. The woman eased through the crowd of girls and made her way directly toward Aline. As Aline tells the story, the young woman flashed her a big smile and said, "You know what? I've been watching you from my car and . . . well, the thing is, I have a school, and I go around looking for girls to launch as models."

Aline says she and her friends just stared back at her. The young woman continued talking. "Don't you want to be a model?" she asked. "Or an actress, or a singer?" Aline couldn't believe what she was hearing—was she really being plucked off the street by a talent scout who wanted to groom her for stardom? Did that kind of thing really happen?

"Well, yes, sure," Aline stammered. "I mean, I can't believe it, but yes—I've always wanted to be a performer. The truth is, I've been writing songs since I was a kid, and I love to sing, and dance—"

"Great," the woman interrupted. "What's your name?"

"Aline."

"How old are you?"

"Thirteen."

"Perfect!" the woman exclaimed.

Aline was surprised: She'd been afraid to tell the truth, certain that her height had fooled the woman and that as soon as she learned how young Aline really was, her interest would cool. Instead, she was even more excited. The young woman scrawled down Aline's phone number and promised to call. If Aline's mother had any objections, the young woman said, she'd come over and speak with her personally.

"Okay," Aline said. "And what's your name?"

"Gloria," the woman answered. "Gloria Treviño."

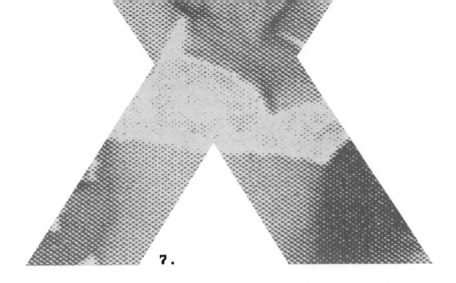

7

The House on
Adolfo Prieto Street

When Aline burst through the door with a giddy smile on her face, Jossie assumed she was tingly from getting a close look at Pablito Ruiz. Then Aline burbled out the news that she'd been picked from dozens and dozens of girls to attend a special model/actress/singer school with Gloria Treviño—

"Who?" Jossie asked. "Who's Gloria Treviño?"

Aline didn't know, either. She was only ten when Boquitas Pintadas made their brief flutter, so she'd never heard of Gloria. But she looked so confident and sensational as she cut through the crowd of chattering girls, Aline told her mother, Gloria had to be *someone*. Jossie would later say that she thought the whole thing was some kind of scam and that her reaction was to forbid Aline to have anything more to do with this Treviño character. "What if they kidnap you?" she'd say she told Aline.

And yet, when Gloria showed up at the house one week later and asked to speak with Aline, Jossie brought her right into the living room and sat down to talk. According to Jossie, Gloria told her that her job was to recruit talented young women for performance scholarships to a special school, where they'd be trained by none other than Sergio Andrade himself. Jossie would later say she had no idea who Sergio was—a statement hard to believe since he had not only been one of the most successful music producers in the country, but *at that moment* he was also working at the same radio station as Jossie. Yet Jossie would say she'd never heard the name before Gloria showed up at her door and had remained skeptical about this whole scholarship business.

Nevertheless, at 11 sharp the next morning, Jossie and Aline were ringing the doorbell at 108 Adolfo Prieto Street for Aline's audition. Mary Boquitas opened the door, and as they entered, Jossie and Aline heard a gorgeous voice echoing from one of the back rooms. It must be Gloria, thought Aline. Although she still was under the impression that Gloria was some kind of talent scout and didn't even know she was a singer, Aline was already so impressed with Gloria's confidence and beauty that she assumed a beautiful voice must be part of the package. But that wasn't Gloria, Mary told them; it was another new recruit, a young teenager from Chihuahua named Ivette Becerra, who had recently joined Sergio's studio with hopes of also enlisting her identical twin, Ivonne. The Becerra sisters were gorgeous brunettes and very talented, Mary confided, but sort of a pain; their father was always coming around the studio, keeping an eye on Ivette.

Gloria came rattling down the stairs. "Mr. Sergio Andrade," she told Aline, rather formally, "is waiting for you in his office." Jossie and Aline headed for the stairs, but Gloria motioned for Jossie to stop. "You'll have to wait down here," she told Jossie. "Aline might get too nervous if you're there." No, Aline protested, she'd actually be more comfortable *with* her mother than without her. Gloria insisted; Aline would have to audition alone. Aline and Jossie stood there confused. It didn't make any sense. If Sergio wanted to test Aline's ability to perform, wasn't it better to have an audience, even if it was her mother? Yet Gloria was unbending; she couldn't explain why Sergio wouldn't permit Jossie to observe, just that it wasn't permitted. That might have made Jossie suspicious— yet even though she'd claimed to not even know who this Andrade was and to have her doubts about the scholarship deal, she's the one who broke the stalemate: Jossie agreed to wait in the lobby. She took a seat and lit a cigarette.

Aline, carrying her little overnight bag, followed Gloria upstairs. She hadn't known what to pack for an audition—actually, she still wasn't sure what she was auditioning *for*, model, actress, or singer—so she'd brought the kinds of things she'd seen the kids wear in the movie *A Chorus Line:* a leotard, some sneakers, and a pair of tights. She also wasn't clear what Sergio expected her to do, so, just in case, she'd stayed up till two in the morning trying to memorize a bouncy tune by Timbiriche, the pop group fronted by breast-clutching, hotpant-wearing bombshell Biby Gaytán. Aline also tried to teach herself how to dance to the Microchip hit "Boomerang." It was a disaster, Aline realized when she had finally crawled into bed a few hours before dawn. She didn't know what she was doing.

Gloria led her into a rehearsal room, where they found the girl whose voice Aline had heard when she arrived. Like Gloria and Aline, Ivette was a slender young girl with a mane of long chestnut hair. Aline began to say hello and was startled when Ivette shot her a dirty look. Before she could wonder why, she heard a man's voice from an interior room calling, "Come in." Aline tried to calm herself down; she didn't want to look like a giggling ninny in front of the man she envisioned as tall, cultured, and elegant, the kind of stylish and piercingly intelligent maker of fashion and culture she'd seen in Hollywood movies.

Instead, she found a guy who looked like a trash collector. He was short, fat, and stubble-faced, wearing shabby, wrinkled clothes and giving off, Aline would say, "a strange vibe." He was friendly enough, greeting her with a smile and shaking her hand warmly, but instead of feeling nervous, something about him made her feel afraid. Sergio began by asking her age, and why she wanted to become an artist. Then he asked her to improvise a little scene—just make up something with whatever she had at hand and act it out. Aline had never improv-ed before, but she gamely tried to crack them up by imitating a movie-comedy Indian. Gloria and Sergio sat there stone-faced.

Next, Sergio asked her to sing. Aline launched into the song she had prepared. Thinking she ought to be emotive, she closed her eyes while she sang and furrowed her brow to express suffering. When she finished and opened her eyes, Gloria's and Sergio's faces were still blank: no smile, no sign of approval or disdain. Neither of them said a word. Not sure what to do next, Aline handed Gloria a tape she'd made of "Boomerang." Gloria put it on, and Aline began to dance, hoping raw energy could make up for whatever was lacking in her singing and acting.

As soon as the song ended, Aline says, Sergio made a gesture to Gloria. Apparently understanding what he meant, Gloria led Aline into the room next door and closed the door. "Aline, you know what?" Gloria said. "For part of the audition you're going to have to take off your clothes." Aline couldn't believe what she was hearing. "It's because we have to see which parts of your body are going to need special exercise attention," Gloria continued.

Aline was petrified. This had never happened in *A Chorus Line*. She refused.

"Don't be afraid," Gloria urged. "No one's going to hurt you. The only ones who are going to see you are Sergio and I. And if you want, I'll leave the room."

"No!" Aline said. "He's the one I'm worried about."

"Don't worry about Sergio," Gloria responded. "It's no big deal for him. For him, it's very normal."

"No," Aline repeated, feeling she was about to cry. "I'm not taking off my clothes."

"All right," Gloria said with an exasperated sigh. "Just go out in your bra and panties. Pretend you're in a bathing suit." That was out of the question, even if Aline had agreed—she'd only recently begun wearing bras, and hadn't put one on that day. Could she wear her leotard? Gloria agreed, handed her a towel, and left the room. Aline stripped, slipped into the leotard, and wrapped herself in the towel. When she returned to Sergio's office, he told her to drop the towel. She let it fall. Sergio had her turn sideways, then three-quarters, and then walk across the room. "OK," he said. "Go get dressed."

The audition was over. Aline picked up her towel and went back to the small side room to change out of her leotard. She was still fumbling into her clothes when Gloria burst into the room. "Sergio really likes you!" Gloria told her. "You've got the scholarship!"

"Really?" Aline said. It was amazing: after botching the improv, after leaving them cold with her song and defying their orders to strip, what could she have possibly done to impress them? The entire morning seemed to be one disaster after another, but Sergio, miraculously, was offering her a scholarship anyway.

"But we do have one thing to request," Gloria continued. "Don't tell your mother everything about the audition. You can tell her you sang, and danced, and did that thing about the Indian, but don't tell her I wanted you to take your clothes off. See, for artists that's the most normal thing in the world, but for people in the outside world, especially parents, they just don't understand. . . ." Worst of all, Gloria added, Aline could lose everything if her mother found out. "She's not going to understand, she's not going to let you come to the classes, and you're going to miss out on the opportunity of a lifetime."

Gloria didn't need to say any more. If she truly was hunting for girls to dominate for Sergio's use, she was about to learn that she couldn't have made a better choice. Only minutes earlier, Aline had been mortified by Gloria's demand that she model naked before the man behind the desk. Now, suddenly, her resentment was washed away by a surge of affection. "Gloria seemed the most beautiful person I had even seen," Aline would later recall thinking at that moment. "I was feeling very tender toward her and saw her as a true friend." Years later, Catherine Hardwicke would zero in on precisely that same bewilderingly fast and powerful transfer of adolescent girl affection in her movie *Thirteen*. "One dynamic she really seems to understand is the intensity of girls' friendships during this time," one film reviewer pointed out. "Finding a new best friend is almost like falling in love, the feeling is so intoxicating and all-consuming."

"Intoxicating and all-consuming." And further buttressing Aline's gratitude and adolescent crush was another, more subtle force: She was also experiencing the strange, paradoxical attraction that some people feel toward their tormentors when pressure is applied, then abruptly removed. When subjected to stress, the human mind instinctively searches for another being to bond with, and the successful brainwasher will make

certain that only one option is available. While it may seem bizarre, stress will often cause the victim to be *attracted* to the brainwasher rather than repulsed. Humans, after all, need warmth and attention, and if the captor is the only one in sight, then the emotional surge is misdirected toward him.

"The need for companionship," Denise Winn points out in *The Manipulated Mind*, "doesn't vanish when guard or interrogator is the only one in the room." Quite the opposite—as stress increases, companionship is needed even more, to serve as an emotional buttress. The brainwasher, ironically enough, becomes "a substitute friend," as Winn puts it.

Dr. William Sargant saw the same reaction in his studies of soldiers. As he relates in *Battle for the Mind: A Physiology of Conversion and Brainwashing,* victims often felt great affection for the captors who treated them ruthlessly (Sargant calls this unjustified affection "one of the more horrible consequences" of brainwashing). Cults and religious revivalists employed that technique to create "instant conversions," while Communist captors were especially adept at applying stress to make prisoners of war renounce their homelands.

And at that moment, Gloria must have seen just how effective stress could be at winning over a girl with fantasies of rock stardom.

"So you promise not to say anything?" Gloria asked.

"I promise," Aline said.

Actually, if Aline had stripped, it might have ruined the entire exercise. What was the point of seeing her naked, after all, since her body easily could be evaluated through her short skirt and braless blouse? What couldn't be seen was something far more critical: How would Aline react to commands? In the face of behavior that she disliked and resisted, could she still be converted to secrecy and compliance? In short, how far could Aline be pushed and still be counted on to keep quiet?

This isn't to say that Aline underwent some kind of snap brainwashing, but the circumstances of her audition, as she describes them, were perfectly suited to both test her receptiveness to mental coercion and "nudge" her in that direction. That may be the *real* reason Jossie had to wait in the lobby: It wasn't important to get Aline naked, but it was crucial to get her alone. After all, if Sergio was only interested in sneak peeks at naked girls, he wouldn't have offered the scholarship to the teenager who *refused* to strip, but would have waited till he found one who peeled with pleasure. Obviously nudity wasn't the goal, just the vehicle—if they wanted Aline to feel stress, what better way than to ask a thirteen-year-old in the middle of the audition of a lifetime to strip off her clothes?

In that light, the whole nudity episode can be seen as just the capper in a series of incidents designed to increase Aline's anxieties. The stress was gradually ramped up, in fact, over a period beginning well before the audition. First, Gloria waited more than a week before getting in touch with Aline; then she threw Aline off balance by showing up at the house instead of calling, as promised. She kept the nature of the audition vague, forcing Aline to worry about what she should rehearse. At the audition itself, Aline was isolated, then asked to improvise a scene, depriving her of any firm grounding, such as a script to read from or a fellow actor to work with. She received no reassurance from Sergio and Gloria, just mute stares, which naturally increased the pressure. Even after Aline agreed to drop her towel and display herself in a leotard, Sergio didn't ease her anxiety with any kind of approval. Only when the pressure was at its maximum—when Aline believed she had muffed the audition and was awaiting the verdict—did Gloria pop in and become her "substitute friend."

The result: In an instant, Aline switched her allegiance from the mother she loved to the singer and manager she'd just met. As she drove home with her mother, she was tempted to talk about the nude-modeling requirement and see her mother's reaction. But as quickly as the thought crossed her mind, she rejected it. "I decided to keep the whole thing a secret," Aline says. "A secret between me, Sergio, and Gloria."

x   x   x

The following Tuesday, Jossie picked Aline up after school and dropped her off at 108 Adolfo Prieto for her first day under Sergio's tutelage. Aline would have classes two afternoons a week, shuttling between dance, acting, and "physical expression" teachers. When she arrived, Aline found Sergio's studio filled with young girls, all between the ages of thirteen and eighteen. Gloria, at nineteen, was the oldest. Aline was surprised to see how many of the younger girls looked and dressed just like her: Nearly all the girls were thin, pretty brunettes with long hair and wearing raggedy, gypsy-style apparel. The similar getups weren't merely imitation, Aline would discover—they were actually the same clothes. Sergio's girls seemed to dress from one communal wardrobe, swapping skirts and tights from one day to the next. Mary would show up wearing a particular blouse one morning, and the next day it would be on Gloria.

"That must be part of the artistic life," Aline figured. The hostility, however, was harder to understand. She had classes with four other girls, and even though they were all more or less her age, they would barely speak to her. Mary, who'd been so friendly on the day of her audition, was now giving Aline the cold shoulder. Even Ivette Becerra, whose father picked her up each night and who seemed much less attached to the studio than the other girls, was treating her as an outsider. As for Sergio, Aline was happier that he *wasn't* speaking to her; the way he raged and shouted at the teachers and other students, she was glad he wasn't paying her much attention. He's rude and unbearable, she thought.

The only one who treated her as a friend, in fact, was Gloria. Between classes, she and Gloria would meet to chat—or rather Aline chatted and Gloria peppered her with questions about her family, her school, and her daydreams. In return, Aline brought Gloria little treats from her school vending machine—candy and bags of potato chips. Gloria devoured the snacks so greedily that Aline, newly conscious of her weight in comparison to all the slim young girls in Sergio's classes, also began bringing Gloria her lunch from school. Gloria happily wolfed down the sandwiches and fruit as well. Aline was amazed at her appetite: Wasn't she being fed at home? Gloria said she was living with an aunt on the outskirts of Mexico City, but to Aline she always seemed ravenous, exhausted, and unkempt. "Artists," Aline thought with a shrug.

Gloria never said much about her personal life during her chats with Aline. She said so little, in fact, that for the first week Aline didn't even know Gloria was a singer—she figured Gloria was Sergio's recruiter and personal assistant. If anything, Gloria spoke more about Sergio than she did about herself; Gloria was always marveling at Sergio's genius, his poetry, his bruised, sensitive soul. After a few days of listening to Gloria's praise, Aline had to confide that she couldn't stand Sergio. She respected his accomplishments and was thrilled that he was going to make her a star, but frankly, she thought he was homely and brutish, and his temper was frightening; he even screamed at Gloria.

No, no, Gloria insisted; Sergio had a wonderful, tender side hidden beneath layers of hurt. Once Aline saw his true nature, she'd realize that Sergio was a wonderful man. His temper, Gloria told Aline, was really pain; Gloria said that Sergio had been badly hurt by the women he'd loved. Look at the proof, Gloria said: Sergio was so kindhearted that he was already talking about personally giving Aline voice lessons. "Do you know what kind of honor that would be?" Gloria asked. "He doesn't give classes to *anyone*. If he picks you for private lessons, that means he's ready to make you his next star—just like he's doing with me."

"You're a singer?" Aline asked incredulously. That was the first she'd heard that Gloria was not just a performer, but a talent whom Sergio was saying would become the greatest star he'd ever launched. The way Gloria acted around Sergio, so servile and attentive, always answering him by saying, "Yes, sir," and "As you wish, sir," Aline had assumed she was his personal assistant, not his prized client. But by that summer of 1989, Sergio had landed a multirecord deal for Gloria with BMG. The record company was so excited about Sergio's rough cut of *¿Qué Hago Aquí?* that it was rushing the album into production and planned to release it by that coming fall. Even though Sergio still had Gloria acting as his personal assistant, she was also rehearsing for the TV appearances and concert tours that would begin when her album was launched in a few months.

To answer Aline's question, Gloria popped a tape of "Dr. Psiquiatra" into a Walkman and plopped the headphones over Aline's ears. Wow! The song was fantastic! Aline couldn't believe that a woman who could sing like that, and was about to have a solo album released by a major label, would take the time to pal around with a skinny little kid like her every afternoon. And the best part was, Gloria was saying that Aline could be the next one making a trip to the Los Angeles recording studio!

"That's why I've got to tell you, you're getting your career off to a bad start," Gloria continued.

"Bad?" Aline asked, suddenly fearful. "What am I doing wrong?"

"You really mucked things up when you wouldn't undress at the audition," Gloria said. "It wasn't professional." Gloria kept explaining: Nudity was no big deal in show business—it was all part of performing. It was an important tool for letting the producer understand what he was working with. What was the big deal—hadn't Aline ever seen a naked woman before? She hadn't? Well, in show business, people get undressed around each other all the time. Sergio was the best, because he never overlooked anything—he had to know absolutely everything about Aline, so he could bring out her strongest traits and hide the weakest.

Finally, Aline said, "Okay."

"Great," Gloria said. "We can make up for your audition right now. Get undressed, and I'll go get Sergio."

Aline slowly began taking off her clothes, dreading the moment the door would reopen. What was Sergio going to make her do? How long was this going to last? It was already 7:30 at night—what if her mother arrived just then to pick her up? She stepped out of her clothes and waited, holding a towel in front of herself.

Sergio and Gloria arrived within minutes. Sergio looked her up and down, studying her with the same impassive gaze he'd had during the first audition. He ordered Aline to drop the towel. He kept his eyes riveted on her. Then, just as he had before, he began putting her through paces: He had Aline face the wall, then show her profile, then walk back and forth across the room. His expression never changed, Aline says; throughout the whole thing, Sergio was stone-faced and staring intently.

A few minutes later, Aline slid into the passenger seat of her mother's car. "How were your classes today?" Jossie asked.

"OK," Aline replied quietly.

X   X   X

When she arrived at the studio the next afternoon, Aline felt differently about Sergio. She expected to be ashamed and resentful; instead, she found herself beginning to like him, much the way her feelings toward Gloria had intensified after the first audition.

"The next day, I began to see him differently," Aline says, and in her own fumbling grasp for comprehension, she hits on an astute insight. "Maybe when someone sees you naked, the two of you develop a little bond of complicity. . . . I began to like him and trust him more."

Sergio called her into his private office that day for a chat. He was friendly and interested in hearing more about the kind of career Aline wanted in music. He told her about some of the songs he'd written, and Aline realized she knew many of them. She'd heard them sung by her favorite singers for years, but never knew they were Sergio's. Her awe increased; her *teacher* wrote "Suavemente"? Aline had understood that Sergio was accomplished and influential, but it only dawned on her now that he was intimately connected to the same singers she had fantasized about. It wasn't just that he could make her dreams come true—in a way, he'd already been in them.

Nearly every afternoon after that, Sergio would find time to pull Aline aside and shoot the breeze for a while. The other girls, Aline says, were quick to notice her special treatment and became even more hostile than before. Gloria, however, thought it was great. While Gloria was eating Aline's lunch one day, she mentioned again how much Sergio had been hurt by women in the past and said it was wonderful that someone like Aline was around to boost his spirits. Gloria said Sergio's heart had once been badly broken, and he'd never gotten over it. It had happened nearly ten years ago, Gloria told her, when Sergio was twenty-seven years old and had fallen in love with a very young singer who, Gloria noted, was the same age then as Aline was now. Sergio and the girl managed to keep their romance secret for a while, but eventually the girl's brother overheard a phone conversation and told their parents. The parents' fury was bad enough, but what really broke Sergio's heart, Gloria said, was the girl's reaction: Confronted by her parents, the girl blamed everything on Sergio. According to Gloria, Aline says, Sergio expected the girl to declare her love for Sergio, and when she didn't, he lost all trust in women forever—overlooking the fact that a thirteen-year-old's shame and fear are hardly the standards by which to measure a mature adult relationship.

Since then, Gloria went on, Sergio hadn't been able to find a love to take her place. Gloria should know, she confessed; she'd been in love with Sergio herself. Aline couldn't believe it—this beautiful, magnetic teenager in love with this ugly, foul-tempered, middle-aged man? Oh yes, Gloria assured her. And how about Aline—was she getting a crush on Sergio, too? Aline couldn't believe Gloria was serious: Sergio was thirty-three and Aline was only thirteen. She'd never had a boyfriend; the closest she'd come to any kind of intimacy was kissing the Michael Jackson poster in her bedroom.

But for the next few days, Aline kept pondering that story about Sergio and the young singer. She thought about Gloria's crazy idea, that Aline might be the girl Sergio had been searching for. She would never do it, of course, but Aline couldn't help wondering what it would be like to be the girlfriend of the great Sergio Andrade, to be on stage singing songs he'd written especially for her. One day in school, she found she'd written Sergio's name all over her notebook.

A few days later, Sergio had brought Aline into his office and had her sit next to him at the piano. He'd just written a new song, he told her, and she'd be the first to hear it. *"Tengo tanto miedo de perderte, antes de poder tenerte,"* he sang. *"Me da miedo que no me hagas caso, y no doy el primer paso."* ("I'm so afraid of losing you, before I've even won you. I'm afraid you won't approve, so I never make the first move.") As he sang, Sergio kept his eyes closed, never looking at Aline. *"Y me quedo contemplándote de lejos,"* he crooned, *"porque no domino el miedo, que me llena el corazón."* ("And so we remain a distance apart, because I can't conquer the fear that fills my heart.")

"I had goose bumps," Aline says. She knew Sergio had written the song for her, and she wanted to show how much she appreciated it. But when Aline asked if she could sing it for her vocal arts exam in a few days, Sergio refused. He didn't just hand his songs over to anyone, he told her brusquely. Aline was seized with embarrassment; she was so ashamed, she recalled later, that she felt just as she had "years ago," as she puts it, "when my father scolded me or spanked me for getting into mischief." Flushed, not knowing if she was resisting a lecher or wounding a saint, she apologized and left the office. Sergio remained silent.

Afterward, Aline tumbled through a series of emotions strikingly similar to the effects of mental coercion. She was "anguished and confused"; she felt worthless and insignificant ("He made it clear that I meant nothing to him"); she was tormented by guilt and felt a compulsion to confess—but since she was afraid to discuss it with her mother and too embarrassed to tell her friends, Aline was cut off from clarifying her feelings with anyone. Anyone, that is, except Gloria. "I needed to confess my feelings to Gloria," Aline says.

Gloria, Aline says, urged her to explore her feelings: If Aline was upset with herself for how she reacted to Sergio, it must mean she was attracted to him at some level. "Go talk to him," Gloria encouraged. "He's *lo maximo*, the best." Aline followed Gloria's advice and went to Sergio's office. He remained seated behind his desk while Aline stood in front of him like a misbehaving pupil and stammered out her thoughts. "It's like, things are happening to me that I've never experienced before," she said. "I'll be very happy, and all of a sudden I'll be sad. . . . This all probably sounds silly to you, but—"

Sergio interrupted, asking who was the lucky man causing her confusion.

"You," Aline whispered.

For a long time, Sergio was silent. Finally, he looked up at her and said, "Are you sure you know what you're saying?"

"I think I do," the thirteen-year-old answered.

"Think about it," he warned her. "I'm a man who has suffered, and I don't want you toying with me." But before Aline could answer, Sergio walked over to the piano and began playing *"Hablando de amor,"* the song that had given Aline goose bumps. When he finished, Sergio confirmed what she'd suspected. "That song was written for you," he said. Then he walked over and kissed her. It was the first time Aline had ever been kissed, she would later claim. Abruptly, Sergio broke off the kiss and walked back to his desk. "Mary!" he shouted. Mary Boquitas came through the door moments later. Sergio ordered her to take his car and drive Aline home. Aline was confused—was she being thrown out again? Only afterward would she realized what that meant: As of that moment, she was Sergio's, so he would decide how and when she would go home.

Two weeks later, Sergio had sex with Aline on his piano bench. They'd been casually chatting in his office after Aline's afternoon classes when Sergio, as he often did, asked Aline if she loved him. "I do love you, Sergio," said Aline, who'd gotten accustomed to the question and was over any shyness she'd had about answering it. But she wasn't ready for what Sergio had in mind next: This time, Sergio told her, she'd need to prove it with a test. He was going to leave the room; when he came back in, he'd know Aline truly loved him if he found her sitting naked at the piano. If she wasn't willing to show him her body, he explained, then he'd know she wasn't willing to open her heart.

Without another word, he got up and left the room. Aline thought he was joking and waited for Sergio to pop his head back in the room with a big "gotcha!" grin on his face. But as the minutes ticked by, Aline began wondering if he was serious . . . and how hurt he'd be if she failed his test of "love and sincerity." Aline was already too familiar with Sergio's dark pouts and icy silences, and she didn't want to feel the misery again of having him shut her out like that. On the other hand, the office door was unlocked—what if she stripped and one of the girls burst in? What if Gloria came in—or her *mother!* Her mother was due to pick her up any minute!

When Sergio reentered the room, he found Aline sitting where he'd told her to, on the piano bench. She was crimson-faced and naked. Sergio closed the door and smiled. He slid onto the bench beside her and began to caress her. Aline "was like a statue," she says, frozen with fear and embarrassment. She was still shocked and rigid when Sergio lifted her and laid her down on the piano bench. It was all part of a test, he told her, a test of her truth and sincerity. When Sergio penetrated, Aline says, she burst into tears. On the ride home with her mother, she was silent. Jossie had noticed Aline's increasing moodiness, but since they'd always been so close, she knew Aline would never keep something serious from her.

Sex, Aline soon discovered, wouldn't be her only test. Sergio began studying Aline's daily behavior and ranking it, hour by hour, as an indicator of her love and sincerity. How she was dressed, the way she greeted Sergio, what time she showed up for her classes—all these and many more were "tests of love," and if Aline failed to measure up in any of them, she got a demerit. "These tests kept getting more and more difficult," Aline says. "Not just to execute, but to understand." If she wore too much makeup, she failed for looking like a tramp; too little, and she failed for not making herself pretty for Sergio.

One afternoon Sergio informed Aline that she'd acquired far too many demerits. As Aline was apologizing in the way Sergio had taught her—dropping to her knees and begging his pardon—he began slipping off his belt. He'd once told her that the day would come when she'd deserve a beating, but Aline had never believed he'd actually whip her. Now, seeing his belt come off, Aline became terrified. "No, Sergio, please!" she implored him. "Please don't hit me!" Before she could finish, he'd begun slapping her with the belt. The more she pleaded, the more he whipped her.

When she got home, Aline had such painful welts on her bottom, she couldn't sit down. She went right to her room, complaining of a headache. Again, Jossie was a bit concerned about how anxious and moody Aline had become since she'd started her after-school star studies. But she just put it down to normal adolescent mopiness: After all, Aline was now thirteen.

Once the shock at her beating wore off, Aline began to think that Sergio might have been right. He'd said it was for her own good, that she needed discipline and punishment if she was going to mature and learn. She shouldn't feel bad about it, Sergio said; he treated Gloria and Mary the same way. If he didn't care about them, he went on, he wouldn't take the trouble. In a way, Aline thought, it made sense: it's exactly what her father would have told her.

Aline had never had a boyfriend, so she took Sergio's word when he explained that scrutiny and anxiety were all part of a healthy, grown-up love affair. But when he got to the part about sex with multiple women, even Aline knew something wasn't right. Actually, it was Gloria who first brought it up. She'd dropped by Aline's house one afternoon, as she had regularly since Aline's incident with Sergio on the piano bench. Her visits were flattering, but a little odd. Gloria was extremely busy at that time, since she'd begun performing in clubs in preparation for her album release. Her live shows were so popular, the buzz about her was already spreading across Mexico. Even before she had radio play or a record to sell, she was becoming an underground celebrity. Still, with all the shows she was putting on and her studio preparation, Gloria still found time to drop in on Aline—always unannounced. Aline loved to see her, but she began to suspect that Gloria was there on Sergio's orders, making sure she wasn't seeing other boys and hadn't told her mother what was going on at the studio.

It was during one of those impromptu visits, while Gloria and Aline were lounging in Aline's room, that Gloria began talking about how wonderful it was to be Sergio's girlfriend. Aline nodded in agreement until she realized that Gloria wasn't talking about Aline but about herself. Yes, she assured Aline, she was romantically involved with Sergio as well. Hadn't Aline realized? Aline was stunned. The next day, she asked Sergio if it was true. Instead of answering, he called in Gloria and Mary. They arrived quickly and stood on either side of him, as if they knew why they were there and exactly what he was going to say.

"If you truly love me, and you want to remain with me," Sergio told Aline, "then you have to accept me with them. Because Gloria and Mary arrived before you, and they're very important to me. You choose." This, as Aline would later recall in her memoir, was the moment when everything began to click into place for her. Though nothing had been said about it, she suddenly understood why so many girls in the studio were sharing each other's clothes and why they'd eyed her so competitively from the moment she'd first come through the door. It also dawned on her that Gloria had lied to her about failing to win over Sergio and about living with some aunt on the outskirts of Mexico City. That's why Gloria always seemed to be at the studio, day and night, and was always dressed in stained, rumpled, passed-around clothes: She and Mary were living there, along with who knew how many other girls, so they'd always be at Sergio's command. The one thing Aline had been right about was her impression that Gloria worked for Sergio as a recruiter. She was a recruiter all right, Aline realized, but not for talent.

All that snapped into focus when she heard Sergio's ultimatum and stared at Gloria and Mary flanking his chair like a pair of lieutenants. Aline could see it all now, and she realized this was the moment to get out. The thought flashed through her mind that she didn't want to be standing beside his chair like Gloria and Mary. And then, Aline says, Gloria and Mary spoke up. Sergio ordered them to tell Aline everything he'd done for them.

"You've fed us," Mary began. "And you taught us so much."

"But you never gave us anything for our birthdays, like you did for Aline," Gloria interjected, her voice both hurt and astonished, as if to ask, "How could Aline be so ungrateful?"

"You even wrote a song for her," Mary added, sounding just as wounded as Gloria. Soon Mary and Gloria were in tears, weeping about how much more Sergio had shown his love to Aline than he had to them. Within moments, Aline was weeping along with them, "like three Mary Magdalenes," Aline says. And once again, in a moment of extreme stress and confusion, Aline felt her affection for Gloria growing. Mary and Gloria seemed "so lonely, so unprotected and desperate for affection," Aline says. Instead of making Aline feel like a victim, they'd somehow made this thirteen-year-old girl who'd recently been pushed into sex on a piano bench feel like she was the most powerful woman in the room.

And so, weeping with love for her two friends, she agreed to stay a little longer and try to make this strange relationship work. Besides, she had to admit that Sergio kept his word: Gloria was beginning to take the country by storm, and Aline was right by her side, just as Sergio had promised.

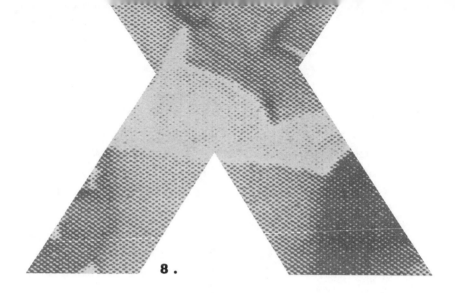

8 .

Song of the She-Beast

"Throw that skinny bitch off stage!"

The hecklers were shitfaced and in full voice as Gloria tried to get through her first song in a small, seedy bar in Mexico City. The louder she sang, the more the crowd screamed for her to shut up. As Gloria describes that night in her memoir, the crowd backed its abuse with action, first pelting her with the lemons from their drink glasses, then with the glasses themselves. It was humiliating, not to mention dangerous. To Sergio, however, it was perfect: You couldn't buy that training for the kind of star he wanted Gloria to be.

A few days earlier, Sergio had called together everyone in the studio. He had both news and marching orders. The news: BMG was about to set a launch date for *¿Que Hago Aquí?* The marching orders: Everyone in the studio, from secretaries to singers, was as of that moment a full-time concert promoter. Sergio wanted them all to hit the streets and find places for Gloria to sing; bars, restaurants, strip clubs, he didn't care, as long as they gave her a mike and put her on stage. "It doesn't matter where, it doesn't matter what they pay, it doesn't matter what hours they make her work," he told them. Once her album hit the shelves, Gloria had to be ready to make a sensation, and the way Sergio looked at it, there was no better training for her than trying to capture an audience who didn't even know who she was.

That's why, on this night, the aspiring diva was in this dive fighting off an angry mob of drunks. The worst part was, Gloria didn't even know the kinds of songs that might catch their interest and shut them up. Other than her meager Boquitas repertoire, just about the only songs she knew were the still unreleased tunes she'd written herself, and there was no way this beer-deafened crowd was going to listen to anything except their most familiar favorites.

"OK, OK," Gloria said. "Do you want me to leave?"

"YESSSSS!" the crowd shouted.

"Well . . ." Gloria said, "GO FUCK YOUR MOTHERS!" And then, since she figured they were going to boo her off stage anyway, she might as well sing what she wanted. She launched into "Dr. Psiquiatra," shouting rather than singing the verses. To hell with them, she thought. While hollering the lyrics, Gloria scooped up fistfuls of the soggy garbage they'd hurled at her—the lemon rinds and wadded napkins and broken drink glasses—and flung it back into the audience. She grabbed a can of soda and doused everyone she could reach. As soon as she finished the song, Gloria bounded off stage before the crowd could mount a counter-attack. She could hear them roaring behind her as the bar owner hurried over. "You were fantastic!" he gushed. "You were the first newcomer they didn't destroy!" The chaos behind her, she now realized, was the once-hostile audience calling for an encore.

Word began to spread about this crazy little beauty with her ripped stockings and tousled hair, coming on stage looking like she'd been in a street fight and acting like she'd start one if the audience didn't bow down and adore her. She was the anti-Boquita, which is exactly what Sergio wanted. Sergio did not repeat mistakes—in his professional life, at least—and he'd seen what happened when he tried to play down his performers' raw sex appeal. He'd packaged the Boquitas as serious musicians and they'd flamed out in months. This time Sergio was going to make Gloria's spontaneity the key to her appeal, and the best way to hone

that—perhaps the only way—was by casting her into the most challenging, unpredictable settings he could find.

Sergio was doing grunge before it had a name, but for him it was more
of a deliberate training program than an organic musical style. He left
nothing to chance when it came to recording—Gloria's songs had been
expertly arranged and painstakingly mastered in the studio—but when it
came to live shows, he sent her out with the minimum possible polish. Her
costumes were pieced together according to her whim that day; her road
crew would often be no more than Mary with a camcorder; her accompa-
niment ranged from slapdash house bands to a screechy boom box; her
playlist often included pop hits she'd learned just that afternoon.

Gloria was so unaccustomed to singing with a live band (she'd only
taken lead vocals on one song with the Boquitas) that in her first solo
show she couldn't figure out who was supposed to end the song, she or the
band. She kept singing "Tristeza" over and over, waiting for the band to
fade out; the band, meanwhile, was awaiting her cue for the last chord.
After forty-five minutes of the same song, the sweat-soaked audience had
quit the dance floor and Gloria's voice was cracking. Finally, in mid-
verse, she just stopped. The audience burst into wild applause, Gloria recalls, "but more out of relief than appreciation."

Her public blunders made for a demeaning and nerve-racking appren-
ticeship, but at least they were grabbing some attention. Gloria was becoming a name at lots of small, windowless, grungy bars; still, she knew
she was better known as a sideshow attraction than a serious songwriter
and performer. Everyone who heard about "La Trevi" wanted to see
what kind of trouble this she-beast in stockings would stir up next. That
was fine with her; Gloria accepted her notoriety with lighthearted irony,
even drawing a cartoon that depicted her as a smiling carnival freak: In
her sketch, she's a cow with an extra leg, next to the caption, *"Pásele a ver
la vaca de cinco patas"* ("Step right up to see the five-hooved cow").

On another night, Sergio got an offer to have Gloria sing in a dollar-a-
dance nightclub, the kind that has largely disappeared from the United
States, but is still popular with single men in Latin America and U.S. border towns. With this crowd, there was no illusion that they were interested in anything except getting a look at a scandalously dressed teenager

and her rumored antics. Sergio shocked even his five-legged cow by accepting the gig. For the first time, Gloria was the most modestly dressed woman in the place. She did her set and was surprised at the warm applause. She was a little less surprised later, when most of the men in the audience offered to pay her to dance. The club owner thought that with a little work she might have a future. "Dress a little more sexy," he told her, "and you could be a hit here."

The lesson from those performances wasn't lost on Gloria, which is exactly the reason Sergio wanted her out of the rehearsal studio and into the line of fire. With the music market overloaded with female soloists, Gloria needed to continually field-test her stage act to see what kinds of stunts would spark a reaction from seen-it-all audiences—and she had to do it before anyone knew who "Gloria Trevi" was. There wouldn't be time to experiment once her album was released: If audiences weren't wild about her in the first month, her promotional money would vanish as fast as her radio air time. That's why, despite the intelligence of her songwriting and her insistence on the title *"artista"* (she never refers to herself as anything else), Gloria was as committed to creating a marketable image as she was to music. Much would later be said about her spontaneity and the brilliance of her onstage improvisation, but whenever some whim of hers worked, it immediately became a scripted part of her "spontaneous" routine. No performance of "Dr. Psiquiatra" was ever complete again without a spewing can of soda.

Finally, in December 1989, BMG started shipping *¿Qué Hago Aquí?* to record stores and radio stations. Gloria had been performing at a grueling pace for months, often sleeping only four hours a night between shows, but as soon as her songs hit the airwaves, she stepped it up even further, appearing at any promotion Sergio could arrange or any festival that would give her stage time. Soon, "Dr. Psiquiatra" was getting airplay and climbing the charts. Within a week, it was No. 5 nationwide.

Not only was Gloria creating buzz in her own right, but her emergence marked the comeback of Mr. Midas. No one really knew why he'd dropped out of the music business; there had been plenty of whispers, of course, but no talkers. In a pattern that would be repeated even after Sergio was arrested, most of the people involved in his scandals preferred to duck publicity rather than tell their tales. Of course, the music beat reporters didn't believe Sergio's story about a "reading, resting, and traveling" sabbatical (as no business writer believes it when a slumping corporate executive suddenly decides to "spend more time with his family"), but once the rumors died down, they were happy to welcome him back. After all, Sergio might disappear, but he never disappointed.

Consequently, reporters began flocking to Gloria's shows. Although she'd never finished high school and had spent the previous three years in virtual isolation, Gloria turned out to have a natural flair for handling both her new celebrity and a barrage of media inquiries. The same techniques she'd developed to captivate a big audience were also extremely effective in a one-to-one setting. She found she could win over a reporter by making eye contact, offering a fresh and unexpected twist on her standard performance, and feigning intense, personal attention. The same skills that made every fan in a ten-thousand-seat auditorium believe Gloria was singing directly to him were just as good at convincing reporters that they were suddenly Gloria's newest, closest friends. Not surprisingly, many articles about Gloria, even after the scandals began leaking out, are surprisingly affectionate. Her enduring popularity with the press extended, by association, to Sergio. What better character reference could a suspected statutory rapist have than this champion of girls' rights?

But the most important device Gloria learned was the old magician's trick of getting reporters to look where *she* wanted them to look. This was especially useful for diverting sticky questions about where Gloria had been for the past three years or about Sergio's past and all the young girls now flowing in and out of his star academy. Gloria learned she could take charge of an interview right from the start by offering a juicy, compelling little anecdote that had the air of confession. If she made the reporters' job easier by feeding them a tale they could use to beef up an article, the reporters wouldn't make their jobs harder by checking to see if it was true. For instance, even though "Dr. Psiquiatra" is about a young woman being ogled by her psychiatrist, Gloria somehow convinced the *Los Angeles Times* that it was inspired by a wild, Dr. Doolittle-esque escapade she had engineered before moving to Mexico City. "The album's first hit, 'Dr. Psiquiatra' ('Dr. Psychiatrist'), was inspired by one of her final acts before leaving Monterrey: the spontaneous liberation of lab animals slated for dissection in her ninth-grade biology class," the *L.A. Times* reported after an interview with Gloria. Portraying herself as the Comandante X of the classroom, Gloria convinced the reporter that as a fourteen-year-old she'd told her school principal, "You're teaching sadism to children. Why don't you make a how-to video instead?" It was a great story that perfectly suited a rebel belle–themed article. Why would a reporter make life difficult by trying to verify it with the principal?

With Gloria supplying a steady stream of controversy and colorful stories, she soon became a media favorite. All the press she was getting, meanwhile, fueled record sales that were far beyond BMG's best expectations. BMG had to ramp up production furiously; unsure how this raw newcomer would fare with her self-written songs and self-produced album, the company had only pressed thirty thousand albums, and they were sold out in days. The record stores were begging to be resupplied, because word had just gotten out: Gloria had just been invited to appear on *Siempre en Domingo*. If she pulled off a decent performance, sales would go through the roof.

"I couldn't believe it!" Aline says. "My fairy godmother, my friend, my sister was going to appear on *Siempre en Domingo*! Who knew how many millions of people in Europe and all of Latin America were going to see her. . . ." And Aline would be right there with her. She went backstage with Gloria to help her dress, then she and Sergio watched from the wings, wide-eyed, as Gloria went running out and, as Aline put it, "ate the stage." Even Aline was astonished by what came over Gloria, wondering for a few moments whether Gloria really had gone berserk from pressure and exhaustion. Gloria was gyrating around so wildly, the spotlight couldn't stay with her. Several times she leapt completely out of camera range.

I'm not crazy, I'm not crazy,
I'm just desperate.

"Are you crazy?" Raúl Velasco asked a panting Gloria when she'd finished. "Crazy for real?"

"No," Gloria responded. "Just desperate."

Raúl Velasco didn't know where this was going. She should have just come back with something safe and sincere-sounding, like "I've known girls with problems and this song is based on their experiences, not mine." But he played along with the improv. "Desperate?" he asked. "Desperate for what?"

"To be happy, to sing, to . . . to . . . to grab your glasses!" Gloria shouted, and she snatched them from his face. Raúl Velasco stood there stunned, blushing and blinking on live TV. Behind him, Gloria could see the faces of the production crew: They were aghast. She began to suspect that this time she might have gone too far, humiliating Mr. Sunday Night before a multinational audience of millions. But once Raúl Velasco recovered his poise, he snapped to the same realization that had made Gloria such a hit among five-legged-cow-loving bar owners across Mexico: This kind of sexy spontaneity was audience magic. As soon as he recovered his composure, and his glasses, Raúl Velasco immediately invited Gloria to come back for the next week's show—an invitation that was quickly withdrawn as soon as The Tiger heard about it.

But The Tiger could growl all he wanted—it didn't matter to Gloria. After her smash performance on *Siempre en Domingo,* Gloria was in demand all over the country. She was a headliner now, and no longer a bar singer with a boom box and a microphone, so Sergio quickly put together a full-scale road crew and began to mobilize. This was Mr. Midas at his best: Once he spotted a trend or got a sense that one of his singers was hot, he knew how to catch hold of the momentum and turn a popular tune into a nationwide hit. He immediately hired musicians and coached them into Gloria's full-time band, and made Aline and Mary, who already knew Gloria's songs and dance moves by heart, into her backup singers.

Actually, Aline says, the backup singer story was initially just a ruse to deceive her mother. Sergio wanted to have Aline to himself on the weekends, and what better way to sweep her off to a hotel than by claiming she was needed on tour with the country's No. 1 singing sensation? But Aline was eager for her chance in the spotlight, and it wasn't long before Sergio gave her a shot, putting her in hot pants and sending her on stage with a tambourine. Her mother wasn't too happy about all the late nights and weekend trips, Aline says, but she was placated by Sergio's good manners and his personal assurances that he'd care for Aline like a daughter.

Jossie's relationship with Aline had never been worse; it seemed they squabbled more than they spoke. Whenever she wasn't off with Sergio or alone in her room, Aline was flaunting Gloria's fame as if it were a down-payment on her own self-esteem and independence. "See?" Aline would say. "Everything Sergio promised is coming true. Glora is famous, she's getting interviewed and appearing on the radio all over the place. And the same thing is going to happen to me, because Sergio told me the very next record he's going to produce is going to be mine." And Sergio made sure Aline never forgot it. On the wall behind his desk he had an enormous calendar marked with concert and recording dates. He'd penciled in a date to record Aline's album, Aline says, but every time she did something to displease him, he crossed it out and moved it back another few days or weeks, depending on the offense.

These punitive postponements were heartbreakingly frustrating for Aline, especially since she rarely understood what she'd done wrong or how she could have avoided it. The more confused and frustrated Aline became, the more she blamed her mother. She couldn't blame Sergio, since he was the one who was disappointed, and she couldn't blame her-self, since she was trying so hard to please him. That left Jossie as the one who was constantly getting between Aline and Sergio—at least, to Aline's thinking. Bit by bit, Aline was destroying the relationship she had with her mother to seize the one offered by Sergio. "At this moment, I hated my mother," Aline would later explain. "I saw her as my worst enemy."

But even Jossie hadn't realized how estranged her daughter had be-come until Aline refused to have a *"quinceañera"* ball—the grand birth-day for fifteen-year-olds, the Latin equivalent of a bat mitzvah, complete with ball gowns and tuxedos and a lavish meal. Jossie had already begun planning Aline's *quinceañera* and was stunned when Aline said she wasn't interested. Aline kept her reason to herself: Sergio didn't want her danc-ing with boys at the party, so he pressed her to have it called off. Then

Aline informed her mother that she would be missing the family vacation in Acapulco so she could stay with Gloria and rehearse. Jossie became so enraged at Aline's defiance that she lost her temper and slapped her daughter, right in the middle of Sergio's waiting room. Sergio quickly interceded. He was so kind and calming, he managed to turn the fight to his advantage. First, he told Aline that she should never, ever disrespect her mother . . . and then, gently, he explained to Jossie what a crucial moment this was in Aline's artistic development. Even though Sergio's secret demands on Aline were causing the rift with her family, in Jossie's eyes he was a good influence on Aline and a benevolent godfather.

Of course, Aline wasn't telling her mother about the less appealing side of her "artistic development": Sergio's insistence on sex, including occasional group sex with Gloria. "The only thing I didn't like about those trips," Aline confides in her memoir, "is what, inevitably, had to happen after each show, when we got back to the hotel long after midnight. Since I always stayed in Sergio's room . . . he'd want to make love to me. He did it, even though I couldn't stand it. It hurt me, a lot. And if that wasn't bad enough," Aline adds, "sometimes it would occur to him to have Gloria join us." That is all Aline would ever say about what happened in bed between her and Gloria; when questioned for details, she would look away and bitterly say, "Imagine for yourself." For a week at a time, the now fourteen-year-old Aline would be on the road with Gloria and her band, thrilling to the applause as Gloria's backup singer, but dreading her return to the hotel in the early morning.

Sergio didn't just dominate Aline in private, with sex and beatings. He also belittled her in public, especially around the other girls in the studio. He nicknamed her "The Camel," probably because of her height and thin, slightly oval face, but it also carried the connotation that Aline was a dumb beast at Sergio's service. It was a terribly embarrassing taunt for a girl who was already self-conscious about her gangly adolescence, but Aline tried to laugh along—even after Sergio placed an ad in the paper reading, "Dromedary camel for sale." Sergio and the other girls were in hysterics all afternoon when callers rang up to ask about the camel. But no matter how badly Sergio made Aline feel about herself, it only intensified how she felt about him. "Despite all the bad parts, all the punishments and humiliation, I adored him," Aline would later say.

It's startling how much Aline's seduction was evolving into a warped version of the prototypical teen escape fantasy. Cintra Wilson, the playwright and cultural critic, examines this iconic desire in her essay "Cock Rock for the Twelve-and-Under: Little Girls and the Unhealthy Way They Love." Wilson zeroes in on the same ego-teetering moment in a young woman's life as Erik Erikson and filmmaker Catherine Hardwicke, yet narrows her focus even further, examining how pop music is specifically marketed to exploit the insecurities of adolescent females. Although her essay was written in 1999, ten years after Aline arrived at 108 Adolfo Prieto Street, it matches Sergio's interaction with Aline so uncannily, he could have used it as a dating guide.

Wilson writes:

Preteen girls want two things: a crazed amount of unwarranted, worshipful attention, and something ridiculously exciting and magical to happen to them suddenly, which would enable them to turn sneering and tall towards their ignorant parents and various preteen enemies and have them all shudder with the recognition that they were critically, mortally wrong in underestimating the preteen girl, and that they will now Pay.

And who will provide that magic? "The teen pop phenomenon." As Wilson describes in half-farcical terms, the fantasy plays out this way: The pop phenom

spirits the girl away from her horrible parents (who die, tragically and bizarrely, soon afterward, leaving the girl with no governing mechanism whatsoever) and establishes an indelible love contract with her, which involves performing songs about her, songs from poems she's written, and even possibly discovering the girl's uncanny singing and tambourine talents. The girl and boy star then live happily ever after, deeply in love, modeling together on the cover of all magazines, and they can buy everything they want, forever, and nobody can tell them what to do.

But just wishing to be swept away by a pop idol isn't enough to make any sane young woman do something self-destructive or irrational, especially not a bright, relatively self-assured girl like Aline. Or is it? Anyone doubting the feverish intensity and logic-override power of a pop idol fantasy should note the audience reaction of any early Beatles, Frank Sinatra, or New Kids on the Block concert.

Sergio was no Ricky Martin, but he'd found a way to turn his seduction of Aline into the perfect teen-girl-escape-fantasy-come-true. Already Sergio had offered Aline wealth, international stardom, and a special identity (albeit shared) as one of Sergio's Girls. At exactly the moment in Aline's life when she was young enough to believe in her fantasies, yet old enough to act on them, Sergio arrived to make them seem real.

Sergio's timing and his technique couldn't have been better, or a coincidence: Years later, nearly every step he followed in the seduction of Aline would also appear in criminal charges filed against him on behalf of other teen girls. It's almost uncanny how perfectly Sergio understood teen girl fantasies and discovered how to exploit them. But perhaps it's not so strange; after all, he had Gloria and Mary Boquitas—two lost, lonely teens—as his constant advisers.

X   X   X

Bat-a-bat-a-batta-bat!

The drummer chattered off a volley, the lights dropped, a spotlight beamed dead center on the stage, and the guitars picked up the rhythm of "Gloria," The Doors' version. The three backup singers—Aline, Mary, and Saraí, one of the new girls—leaned into their mikes and chanted "G!...L!...O!...R!...I!..."

Gloria leaped into the spotlight, a frenzied blur of angry hair and ruined clothes, fighting the air with her fists as she screeched: *"GLOOOOORRRRRIIIIAAAAA!"*

"G . . . L . . ."

Gloria was down on her knees, tearing at her shirt, looking like she was delusional with fever and ready to rip off her clothes, screaming: *"GLOOOOORRRRRIIIIAAAAA!"*

That was usually the calmest moment of the night. Gloria's shows would start around 9:00 and go until 1:00 A.M. . . . 2:00 A.M. . . . until either she or the roaring crowd was hoarsed into silence. By the end of its first week on sale, *¿Qué Hago Aquí?* was No. 1 in the charts, and concert promoters throughout the country were calling Sergio every day, promising to fill any venue he wanted, for as many shows as he wanted, on any night they could get the new Mexican sensation. Two million copies of the album would be sold, and wherever she performed, Gloria was selling out the house.

After she croaked out her last encore of the night, Gloria would collapse in the arms of her roadies. "Because of the way I sang, danced, and ran around, I'd finish the show soaked in sweat and Coca-Cola," Gloria would say. "Security crews would rush me off in their arms, with barely any clothes on, since my skirts, shirts, jackets, and nylons were torn apart, victims of my desperation and tantrums." She'd be hustled through the back of the arena and directly outside without changing: They'd learned that if Gloria didn't vacate the premises immediately, the police would have to battle her way out. Fans would pour out of the concert hall and swarm every car in sight, blocking all the exit streets as they searched for a glimpse of Gloria. Often police would surreptitiously escort Gloria into an ambulance and slip her out under police guard.

During these early shows, Gloria developed what would become her signature routine: She'd kneel and croon to the closest muscled hunk in the audience, then pull him on stage. As he stood there, thrilled and a bit confused, Gloria would dance and rub up against him, bit by bit easing him out of his shirt. She would continue playing out the seduction scene, convincing him to step out of his pants. But once she had her victim down to his underwear, Gloria would grab his belt and start lashing at his back. Then, after she'd abused and embarrassed him, she'd push him down until he was lying on his back on the stage and press her body against him, miming sex. If he tried to flee before Gloria allowed him, she'd grab him by the shorts; she was running the show, so leaving before she permitted would cost the last shreds of both his dignity and underwear.

"I love to see men in the role of women," Gloria explained to a reporter for *Más* magazine. "I love to see the look on their faces when I push them to the floor. When they feel like little women about to be raped. They have this expression on their face of 'No, no, no!'" Of course, this act was no longer a surprise after a few performances, but Gloria had no trouble finding men to play along with her rape fantasy. "I think that when guys are in our position, the roles are reversed," she continued, suggesting that excessively macho men really savored the experience of a little submission. "Now it's the man who's on the bottom. And me, a woman, is stripping off his clothes. A woman seducing them, and trapping them. Sometimes I take off their belts and whack them, because many times they've been guilty of beating women. The next time they're with a girl, I bet they'll be a lot sweeter—because now they know how they feel."

Critics quickly pointed out that Gloria's claim of striking a blow for women's rights was preposterous: If her goal was to teach humility, they said, it's doubtful that any man who had just been publicly humiliated by a woman would feel more kindly toward his wife. OK, Gloria said—in that case, maybe I'm just putting on a peep show for the ladies. "I do it because, number one, I like it," she retorted. "And two, because it amuses me. Besides, it gives the girls an eyeful. They get to see a naked guy on stage."

Looking back, the real question is whether this onstage whipping routine was actually inspired by what Gloria experienced every day in Sergio's studio or, even more bizarrely, was stage-choreographed by Sergio himself. The belt lashings, the humiliation, the physical domination of a defenseless person—all this, according to Aline's memoir, was exactly what Sergio was doing to his teen girl protégés.

It was strange that in all the scandalous buzz surrounding Gloria's behavior one key question was lost: No one asked Gloria just how she knew that women are often whipped with men's belts and suffer spousal rape. No one seemed to wonder how a teenager from a middle-class family seemed so knowledgeable about domestic abuse. Had she suffered this personally? Had her mother been beaten? Did she know girlfriends or relatives who'd been abused? Instead, the debate focused on whether the routine was "proper" or "improper," and whether Gloria was helping women or hurting them by carrying on this way. Undeniably, domestic abuse is a widespread horror; anecdotally, it's considered particularly prevalent in Latin America. But the question lingers: Was it just a coincidence that Gloria's performances so eerily mirrored Aline's account of what Gloria and the other girls were personally experiencing at Sergio's hands? Gloria seemed very certain that men lash the women in their lives with their belts—perhaps, from the perspective of Sergio's star academy, she truly did have reason to know.

Perhaps the hidden world of 108 Adolfo Prieto Street was being acted out before the eyes of millions of her fans. Already Gloria had written two new songs secretly based on her troubles with Sergio and Aline, and now those troubles might be creeping into her stage expression as well. No one would know—except the three teenage girls chanting out the letters of her name and the obese, silent man watching from the wings with his arms folded.

By the summer of 1990—barely six months after Gloria's star-turning moment on *Siempre en Domingo*—Sergio was getting anxious. Three of Gloria's songs held the top three positions in the charts and her popularity was soaring by the day, but Sergio knew how fast that could end. She was playing a dangerous marketing game by relying so much on her looks, style, and charisma—at any moment, another sensation could come along with hotter looks, a funkier new style, and at least as much charm (no matter how extreme the worst-case scenario, it was impossible to imagine anyone beating Gloria in the personality category). Sergio also knew that imitation could halt Gloria's trajectory just as quickly: If Gloria started a fad of Trevi copycat singers, it wouldn't be long before TV and the fan mags became gutted with wild-haired look-alikes in torn clothes, all of them diluting Gloria's image and siphoning off her fan base. In a week Gloria could become "one of " instead of "the one."

Like Madonna, Gloria would have to constantly renew her image before her fans had adjusted to the old one. Sergio had to make sure there would always be more Gloria news—and especially more Gloria products on sale. He had plans for a Gloria comic, which she'd draw herself, and Gloria movies, and a special little Gloria surprise—a breast-bulging pinup calendar—which Sergio predicted would outrage half the country and earn millions from the other half. But before any of that could be more than a fantasy, Gloria had to prove she was more than a hairdo and a few lucky hits. She had to prove she could keep supplying substance, not just shock.

So in August 1990, Sergio stunned the concert promoters who were still begging for show dates by announcing that Gloria was taking a break from the road. Sergio had decided the time had come to record Gloria's second album; Gloria had already written a notebook full of new songs, and Sergio knew how good they were. He was also excited about a tune that had been written especially for Gloria by Mary Morín, a first-time songwriter and Gloria wannabe who'd been captivated by Gloria's swagger. Called "Pelo Suelto" ("Untamed Hair"), the tune had the potential to become Gloria's image-defining anthem, not to mention another No. 1 hit. Sergio was hot to get this second album out fast; conventional wisdom dictated that he wait until sales of the first began to lag, but with such great material to work with, Sergio was betting that an early release would change Gloria's current image from novelty act to serious artist.

At least, Sergio hoped so. The Church and legions of Mexican parents were praying that she'd fail and fade away, the sooner the better. Top political leaders, especially in the conservative PAN (National Action Party) which would soon make Vicente Fox the nation's president, were loudly railing against Gloria's "lewdness." PAN campaign workers in Juárez were caught tearing down posters announcing a Gloria concert. With opposition like that, Gloria's second album had to be an absolute killer.

x   x   x

So why was Sergio treating the recording session like a sorority spring fling? This would be one of the greatest challenges of Sergio's career, not to mention a critical test for Gloria, but instead of secluding themselves as they'd done so successfully before, Sergio and Gloria were planning to cart along their entire chaotic entourage to Los Angeles. They were going to uproot nearly the entire star academy, bringing not only Mary, but Aline and Ivette and Sonia, and Gloria's young cousin, Mariana, plus the boy band, Clase 69. Even Crystal had patched things up with Sergio and was coming along for the trip.

Sergio had little choice. The only thing he'd ever been able to dangle before the girls to win their obedience and silence was the promise of a recording session. He couldn't put them off forever, especially not after the explosion of Gloria-mania that had come from her first attempt. For the girls in Sergio's star academy, Gloria's success proved that the fantasy Sergio was selling was real: One of them had gone to Los Angeles and come back a superstar, so why not the rest of them? The secret of Gloria's success, they were certain, wasn't Gloria; it had to be Sergio. Gloria had been a nobody before that trip, but Sergio had been Mr. Midas for years. The more records Gloria sold, the more the other girls pushed Sergio for their chance. It was terrible time management, of course—since the whole operation now depended on Gloria, it was foolish for Sergio to distract himself in the studio by shoehorning in three mediocre novices and a past-her-prime ex-girlfriend—but nevertheless, he announced that during Gloria's down time, he'd also roll tape on Aline, Crystal, Sonia, Mariana, and Ivette.

On the other hand, why was Sergio also carting along this boy group, Clase 69, if he was reportedly so vigilant about keeping his girls away from any other men? Clase 69 had another, nonmusical purpose, Aline explains: They were the star academy "beards," a group of handsome young men who could serve as public boyfriends for Aline and the girls. "I really liked two of them, Eduardo Méndez and Flavio César," Aline recounts in *Aline: La Gloria por el Infierno.* "I pretended to my girlfriends at school that Flavio was my boyfriend, and they believed it. There was no way I could tell them the truth, that my real boyfriend was Sergio Andrade, a gentleman who looked like my father." Aline actually did have a crush on Flavio, and kept a photo of him hidden in her locker at school, where Gloria and Mary wouldn't happen upon it when they visited her at home. But she almost never spoke to him when they passed in the studio: "Sergio would never allow it." Needless to say, the boys of Clase 69 performed their duties and kept their distance. Sergio fulfilled his part of the bargain by recording their album; shortly after they returned to Mexico, however, Clase 69 dropped into obscurity and disbanded.

Sergio, meanwhile, had his own beard: Mariana, Gloria's stunningly beautiful seventeen-year-old cousin from the U.S. border town of McAllen, Texas. Even though she had lived nearly all her life in the United States and spoke broken Spanish, Mariana thought she had a chance at duplicating her cousin's success as a Latin pop star. Gloria brought her to Sergio's star academy, where Mariana was offered a deal: Sergio would coach her and produce her record, if Mariana agreed to pose as Sergio's girlfriend whenever Aline's mother was around. Mariana agreed.

"I don't know if she ever really was involved with Sergio," Aline wonders in her memoir. "Such a gorgeous girl! The prettiest face I had seen in my entire life: very pale, with dark hair and a tiny nose . . . a model!" (Aline wasn't alone in this opinion; an NBC television executive who later aired footage of Mariana when she opened up about her cousin called her "the most beautiful non-celebrity" he'd ever seen. Mariana would later have her own horrific stories to tell about Sergio—not to mention a saga that would be as strange and as mysterious as her famous cousin's.) When Jossie stopped by the studio to pick her up, Mariana was supposed to rush over and begin cuddling up to Sergio.

But mostly these precautions weren't necessary. Jossie was rarely seen around the studio anymore. She would later portray herself as a hyper-vigilant mom who'd been hoodwinked by a master con artist, but by the summer of 1990 Jossie wasn't much involved in her fourteen-year-old daughter's life. In the year since Aline's audition, Jossie had stopped working at the radio station and had begun her own ceramics business, which was growing fast and demanding a lot of her time. Conveniently, Sergio offered to have his personal chauffeur shuttle Aline between middle school and the studio, then drive her home at night. Jossie accepted, pleased at the time that one of the most successful men in the Mexican music industry would dedicate his private driver, and so much of his time, to a middle-school girl who had yet to sing a note in public. Now that she wasn't transporting Aline anymore, Jossie barely saw her; they only had a few minutes together in the mornings and late evenings.

One afternoon, Sergio called Jossie with a request. Aline was about ready to cut her first record, Sergio told her, so she'd need a passport for the trip to Los Angeles. Also, Sergio continued, once Aline had a passport, he should probably hold on to it; he'd have to have it on hand when he booked the tickets. Oh, and by the way, Sergio concluded, Jossie would need to sign an affidavit giving him guardianship of Aline for international travel. Again, it might have struck Jossie as a bit odd that a man who was in the midst of managing the hottest new sensation in Latin America would take time out to personally make his backup singers' travel arrangements, not to mention producing, arranging, and recording an album for a fourteen-year-old who had never played an instrument, written a song, or done anything more than shake a tambourine between two other girls.

But somehow it didn't.

Right around the time Jossie was handing over Aline's passport and granting Sergio legal guardianship, another mother was having a very different reaction. For some time, Ivette and Ivonne's mother, Emma de Becerra, had been uncomfortable with the stories Ivette was telling her about life in the studio. The other girls were "a little strange," Ivette told her; Gloria, Mary Boquitas, and Aline acted like Sergio's slaves and never did anything "unless Sergio first gave them permission." Consequently, Emma had her guard up when Sergio called and asked her to sign the same kind of guardianship affidavit he'd gotten from Jossie. Emma refused. Sergio became furious, she'd later say, screaming that "she'd better sign it, or else." Emma was so appalled by Sergio's tantrum, she decided to get her daughters out of the school and end their relationship with Sergio. Ivette would not be making the trip to Los Angeles. (Within a year, Ivette and her twin sister, Ivonne, would have a new album out under new management. Coincidentally, they'd be featured in a 1991 issue of *TVyNovelas* with Gloria on the cover.)

Yet Jossie accepted Sergio's vagaries about where he and the girls would be staying in Los Angeles; when Jossie asked for the phone number of their hotel, Sergio said he wouldn't pick a hotel until he got there. Jossie delivered the passport and guardianship affidavit to Sergio. She was focused, Jossie said, on proving to Aline that she trusted her. Besides, she was going to be out of the country herself that weekend; she had a ceramics conference in San Antonio, Texas.

Before Aline left, however, Jossie reminded her to call home with a contact number as soon as she arrived in Los Angeles. Aline agreed, and soon she was settling into Sergio's car to begin the trip. But instead of heading to the airport, Sergio took Aline back home to his mother's house. It was a bizarre scene, Aline recalls; Sergio's mother was a silent, frighteningly dour woman who only glared at her. Why on earth would Sergio take her there?

But even though he was now a middle-aged man who owned at least four homes, Sergio kept a bedroom in his mama's home and still liked to bring girlfriends there to have dinner and spend the night, just as he had with Ga-Bí years ago. This time, though, he was pushing it: Sergio was still married to a nineteen-year-old and was now showing up with a fourteen-year-old. But instead of hiding these extramarital romps from his elderly, very Catholic mother, Sergio apparently wanted to be sure she knew about them. Maybe, in a way even he didn't recognize, Sergio saw his affairs as something his mother would be proud of: Even though he was an international success and at that moment was being applauded as the creator of Mexico's most talked-about celebrity, maybe Sergio still had to show his mother that her awkward, chubby son could bring home a prom date.

There was no glory in it for Aline, however. The next morning was her fifteenth birthday, and instead of awaking to the excitement of a huge party and piles of gifts, she found herself in the home of her thirty-seven-year-old boyfriend and his silent, glaring mother. It was a depressing contrast to the celebrations her friends would enjoy for their *quinceañeras*, but at least Aline was able to put it behind her later that day, when she was finally seated between Gloria and Sergio on a plane bound for California.

As soon as they arrived, Aline says, Sergio began rushing around to get his girls situated. Instead of putting a road manager in charge, Sergio insisted on dictating all the girls' activities himself. He personally checked them into a Best Western hotel, then doled out room assignments, coordinated Gloria's shopping trips with her recording schedule, and gave each girl just enough money for a single meal, which meant they couldn't stray from him for more than a few hours. Finally, he coached Aline on how to handle her mother and stepfather. "Don't let them know the name or phone number of the hotel," Aline says Sergio told her. "Tell them I need you to concentrate on your album, and you can't be getting calls at all hours." Aline made the call according to instructions; luckily, she says, her stepfather bought it.

Sergio was spending so much effort managing his girls, it didn't seem he'd have energy left to record one album, let alone six. But once he got to the studio that night, Aline says, Sergio turned into a different man. He liked the midnight-to-dawn hours because the studio was not only cheaper, but also deserted and free of distractions. Sergio would clap headphones over his ears, and for the next eight hours he was unapproachable. He was completely absorbed in the music, never cracking a joke or a even smile, snapping at anyone who broke his concentration. Still, even though Sergio demanded uninterrupted focus, he also insisted that Mariana, Aline, and Mary remain with him all night. Even though Gloria was recording her solo tracks and there was nothing for the other girls to do, the three of them had to sit in silence while Gloria attempted take after take. "We were dying," Aline says. "Those hours seemed interminable."

Sergio must have been going through his own special kind of torment. Much later, from behind the bars of a Brazilian prison, he'd depict these days with Aline, Gloria, and the rest of his ever-expanding harem as "every man's fantasy," but the truth is, he paid a day-to-day price for it in sheer irritation and boredom. During those September studio sessions when his creative synapses were crackling and he knew—he just knew—that he was working on a masterpiece, who could he talk to? Who was there to stimulate his mind, share his ideas, entertain him with the sharp snap of wit?

No one. Sergio had no pals, partners, or collaborators; he didn't seem to have any men in his life—or mature friendships of any kind, for that matter. Over the last few years he'd surrounded himself exclusively with a chattering clan of girls who were, for want of a kinder word, bimbos. None of them had attended high school; none of them had interests that extended beyond Sergio, celebrity worship, and themselves. None of the girls were even all that interested in music (apart from Gloria, who did have a gift for songwriting). What they wanted was stardom, and pop music was as good a trampoline as any. Better, actually, because as Aline was discovering on the eve of cutting her first album, pop music didn't really require much experience, or any particular talent.

Why, it didn't even require much of her attention: When Sergio relaxed a bit at the mixing board and tried to teach Aline his craft, she zoned out. "Sometimes Sergio explained things to me," Aline recalls, "but I didn't understand anything he was talking about. . . . Those nights were *sooo* boring!" For a man who'd studied philosophy and classical music, a poet and composer whom even his enemies called brilliant, this had to be the bitter flip side of his sex fantasy: night and day, he was surrounded by bored, uncultured, attention-starved teenage girls.

Still, during work hours, Sergio's stamina and dedication to the job were amazing. Sergio would stay at the mixing board till dawn, Aline says, then head back to the hotel and start making business calls to Mexico and New York, where the workday had already begun. After only a few days at Sergio's pace, Aline was woozy with fatigue. She wasn't allowed to sleep until Sergio was ready to go to bed, and even then, he'd only rest a few hours. Aline became so sleep-addled that one morning she accidentally violated one of Sergio's strictest orders: She answered the phone.

"Aline?" said the voice on the other end of the line.

"Mamá?" Aline replied, startled. How on earth did her mother find out where she was?

"What are you doing there?" Jossie demanded. "Isn't that Sergio's room?"

Aline stammered out a denial. No, no, she said; the hotel must have connected her to the wrong room. Jossie heard out Aline's explanation, but it was her voice Jossie was listening to: Her daughter sounded confused and panicked. Even as Aline was talking, Jossie had decided what to do: She let Aline think she believed her, then she hung up the phone and went straight to the airport. By that afternoon she was in a Los Angeles taxi, heading toward the Best Western Hotel.

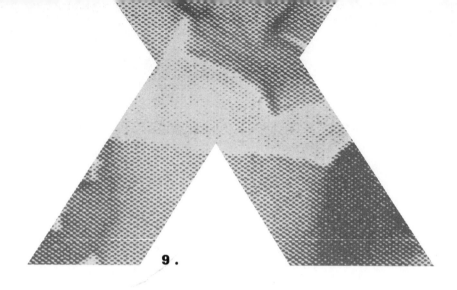

9 .

La Chica Fea

*H*ow rotten a mother was she? In other words, why did it take Jossie an *entire year* before she finally began to question what her daughter was up to? Wouldn't a responsible parent have cracked down long ago, as soon as her daughter began coming in five hours later from a two-hour music class and vanishing every weekend in the company of a middle-aged man with a scandal-tainted past and the most sexually notorious celebrity in the county? Of all people, Jossie should have been alert to the dangers, especially given her own history. From the time she was a little girl, Aline had heard the story of Jossie's secret courtship with the older man who'd swept her off her feet. It was The Greatest Love of All, according to how Jossie described it. So shouldn't she have suspected Aline might follow in her footsteps?

Perhaps. But consider the alternative. Was it more likely that a top music producer who specialized in female performers saw some latent talent in Aline—or that a cunning pedophile had enlisted a superstar singer, the singer's cousin, and his own wife in a complicated, yearlong conspiracy to trick her gangly, rather unremarkable-looking young daughter

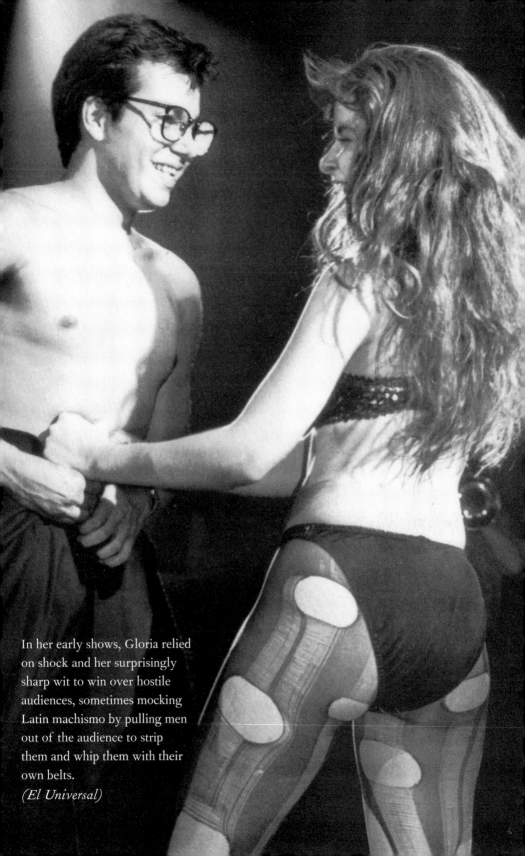

In her early shows, Gloria relied on shock and her surprisingly sharp wit to win over hostile audiences, sometimes mocking Latin machismo by pulling men out of the audience to strip them and whip them with their own belts.
(*El Universal*)

In her last big chance, Gloria became "La Atrevida," by combining angry feminism and raw titillation. *(Flor Cordero)*

Gloria was banned from television after her stormy TV debut, but her live shows were making her an international sensation. Concert promoters were so desperate to lure her that they paid with suitcases full of cash. In this performance, the ever-shadowy Mary Boquitas dances behind Gloria. *(Miguel Velasco)*

"God was in a naughty mood when he made my body," Gloria declared, and proved it with her first pinup calendar in 1992. Because she was promoting herself as a role model for girls and a champion of oppressed women, Gloria claimed the nudie poses were empowering. By the mid-'90s, however, younger and younger girls were appearing in the background. (*Miguel Castillo*)

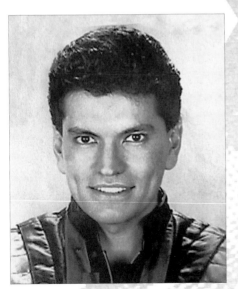

"He was a beautiful man when I knew him," says Sergio's former lover, the singer Ga-Bí. During his own singing career, the young Sergio Andrade combined piercing eyes, a blinding smile, and exceptional songwriting talent. After he began managing young female sensations, however, his weight shot up and his appearance deteriorated. (*Judith Chávez-Parks, "Ga-Bí"*)

In this photo, fourteen-year-old Karina Yapor bears a startling resemblance to the young girl once known as "Squaw Treviño." After Karina disappeared and abandoned a baby in Spain, her parents launched a national manhunt for the singer, her manager, and the lost girls. *(El Universal)*

Aline Hernandez, the child-bride who ignited the scandal. Aline married Sergio at thirteen, fled at seventeen, and at age nineteen told the story that would suddenly make Gloria and Sergio disappear, along with nearly a dozen clan girls. *(Grosby Group)*

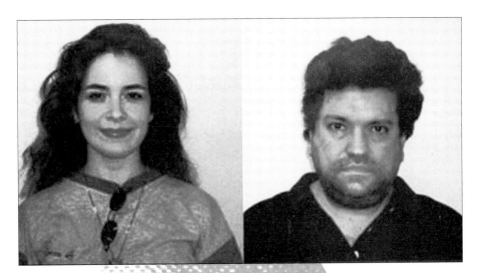

After disappearing for nearly two years, Gloria and Sergio were finally spotted on a street in Rio de Janeiro. With them were the three missing de la Cuesta sisters; two of them were pregnant. There was no sign, however, of Gloria's newborn daughter. Gloria made sure to freshen her makeup before the mug shots were taken.

Mexico was shocked to wake up one morning and find its favorite pin-up girl on a wanted poster, next to the famous record producer known as "Mr. Midas."

SE BUSCAN

Sergio Gustavo Andrade Sánchez   Gloria de los Angeles Treviño Ruiz

Even though she couldn't promote her albums on television, Gloria quickly shot to the top of the charts. Weeks after the release of *¿Que Hago Aqui?*, Gloria had the top three singles in the country, making her the Mexican Elvis. *(Courtesy of the author)*

Unlike Madonna, Mariah Carey, and other pop divas who failed as movie stars, Gloria was a smash success. Her first two films broke box office records. Secretly, they also helped create a false image of Gloria's life, since they were supposedly drawn from her true experiences. In all of her films, Gloria posed as a surrogate big sister for pretty young girls. *(Courtesy of the author)*

Rarely a month went by without a new Gloria outrage, which led to more Gloria magazine covers. By the mid-'90s, she was one of the most famous living Mexicans in the world, and the most imitated woman in Latin America. *(Courtesy of the author)*

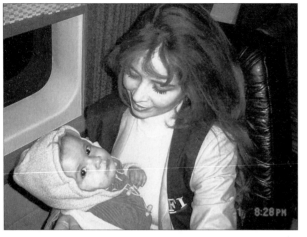

Gloria and her "miracle baby," Ángel Gabriel, who was somehow conceived in an all-women's cell block with no conjugal visits. Although Ángel Gabriel was supposed to prevent her extradition, he and Gloria eventually were flown back to Mexico. *(El Universal)*

Gloria finally agreed to return to Chihuahua to face charges in Mexico's trial of the century. Her son would spend the first two years of his life in jail cells. *(El Universal)*

into sex? Instead of being more skeptical and asking herself why Sergio would fill her daughter's head with promises of stardom, Jossie asked herself, "Why not?"

It's what Sergio did; that was his gift. Who'd heard of Crystal before Sergio began managing her? Who knew Lucerito could really sing and not just look pretty next to a piano? So didn't it make sense that Mr. Midas might have seen something in Aline that was invisible to the untrained eye—otherwise, why would he bother? "What if Sergio really was getting ready to make her record?" says Jossie, recalling her thinking at the time in Aline's memoir. "What if I derailed her future, this great opportunity before her? What if I was just imagining things that weren't really going on?"

But what finally stung Jossie into action was the message Aline had left with her stepfather when she called from Los Angeles. As soon as Jossie got home from San Antonio and heard that Aline wouldn't leave a phone number, on Sergio's orders, she knew something was going on. Perhaps to compensate for her previous permissiveness, this time Jossie's response was extreme and immediate. She tried calling the Adolfo Prieto Street number, but no one answered. She tried calling hotels at random around L.A., but none had a Trevi or an Andrade registered. Then, as Jossie simmered and wondered what to do next, she suddenly remembered a conversation she'd once had with Aline about the studio where Sergio had recorded Gloria's first album. The name was unforgettable because it matched Gloria's success so perfectly: Milagro Sound—the sound of a miracle.

Jossie called a cousin in L.A., who got her on the track of Milagro Sound. By that time, it was three in the morning in California and nearing daybreak in Mexico City, but Jossie called the studio anyway. She had just missed Sergio, someone at the studio told her; he must have gone back to the hotel. By chance did they know which one, Jossie asked. They did—and Sergio's room and phone number to boot. Jossie was furious when she punched in the numbers, ready to blister Sergio for making her worry—but when she heard Aline's sleepy voice answering the phone in Sergio's room, she went cold. "I felt my soul hit the floor," she recalled. This was even worse than Jossie had imagined. She'd been upset that Sergio was ignoring her concerns and was treating her middle-school daughter like a roadie, but she never dreamed he was sleeping with her. That's why even though she hadn't slept all night, she went straight to the airport and got on the next flight to Los Angeles.

Jossie was standing outside the hotel, pacing and smoking a cigarette, when Sergio and the girls came strolling back from lunch. They were shocked, Jossie says, but recovered enough to greet her and feign delight. Then, Jossie says, Sergio launched into a barrage of happy talk, congratulating her on showing up just when Aline was about to go into the sound booth and start recording. Everything was going great, Sergio told her, just great! Gloria's record was just about finished, and next up would be Aline's, which Sergio was certain would be just as big a smash as *¿Qué Hago Aquí?* But he'd explain more about that later, he told Jossie. Yes, he could see she wanted to speak with him, but right now he had to go. First thing tomorrow, OK?

"He didn't even give me a chance to complain," Jossie says. More likely, though, he trumped her from the start with the one argument she had no answer for: What if Aline's ticket to wealth was about to be punched? How, then, could Jossie refuse? Aline swore vehemently that she'd been sharing a room with Gloria and Mary, that Mariana was Sergio's girlfriend, and would Jossie please, *please stop embarrassing her* and go home. Jossie wasn't giving in that easily; she checked into the hotel and told Aline to gather her bags. Aline was staying with her until Jossie had a chance to sort things out with Sergio. If she wasn't convinced by what she heard, Aline was on the first flight home with her.

But when Jossie knocked on Sergio's door early the next morning, no one answered. She tried Gloria's room. Oh, Sergio's gone, Gloria told her. He had to go back to Mexico on urgent business, Gloria said, and he wouldn't be back for three or four days. Jossie was stunned, then furious. OK, she told Gloria. I've had enough. I'm taking Aline home with me today.

"But, señora, that's impossible," Jossie recalls Gloria telling her sweetly, in a tone of mock regret. "Sergio still has Aline's passport." Sergio always held all the girls' papers, Gloria explained, and since he hadn't returned Aline's, he must have accidentally taken them with him. It looked like Aline would have to stay until he got back.

And that, Jossie says, was the beginning of Sergio's multipronged attack on her sanity. Jossie vowed she wouldn't leave California without Aline, but instead of arguing back, Gloria merely shrugged. As you wish, señora. For the next three days, Gloria and the other girls were polite but dry, treating Jossie like a neurotic old woman who had to be tolerated while they went about the professional, no-nonsense business of recording an album in collaboration with a respected producer. Aline, on the other hand, was in a rage, accusing Jossie of humiliating her with perverted suspicions and blackening the name of a man who had only been good to them. After a day or two of this treatment, Jossie felt her moral outrage wobbling; she had to wonder if maybe she was making a mistake.

Which was exactly Sergio's plan, Aline says. He had never gone back to Mexico at all. The entire time Jossie was fretting at the Best Western, Aline claims, Sergio was hiding out in a nearby apartment he owned, then slipping into the studio by night to work with Gloria. He was doling out specific instructions to the girls about how they should handle Jossie, Aline says—gentle bewilderment from Gloria and Mary, self-righteous anger from Aline—as part of his strategy to sap her confidence and blur her moral certainty. He was also doling punishment, Aline says: As she feared, Sergio blamed *her* for Jossie's ambush appearance. The first time Gloria and Mary took Aline to see Sergio in his hideaway, Aline says, he slid off his belt and whipped her for letting Jossie know where they were staying. He kept lashing at her, Aline says, even though she wept and pleaded that it wasn't her fault. But rather than driving her away from Sergio, the whipping only hardened Aline against Jossie—when she got back to the hotel, Aline says, "I hated her more than ever."

Three days later, Sergio reappeared at the hotel. Finally, Jossie had a chance to recover her daughter's passport and take her home, not to mention giving Sergio a piece of her mind. Jossie met Sergio in his room and she . . . crumbled. By the time they were face-to-face, Jossie says, her anger had melted into little more than a vague sense that something wasn't right—and she couldn't even tell anymore if Sergio was to blame for that feeling or her own paranoia. Sergio, for his part, acted the exact opposite of a man with something to hide. He listened to Jossie's faltering complaints with a stony expression and answered them with courteous condescension: If the señora is dissatisfied with the free professional training her daughter is receiving, then by all means, take her home. It would be a pity, he sighed, since Gloria was nearly done with her album and Aline's album would be next, but if the señora has some kind of problem . . . What was the problem again, that Aline forgot to leave a phone number? I see. But she did call, correct? So what exactly is the problem, since she called as promised?

By the time Sergio had finished, Jossie says, she had withdrawn her objections and had begun apologizing for bothering him with her paranoia. She didn't cave completely—not at first. No matter how convincing Sergio had been, no matter how deftly he had flip-flopped her feelings from outrage to shame and confusion, she still held her ground on one point: She was going to stay in Los Angeles until this album was done and keep an eye on Aline.

Oh, of course, Sergio said; it would be great to have you as part of our family. However, he was quick to add a condition: She couldn't come to the studio. That would make the girls far too self-conscious, he said, and ruin the session. Better if she waited at the hotel while Aline was at work. Would that be OK? Jossie agreed.

But the problem, as she soon discovered, was there was no telling when Aline would show up. Often she'd be gone nearly the entire night, and Jossie had no way of knowing if she was truly in the studio or off somewhere with Sergio. So for the next week Jossie sat in her room at the Best Western, smoking cigarettes and brooding, wondering when Aline was going to return and whether Sergio had duped her. When Aline did appear, her behavior was so distasteful that Jossie had moments of wondering why she was working so hard to protect such an ungrateful brat. Aline avoided speaking to her, and whenever she did, it was in a tone of disdainful condescension. Even on the morning of Jossie's birthday, Aline wasn't any warmer. As usual, she left without saying anything, leaving Jossie to spend the day alone in the hotel, smoking and watching TV.

Sergio's plan, as described by Aline, was working. "I was sick of such a miserable, humiliating experience," Jossie would say. "More than irritated or angry, I just felt sad, lonely, and uncertain what I should do, if it was better to stay there or trust in Aline's judgment." Most confusing of all was Aline's anger: even though Jossie was there to protect her, Aline treated her mother with nothing but disdain and unconcealed loathing. Maybe, Jossie started to think, maybe Aline was angry because she was right—maybe Jossie *was* blowing things out of proportion. Maybe Aline's rudeness was a result of hurt feelings; if Aline truly was behaving herself and wasn't involved with Sergio, then perhaps Jossie was infuriating her by not giving her praise and credit she deserved for a job well done. Those doubts began to eat at her, Jossie would later say. That, at least, would be her explanation for leaving. Within two weeks, Sergio had succeeded: Jossie checked out of the Best Western and went home, leaving Aline behind.

Without her mother around, Aline says, Sergio immediately moved to reassert any control he might have lost during Jossie's occupation of Aline's room by punishing Aline as he pleased. One morning soon after Jossie had left, Aline says, she and Sergio returned to the hotel from another endless night in the studio. Aline accidentally drifted to sleep while Sergio was off talking to Gloria and Mary. When he came back twenty minutes later, Aline woke up and knew at once she was in trouble. Aline braced herself for a whipping, but Sergio had something else in mind. This was a terribly hurtful thing she'd done to him, he explained; closing her eyes on her boyfriend was tantamount to turning her back on him. To be so rude to the man who loved her, she must not have known what she was doing, he continued. But he knew a way to make sure she understood the next time. Sergio dragged her to the bathroom, Aline says, then pushed her inside and told her to strip off her clothes.

Aline obeyed. Sergio pointed to the floor and said that if she couldn't control herself better than a dog, she should sleep like one—under the toilet. The details of this naked incarceration, of course, are identical to the ones Rubén Aviña claims he heard from Gloria when she was describing her treatment at the hands of an anonymous, sadistically controlling boyfriend—a boyfriend she claims to have lived with during the same period when, she'd later say, she'd fallen in love with Sergio. Aline curled up on the cold tiles and cried herself to sleep, just as Gloria reportedly had. A few hours later, Sergio unlocked the door and said she could come out, but she still didn't deserve to share his bed: Aline could sleep on the floor. "That became sort of a habit with us," Aline comments. From that point on, whenever Sergio was displeased with her, he'd send her to the floor to learn her place.

It was cruel and humiliating but, of course, Aline deserved it. At least, that's what Sergio had gotten her to believe. He'd found a cunning new way to make Aline submit, and the best part was, it didn't depend on threats or bribery. He was a little limited in those regards anyway: Since he'd already used the recording as bait, he couldn't now turn around and use it as a threat. If he did, he'd be boxed in. If he kept threatening to kill the recording, Aline would eventually realize he was bluffing; if he did kill it, on the other hand, she'd be gone. Sergio knew that if he ever blew up and said, "That's it, Aline—no album!" Aline would, in short order, be on the phone to her mother and most likely to the police.

No, he needed some hold on her that she would never question—and when he got her into the studio, he found it. Once Aline got a firsthand look at how difficult it was to record a professional-quality song, she realized just how limited her own talent and experience were. It was one thing to fantasize about becoming a star back on Adolfo Prieto Street; it was another to stare at a microphone in a soundproof box and be told, "OK, go do it." Aline began to doubt her ability as a singer, which Sergio quickly turned into doubts about herself. If she wasn't a good singer, it was because she wasn't a good person. She wasn't disciplined enough; she wasn't hardworking enough; she wasn't *obedient* enough. If only she'd listen to Sergio and do what he said—*everything* he said—maybe Aline would improve.

Gloria and Mary reinforced this doctrine, Aline says. "I ended every conversation with them believing they were right about everything, including Sergio's punishments," she says. "They were for my own good, because I deserved them and because they were the only way I would mature as a person and grow as an artist." Gloria, eerily, would say almost the same words when she told the story of Sergio punishing her by making her run around the Chihuahua cathedral: "It was for my own good." Sergio's syllogism had been neatly tied together: Aline had been persuaded that being a good singer was the same as being a good person; and being a good person, as every good Mexican Catholic knew, meant making amends for your sins and taking your punishment. Being a good singer, therefore, meant being punished.

Much later, after Sergio's clan had been exposed, public opinion would immediately and lastingly assume that Sergio's hold over the girls began and ended with the lure of stardom—that they stayed with him because they wanted to be famous. The truth, however, is both that simple and much more complex. As Aline's relationship with Sergio was already demonstrating, Sergio convinced the girls that if they endured his demands, they'd be not only famous, but *better*. They'd be better people, true artists who'd suffered and were therefore worthy of fame. How could they doubt him? After all, hadn't Gloria suffered and lived on the streets and come out of it with a full songbook and a new persona? She had suffered and found redemption; so could they. It was an easy rationale for Sergio to establish, because it immediately resonated with these Catholic girls who'd been raised with the story of Christ's suffering on the way to glory.

And by suffering, the girls would also be worthy of the thing that made Aline so obsessed by fame in the first place: love. Just like Gloria, Aline was searching to fill the ache in her life created by a self-absorbed mother and a missing father. Somehow the need to be loved by one person had been transformed into the need to be loved by everyone—and the one who could make them worthy of all this love was Sergio. When it comes to listing the reasons why she didn't run for home after Sergio locked her in the bathroom, Aline doesn't mention fame at all; it's all about being loved and being needed: "Sergio told me that he loved me, that he needed me more than ever, that if I went with my mother, I ran the risk of throwing away everything we'd achieved together." *Sergio needed her.* . . . The more power Aline sacrificed to Sergio, ironically, the more she gained. For the first time, she was experiencing the power of being needed.

But while Sergio was busy reestablishing this dynamic with Aline after her mother had left town, another parent was arriving at the Best Western in search of his daughter. Gloria's cousin, Mariana, had called her father in Texas and asked him to come, right away, to take her home.

Something must have been seriously wrong for Mariana to want to leave just then, after she'd already recorded the first few tracks of her album. And why, as Gloria would later claim, wouldn't Mariana tell anyone what was wrong—not even the cousin she idolized? "Mariana didn't say anything to me," Gloria insists. "I felt bad for her after I heard some tracks from the album she had abandoned—it would have been a hit." Just as strange was the fact that Mariana needed her father to escort her; what made her feel that she couldn't sneak away and go to the airport on her own?

Even Aline, who'd become good friends with Mariana, wouldn't find out what happened until after her own story became public with the publication of her memoir. That was especially odd, since Gloria would later suggest that Aline's mother had something to do with the mysterious change in Mariana's behavior. "Ever since *la señora* Jocelyn showed up in Los Angeles," Gloria would contend, "Mariana had been in a tailspin, eating more and more and getting fatter by the day." Mariana was doing great before Jossie showed up, Gloria says: "Sergio was working on Mariana's album, he'd talked to her about what she should wear and gave her money to buy clothes. Mariana's personality was getting worse by the day, and her attitude was strange and dark."

It's a perplexing comment, since Gloria doesn't follow up by offering the slightest reason why Jossie's arrival would have any impact on Mariana. It seems more likely that she's taking a wild swing at neutralizing two critics by pitting them against each other. She'd have a good reason for depicting Mariana as unstable and coercible: When Mariana finally spoke, her story would be especially damning to Gloria. Mariana's version of what was going on in the Best Western that September, and why she urgently needed her father to take her away, wouldn't come out until a few years later, when Sergio and Gloria were behind bars in Brazil and Mariana, for the first time, was talking to detectives in Texas about her famous cousin.

"He beat me up and abused me, and I saw my cousin standing there watching," a tearful Mariana, going by the name Brandy, would say in a February 2001 special on the NBC-TV newsmagazine show *Dateline*. According to Mariana, she was sixteen when Gloria encouraged her to come to Mexico City and attend Sergio's star school. The school was "very legit, very legit," Mariana acknowledged, and she was thrilled with the instruction she was getting. Sergio was turning her into a finer singer than she'd ever imagined possible, and she was amazed that Gloria, her gorgeous, glamorous cousin, kept saying that a face like Mariana's, with those lovely hazel eyes framed by silky black hair and a spray of freckles across her nose, was more beautiful than her own and just made for album covers.

But after she'd been in Mexico City a few months, Mariana said, Sergio came into her room one night and sat on the edge of her bed. She didn't like what she saw in his eyes and pulled away from him. Sergio pulled her back, she said, and when she resisted, he smacked her across the face and heaved his heavy body on top of her, holding her down. Just as he was pulling off her nightclothes, Mariana said, she thought she was saved: Over Sergio's shoulder, she could see Gloria entering the room. Mariana said she called out to Gloria for help, but her cousin just stood in the doorway, watching. The next morning, Mariana went home to Texas. She was too ashamed to tell her parents what happened, and a little afraid that no one would believe that Gloria, the pride of the family, could have acted so despicably. Amazingly, Mariana continued, Gloria called a few weeks later, bubbling with excitement and saying Sergio had landed Mariana a record deal. Mariana had to come join them in Los Angeles *at once* and record her songs, Gloria said, acting as if nothing bad had ever happened.

"I didn't want to go," Mariana said on *Dateline*, "but my father made me." (Her account differs slightly in this regard from Aline's, which has Mariana traveling with the clan from Mexico City.) Because she hadn't told her family anything about the alleged rape, Mariana said, they didn't understand why she was balking and they insisted she take Sergio up on his offer. And it was so tempting. . . . So Mariana convinced herself that Sergio's attack had been a mistake, a one-time incident that wouldn't be repeated, and she got on a plane for California. A few nights after she arrived, it happened again. This time, Mariana said, Gloria was in the hotel room with her when Sergio raped her. This time she did tell her father, who came and brought her home. When she asked what she should do,

Mariana claimed, her grandmother told them all to keep quiet. "After that, I contemplated suicide many times," Mariana said. She was too afraid of being cut off from her family if she spoke up, Mariana said, so she kept quiet.

It's amazing that despite all this drama—despite the covert operations Sergio was directing from his hideaway, the arrival of inquisitive parents, the flight of Gloria's cousin, and the constant girl trouble Gloria was handling back at the hotel—Sergio, somehow, actually managed to complete *Tu Ángel de La Guarda* on schedule. In less than two weeks, Gloria had clean takes on the ten songs she had written for the album, plus the two new ones Sergio had commissioned. Sergio's choices were fascinating: not only did his two songs nicely complement Gloria's creations, but they reflected the two dominant and contrasting sides of Gloria's character. The question lingers: Just the way Gloria claims she embedded secret references to Sergio and Aline in two of her songs, was this Sergio's way of telling Gloria that only he knew who she really was?

"Pelo Suelto," the contribution of Gloria-wannabe and sometime backup singer Mary Morín, is proud and free-spirited:

> *I'm always going to be*
> *the way I want to be.*
> *I'm going to free my mind*
> *from any complexes*

"La pasabas bien conmigo" ("You Had It Good With Me"), on the other hand, by Oscar Mancilla, is shadowy and rather sinister, a ballad of angry love and deception with a tone similar to the ultimate stalker manifesto, Sting's "Every Breath You Take." In Oscar Mancilla's verses, an ex-girlfriend tries to browbeat her former love into at least admitting their affair. Gloria begins in a wounded, angry tone that matches the self-abasement of the lyrics: *"I know I'm uglier than the girls you go out with. . . ."*

The girls' voices, which have been harmonizing behind her, suddenly swell, rising in power to repeat the word *"Nadie, nadie, nadie"* ("nobody,

nobody, nobody"). The chorus is symbolically perfect: the voices represent an army of rejected girls, nobodies, with Gloria as their leader.

Finally, Gloria releases her pain in a shout that's so tortured, so angry and plaintive, it's easy to imagine it echoing inside an empty house, where no one would hear her, and no one would care:

> . . . *and you never can dennnnnnyyyyyyyyy*
> *YOU HAD IT GOOD WITH ME!*

It's easy to guess where Gloria found the pathos she poured into Oscar Mancilla's verses. At the same time that she was learning the song, she was helping Sergio carry out a plot to continue his secret love affair with Aline. Much later, she would look back on those weeks in Los Angeles and recall that even while she was helping Sergio deceive Aline's mother, Gloria was gazing at her short, sadly obese and desperately scheming manager and thinking, "I also love you, like no one has ever loved anyone before."

And in her own disturbed way, she was about to prove it.

x   x   x

Sergio kept his promise. As soon as the last track of *Tu Ángel de la Guarda* was completed, he began prepping Aline, just as he had Gloria and Crystal and Lucerito before her, coaching her with exact instructions on how to hit her notes and articulate her lyrics. He assembled eight songs for her, and reworked two she'd written herself. After weeks of being treated like a dog and whipped and insulted, Aline wasn't left with much confidence in herself, but Sergio had left no doubt in her mind that if anyone could make her sound good, it was he.

But once Aline was in the booth and began to sing, her doubts melted away. She was having the time of her life! And the more she sang, the more she was overcome with emotion for the man watching intently and conducting her through the soundproof window: "During this unforgettable process of recording, with Sergio signaling me directions for how to interpret the verses, I felt more love for him than ever before." Little wonder: Aline was alone in the spotlight, finally getting all the attention she'd ever craved from her idol, Gloria, and the dominant man in her life.

There was one lingering disappointment, however: Sergio insisted that Aline's album be called *Chicas Feas (Ugly Girls)*, after one of the bouncier tracks by Carloz Vargas. What if the association stuck, Aline fretted, just like Sergio's dromedary joke? What if she became known everywhere as the ugly girl? Gloria and Mary were already taunting her with jokes, and Sergio was using it as a nickname. "Anyone seen *la chica fea?*" he'd ask, setting the other girls into a torrent of giggles. Sergio, at times like these, seemed torn between glamorizing Aline and humbling her: He worked relentlessly for nearly two weeks in the studio to mix and arrange her album, but on the night before her photo shoot, Aline claims, Sergio ordered her to spend another miserable night on the cold floor without a blanket. The next morning, she truly was "Aline, *la chica fea.*"

With the two main albums in the can and Mariana gone from the clan, that only left Clase 69 to deal with. Sergio decided to bring the girls back to Mexico for a brief visit. He wanted to get Gloria's album ready for distribution as soon as possible, and he figured Aline had better go home for a few days to keep Jossie calm. Besides, she was due to begin high school in a few days. Then they'd be off again—to Los Angeles, then a quick spin around Mexico to set up promotions for *Tu Ángel de la Guarda*, back to Mexico City for Aline to appear a few days in school, and off once more to launch Gloria's latest concert tour.

But when Aline arrived home, as she relates in her memoir, she found Jossie armed with new determination—and new locks on the door. "This is it," Jossie told Aline, clicking the front door of the house shut behind them and pocketing the key. "This thing with Sergio is over." She had changed all the locks in the house, Jossie informed her; from that moment on, Aline would not leave the house unless Jossie was with her. There would be no more star school, no visits from Gloria, no phone calls from Sergio. If Sergio still wanted to release Aline's album, fine—but Jossie would personally accompany her to every rehearsal and every public appearance and bring her home afterward. Whatever Sergio was up to with her fifteen-year-old daughter, it ended here.

Aline couldn't believe it—here she was on the brink of stardom, and now she was *grounded?* She screamed insults at her mother, flying into a rage that only ended with a slap. Aline reversed tactics; she tried begging, arguing, and negotiating, but Jossie was unbending. Every time she had compromised before, she'd ended up feeling she'd been fooled. This time Jossie was dropping the iron curtain. Once school began, Jossie would be dropping Aline off in the morning and picking her up in the afternoon. To ensure Aline had no contact with Sergio, Jossie forbade her to answer the phone.

The next morning, Gloria tried calling Aline, but Jossie wouldn't put her through. A few hours later, Gloria showed up at the front door. Jossie couldn't believe it—this was Latin America's most famous young star, running around like a bike messenger between a high school freshman and her middle-aged manager? Jossie yelled downstairs for Isabel, the family's domestic helper, not to let her in. Then Jossie went outside herself and let Gloria have it. If Gloria was going to lower herself to doing Sergio's dirty work, Jossie decided, then she was going to have to take what was coming. "You can take that album of hers," Jossie shouted at her, "and go to hell!"

For three days, Jossie kept Aline cloistered. On the third day, when it seemed Aline had calmed down a bit, Jossie let her out of the house for the first time to make a short trip to the grocery store with Isabel. On the fourth morning, Jossie got up early to drive her husband to work. She carefully locked the doors behind her and was back in less than an hour, plenty of time to make Aline's breakfast before she woke up.

Except Aline was gone.

At the same moment that Jossie was returning to the house, Aline would later reveal in her memoir, she was running down a nearby street toward a taxi. Waiting for her inside the cab was Mary Boquitas. Aline tumbled in, breathless, and the cab squealed away. The day before, while Isabel was distracted at the grocery store, Aline had slipped away to a pay phone and made a frantic call to Sergio. They arranged to meet at a certain corner, during the thirty minutes Jossie would be out of the house the next morning. As soon as her mother left, Aline began tearing through the house looking for a spare key to the new locks. She found one hidden in the kitchen, and with just minutes to go before her mother arrived, she slipped out the door and took off at a sprint.

Sergio had arranged a hideout, Mary told Aline as the cab sped away. Nora, the ex-wife who was still working as Sergio's office assistant, had agreed to conceal Aline while Sergio figured out what to do about Jossie. Shortly after they arrived, Sergio turned up at the house and found that his current teenage wife and his former teenage wife were giving romantic advice to his runaway teenage girlfriend. "We have to deal with this intelligently," Sergio announced, ignoring the fact that the current scene suggested it was far too late for that.

But Sergio did realize how much trouble this could mean—for him, that is. If we're not careful, Aline recalls him saying, your mother will have me charged with kidnapping. Sergio soon came up with a plan: First he'd send his aging mother over to Aline's house to beg Jossie not to call the police. Then Sergio would go himself. When he arrived, he found Jossie's entire family assembled, but before they could attack, he made an announcement: He and Aline wanted permission to marry. "I was stunned," Jossie said later. "I was completely against it." But not so much against it to prevent her daughter, several weeks later, from stepping before a municipal justice to become the fourth Mrs. Sergio Andrade.

"Are you aware of what you're doing, marrying a man twice your age?" Jossie had asked her for the last time.

"Mamá, you have to understand," Aline had replied. "I'm in love with Sergio Andrade."

Sergio and Aline were married in a civil ceremony in a small restaurant on November 19, 1990. Luckily, Mary Boquitas hadn't objected when Sergio asked to fast-track their divorce; he managed to become single again just days before the wedding. Aline's mother and stepfather were there, as well as Sergio's attorney. Aline received her wedding toasts with a champagne glass of Coca-Cola; she was still too young to drink. One observer said she looked less like a bride and more like a girl receiving First Communion.

Unfortunately, Gloria and Mary could only stay for fifteen minutes of the reception before they had to take off for a show. They didn't turn up at all for the mass two weeks later. Somehow, in the midst of cajoling

Aline's family, planning two wedding ceremonies, and processing his third divorce, Sergio had still found time to supervise the release of Gloria's album. Within one week, *Tu Ángel de la Guarda* had rocketed to the top of the charts, leading all other albums in sales and radio requests. Gloria and Mary went on tour immediately, promoting the album and singing in small arenas across the country. As Trevi-mania began to sweep the country, Sergio soon understood that the usual five-thousand-seat auditoriums wouldn't do anymore; the message sank in during a show in León, when Gloria began "Pelo Suelto" and was drowned out by a capacity crowd that shouted out every word of the song.

Sergio could barely spare the time for the wedding; a honeymoon was out of the question. Offers were pouring in from concert promoters across Central and South America and Latino-rich corners of the United States who promised that with Gloria's name they could easily fill twenty-thousand-seat arenas. "We insisted they pay us in cash, before the show," Gloria says. Even on those terms, promoters eagerly signed on. "Suitcases full of money were showing up all the time," Gloria says, "to the point where the sight of them used to crack me up." Times had certainly changed: The homeless girl with the *pelo suelto* who, twenty-four months ago, was eating pig's-eye tacos and begging for pesos from dog-walking dowagers was now making light of her daily avalanche of cash.

The newlyweds immediately flew off to join Gloria and Mary for their next show. Even though Aline's own album was recorded and nearly ready for release, Sergio ordered Aline back into her hot pants to resume her spot behind Gloria as a backup singer. The demotion was frustrating, and a little humiliating. Wasn't Aline supposed to be Sergio's Next Big Discovery, the next Gloria Trevi? Then why was she still stuck in the background, shaking a tambourine and shouting out the letters of another singer's name? Aline didn't get it—until, she says, Sergio spelled it out for her.

"He wanted me to find more backup singers," Aline says. "He said he couldn't pull me out of Gloria's band until someone was found to replace me." That would be Aline's job. If she wanted to see her record released, she'd have to get out and start recruiting. Suddenly, her own introduction to Sergio's star school made perfect sense: So *that's* why Gloria was lingering outside the radio station while dozens of girls were lining up to see Pablito Ruiz. It was no coincidence, Aline suddenly realized: At that time, Gloria was waiting for her own first album to be released. Sergio must have made the same deal with Gloria—first find another girl to take your place, then we'll see about getting your record out. Likewise with Mary Boquitas—as long as Aline had known her, Mary had been waiting for a shot at her own solo album while serving as Gloria's backup singer and top lieutenant at Sergio's star school. This must be the routine—first you serve Sergio, then Sergio serves you. You don't get what you want until Sergio gets what he wants. If she didn't want to linger in purgatory as long as Mary, she would have to be even more obliging than even Mary had been.

What Sergio wanted was . . . well, Sergio never really said. Nothing was ever explicitly demanded: Sergio never told Aline to get him a young girl to have sex with. Sergio, as Aline recalls, just told her to find someone "appropriate." But to Aline, there was no mystery about the kind of girl Sergio was looking for: He wanted one who would look like Aline, act like Aline, and, most important, obey like Aline, and until she found the properly compliant candidate, *Chicas Feas* would remain locked in Sergio's desk drawer. This time Sergio could threaten to kill Aline's album with nothing to fear, since the danger of her running home and telling her mother had ended the day she said "I do."

So just a few weeks after her marriage, Aline began scouring the country for Sergio's next girlfriend. Gloria, curiously, confirms this in her jailhouse memoir, although she suggests Aline was the instigator. "Aline was proposing backup singers left and right," Gloria states. "She was urging him (Sergio) to choose one to take her place in my band, so he could make definite plans to launch her as a soloist." While Aline might not have been able to articulate Sergio's specifications, Gloria had no trouble rattling them right off. "The requirements," she says, "were youth, good looks and voice. That's why Aline was inviting every half-way decent-looking girl that crossed her path to come audition."

Being young then was the number-one requirement, followed by beauty. The ability to actually sing came last, while training and experience didn't even make the rankings. Youth was something Aline was dangerously close to losing herself, and that, more than the need for another voice in the chorus, probably explains why Sergio chose this moment to dispatch her on a girl hunt. It might not have dawned on Aline yet, but Gloria and Mary knew from personal experience just how close Aline was to the far side of the hill. Even though Sergio and Aline had just been married weeks before, Aline was fast approaching her sixteenth birthday—exactly the age when Gloria and Mary had both been cut loose by Sergio. Sergio had made Mary a Boquita at fourteen, married her at fifteen, and demoted her to star school lieutenant and secondary sex object at sixteen. Likewise with Gloria—she beat out dozens of competitors for that last spot in Boquitas Pintadas at age thirteen and had a place in Sergo's heart, not to mention a bed in his office, for the next two years. But once Gloria turned sixteen, she was out on the street. She only caught Sergio's eye again when she had something to offer besides herself—a notebook full of sure-hit songs and a fat inheritance check to record them with.

Aline had some far-reaching help with her recruiting mission: Sergio had begun a fan magazine called *Las insólitas, increíbles e inverosímiles aventuras de Gloria Trevi (The Amazing, Incredible, Scarcely Believable Adventures of Gloria Trevi)*.

Las Aventuras looked more like a comic book than a magazine; it was mostly photos and cartoons, and was clearly aimed at preteens. Gloria drew the comic strips herself, in her usual little-girlish style: Typically, she depicted a round-faced girl with big round eyes getting in trouble in school, or flirting with a classmate while lots of red hearts floated around their heads. There were some song lyrics ("Play *Pelo Suelto* yourself!") and, in the first issue, a full-page photo of the well-scrubbed and very soon-to-be-forgotten faces of Clase 69. The rest of the magazine was devoted to photos of Gloria either singing or modeling skintight clothes, or posing with fans. These fans were always girls, and they always looked no older than twelve.

In one issue a strange feature appeared. Sandwiched between fan photos of young girls dressed up like Gloria in short skirts and ripped nylons and ads for Gloria's upcoming bikini calendar was a full-page drawing of a beautiful naked woman with one of her nipples bare and a hand over her crotch. Running down her back and behind her rump were a series of questions:

> *Have you had sexual relations?*
> *Why? If your answer is "No," write and tell us the reason.*
> *How often do you make love?*
> *How old were you when you first had sex?*
> *With whom?*
> *How did it feel?*

The only label above this list was the word *TEST,* and this vague explanation: "You might be asking yourself, 'Why are they doing this?' Well, because we want to do a complete survey of real sexual practices among the young people of our country and that way be able to help answer any questions they might have." It followed an article about HIV/AIDS, and was ostensibly a quiz designed to help educate girls about sexually transmitted diseases. But it had an oddly bossy tone ("We've received very few answers, so listen up: Get moving and send us your responses!"), and there was no indication of just how Sergio and Gloria planned to use the letters they got. Were they going to publish the results, or fund research, or start a sex advice column? There was no clue—and no hint why a twenty-year-old pop singer-turned-amateur AIDS researcher and her manager would need to know "With whom?" and "How did it feel?"

There was one other special item in several early issues of *Las Aventuras:* a contest called "Los Coros de Gloria" ("Gloria's Backup Brigade"). Any girl who wanted to audition to become one of Gloria's backup singers was asked to submit two photos—a head shot and full body shot—plus an audio or videocassette of them singing. The winners, according to the contest, would get a chance to travel, rehearse, and appear onstage in a real concert with Gloria Trevi. Plus, the lucky girls would enjoy "a good salary, a magnificent working environment and the possibility of launching their own careers as professional singers."

The contest was a strange deviation from Sergio's usual meticulous professionalism. Every other aspect of Gloria's music was under his strict supervision—he approved or rejected all her songs, rewrote lyrics, selected the studio musicians, personally mixed and arranged every track of her records, and screened and hired every member of the band. He even wrote the allegedly "personal" introduction for Aline's album ("Ever since I was a little girl, I felt the need to write little stories and sing, sing, sing."). Yet when it came to boosting and complementing Gloria's voice with a harmonizing chorus of seasoned professionals, Sergio was willing to ignore the deep pool of experienced talent now available to a star of Gloria's caliber and pick, instead, some random teenager based on her Polaroid and Memorex.

Not surprisingly, the tapes came pouring in, and Gloria began hearing a new kind of teen scream as she was hustled out to her limo after a concert: Instead of autographs, girls were now begging for a personal audition. And if they had the right look, Gloria or Aline or Mary made sure they got it. Gloria brought in Andrea, her childhood friend from Monterrey. Mary Boquitas brought in Gaby, a twenty-year-old from remote Tamaulipas, but Sergio didn't much care for her. The De la Cuesta sisters appeared on their own. Gloria recalls being in the middle of a photo shoot with a mariachi band one afternoon at the star academy when she was called to Sergio's office. Sergio and Aline were talking to two very excited girls. They had a third sister, the girls said, but she was kind of young . . . Sergio asked to meet her as well.

Aline landed the best recruit of all, Marlene Calderón. Aline spotted her during a talent show in Los Mochis. When Marlene approached Aline for an autograph after the show and blurted out how much she'd dreamed of becoming famous, it suddenly flashed on Aline: "Sergio would really like this girl." Marlene was thirteen years old—perfect. Aline briefed Sergio when she got back to Mexico City. "Well, send for her!" she recalls him responding. He dispatched Aline and Andrea to return to Los Mochis and bring Marlene back for an audition.

Aline wasn't in the audition room, and she never asked Marlene if she'd had to strip naked. But she was there when Sergio approached Marlene's mother and broke the news that Marlene had won a scholarship—if her mother would permit her to leave home and come live at the star academy. "He repeated exactly what he'd told my mother, years ago," Aline recounts. "The same old story." Except this time Sergio had proof—he'd turned Gloria into a superstar, and Aline was already appearing on TV in anticipation of her album release. One week later, Aline and Andrea returned to Los Mochis to escort Marlene back to Mexico City. Marlene's mother clung to Aline, begging her to take care of her baby.

"If that poor woman had known in that moment that it was all a trick and everything that was awaiting her daughter . . ." Aline would later say. "And it was my fault." There were two major differences between Aline and Marlene, however: Once Marlene arrived at the star school, Aline says, she submitted almost instantly; and unlike Aline, who didn't know about Sergio's ongoing relationships with Mary and Gloria until after she'd fallen for him, Marlene knew Sergio was married to Aline, but didn't seem to care. "Everything was the same as with me, except she fell more quickly," Aline says. "Within one month, she was completely installed in 'the system,' meaning she knew what went on in the office, who was who, what her obligations were, and what her role was in 'the game.' She began going out with Sergio—that was obvious. He had her in his office all day, and she was by his side at all times. He'd begun to punish her, just like me. . . ."

By mid-1991, Aline had basically pimped a thirteen-year-old schoolgirl for her middle-aged husband and was standing by while they disappeared into his office for sex. But Sergio's bed partners weren't limited to his wife and his new girlfriend—according to Gloria's own count, Sergio was having sex with at least five other members of his growing clan, including longtime clan member Sonia Ríos; new recruit Wendy Castelo; Katia de la Cuesta; Gloria's childhood buddy Andrea; and Gloria herself, at least on her most recent birthday. ("He caressed me . . . with force and ownership," Gloria would relate. "Then we made love until we fell asleep.") Those were only the girls she was *certain* he was sleeping with. "I suspected he was having other little adventures," Gloria adds, "though I couldn't be sure."

But Aline had gotten what she wanted—*Chicas Feas* was hitting the record stores and inching a bit up the charts, in no small part due to Sergio's master string-pulling. First, Sergio put Aline on the cover of Gloria's magazine, and then, according to Gloria, he began working a little squeeze play on the music directors of Mexico's biggest radio stations. With Gloria to use as leverage, she says, Sergio could strong-arm radio stations into listing Aline's title track among their Top 5 Most Requested. If the station's music directors didn't want to help Aline, well . . . maybe Gloria wouldn't be available for that station promo after all. The strategy worked like a dream, Gloria would later claim; Sergio was even able to convince Raúl Velasco, and astonished Aline by getting her on *Siempre en Domingo*.

Her appearance on the show, however, turned out to be sadly unremarkable except in one regard: the difference between her style and Gloria's. Unlike her mentor, who "ate the stage" when she got her chance at live TV, Aline was so overwrought with emotion that she barely managed to warble her way through *Chicas Feas* before she began weeping. It was strange, and a little sad: Despite spending two years studying under Mexico's hottest star maker and Mexico's hottest star, Aline came across like any other maudlin, sob-choking, female balladeer—exactly the kind of singer, Sergio often warned, who wouldn't stand a chance anymore in the evolving Mexican music industry.

But despite her wet eyes on stage, Aline was hardening in other ways. According to Gloria, Aline had turned into something of a sexual adventurer herself; once, Gloria says, she wandered into a bedroom and found Aline in bed with Sergio and Katia de la Cuesta. By Aline's own admission, she wasn't bothered anymore by Sergio's punishments or her own guilt about luring Marlene into the star school. "This was much more than I had even dreamed of," she relates in her memoir. "The other thing, the ugly part, didn't bother me that much anymore. Everything has a price in life, I figured, and I'd paid for what I'd gotten."

And when she was no longer getting what she paid for, she left.

Chicas Feas wasn't selling, despite Sergio's covert promotional operations, and Polygram Records canceled Aline's contract. Aline was eager to pursue other music companies—"How about BMG? They took a chance on Gloria!"—but Sergio had far more urgent projects to take care of, not to mention a growing amount of personal debt to service. Gloria was filming *Pelo Suelto,* a star vehicle based on a glamorized version of her life. When Sergio wasn't supervising the film, he was working hard on Gloria's third album and her first pinup calendar. Plus, he had to get cracking on Mary Boquitas' long-promised album, and it wouldn't be long before he'd need to get something going for Marlene and Wendy. At least Katia and Karla de la Cuesta seemed content as Gloria's backup singers, but who knew how long that would last?

Even if Sergio did have the time to take another stab at making Aline a star, would he have bothered? Mr. Midas rarely made the same mistake twice, as he'd once warned Gloria. Aline had had her chance, and besides, that past September, she'd turned seventeen. And so, right before Christmas 1992, while Sergio and Gloria were appearing at a music festival in Chile, Aline climbed into the king-size bed that she'd been sharing with Andrea and Katia. Around 2:00 A.M., long after the other two girls had fallen asleep, Aline eased her way out of bed, grabbed a small bag she'd hidden in the closet, and slipped out of the house. By 2:30 in the morning, she was sitting in her mother's kitchen drinking warm milk with egg and cinammon.

She'd left behind a note for Sergio. "I promise I won't say anything," Aline had written.

And she wouldn't—for a while.

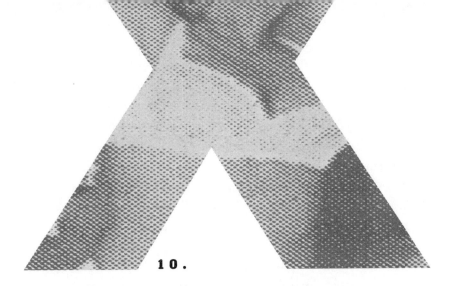

10

"What's the Big Deal About Virginity?"

arina Yapor was seven years old and playing with her dolls on the living room floor when something her parents were watching on TV caught her eye. Soon she'd abandoned her Barbies and was mesmerized in front of the set. Wow—that had to be the coolest girl Karina had ever seen! The way she sang, and danced, and goofed around—she was just like the wild kids in school the teachers always yelled at but secretly liked. Look at her now—she's grabbing Raúl Velasco's glasses!

Karina already had a role model at that point: Malibu Barbie. But after that Sunday night, she become devoted to Gloria. It wasn't that much of a switch, really: according to the movies that Karina rushed to as soon as they started coming out, Gloria Trevi lived in a little pink RV, like Barbie's Vacation Camper, and buzzed around on a cute mototcycle with a sidecar, just like Barbie and Ken, and was always changing into pretty outfits and bikinis and having fun adventures. Gloria was an action doll come to life—she was Monterrey Barbie! But the best part was she was less grown up than Barbie; you could tell that from her movies, the way she was always playing and palling around with little kids, and from all those comics she drew in her magazine.

When Gloria gave a concert in Chihuahua in 1990, Karina's hometown, Karina not only got permission to go, but managed to get onstage. Karina was tall for her age and very pretty—in fact, she looked strangely similar to Aline—which is probably why Aline and Mary Boquitas spotted her from the stage when Gloria invited fans to come up and sing "¿Qué Hago Aquí?" with her. Once on stage, all the other fans just stood in place and sang, but not Karina. She bolted straight for Gloria, grabbed her in a hug, and didn't let go until the song was over. Gloria just smiled and kept on singing.

After that night, Karina became sort of obsessed. She began dressing up in whatever old clothes and junk jewelry she could scrounge from her mother, trying to mimic Gloria's street-chic style, and got so good at imitating her idol that her friends at school began calling her "Karina Trevi." At first, Karina's mother disapproved of Gloria's fresh mouth and some of the awful things she said about sex, which, fortunately, flew right over her daughter's head. But then Teresa Yapor read a magazine article about the terrible relationship Gloria had had with her mother while growing up, and that gave Teresa a twinge of sympathy for the star: Teresa was very close to her son and daughter, and she felt bad for the mother who'd lost a daughter and for the teenage girl who'd grown up without parents.

As for her husband—well, Miguel Yapor could care less. For the past few years, he'd been drawing more and more into himself. He'd once been a striking man, lean and tall, with a lady-killer mustache and a hearty laugh. But a few years after Karina was born, he began feeling spasms in his legs, which turned into blinding pain in his lower back. Soon he could barely walk. Miguel was diagnosed with a degenerative neuromuscular ailment that would gradually weaken him and finally confine him to a wheelchair. The disease took its toll on Miguel's relationship with his wife and two young kids, and on the small upholstering business he ran with his brother. Money, never in abundance, got tight. Fear and pain ate into Miguel's personality, making him morose and often silent. Sometimes it was as if he weren't even there.

So Teresa worked extra hard to stay involved with Karina. Whenever Gloria came to Chihuahua to perform, she would cart Karina around so she could get a glimpse of her hero. Karina was always in the throng as

Gloria exited her limo, and she was always bringing special treats to Gloria's hotel, once even delivering a homemade pineapple cake to the head of Gloria's security detail. It wasn't in vain—through little gestures and focused smiles and occasional personal comments, Karina got the feeling that Gloria noticed and remembered her. And finally, on October 8, 1994, twelve-year-old Karina found out she was right.

As Karina would later testify in court, she and her mother had gone to the Chihuahua airport with a mob of other fans to welcome Gloria back for her latest concert. They spotted Gloria in a side room being interviewed by a crush of reporters. Karina grabbed her mother's hand and tried to pull her inside. Just as a security guard was stopping them, however, Gloria caught a glimpse of Karina over the reporters' heads and signaled to the guard to let the Yapors in. Once the reporters filed out, Karina found she and her mother were alone with Gloria and four members of the clan: Mary Boquitas, Marlene Calderón, Katia de la Cuesta, and another new girl, Gabriela Holguín.

"Look how big you've gotten!" Karina recalls Gloria telling her. "You've grown so much, you're almost taller than me." Karina couldn't believe it—not only had Gloria recognized her, but it seemed she'd been keeping an eye on her for a long time. And then Gloria stunned her with an offer: When she returned to Mexico City in a couple of days, she said, she wanted to bring some photos of Karina with her. She always needed more girls in her group, and her manager was also looking for fresh talent to launch as soloists. If her manager liked what he saw from Karina's pictures, Gloria said, she would recommend that Karina be brought to Mexico City for an audition. If she passed the audition, she would be given a special training scholarship and her parents would be paid a salary on her behalf of two thousand dollars a month. There might also be a part for her in Gloria's latest movie, which would be written and directed by her manager himself, Sergio Andrade. There were a couple of rules, though: Karina would have to move to Mexico City and live with the other girls in training; she had to be ready to travel a lot; and most important, no parents would be allowed. Sergio had found that they interfered too much with the girls' concentration.

So—were they interested?

Four days later, Karina and her mother were on a plane to Mexico City.

How could they turn it down? By 1994, Gloria was probably the best-known living Mexican in the world, easily rivaling international soccer sensation Hugo Sánchez and certainly outranking recently elected President Ernesto Zedillo. Salma Hayek was barely known then, having just made her Mexican film debut in the respected but little-seen art house film *El Callejon de los Milagros* (titled "Midaq Alley" in English). Selena, the Mexican-American singing sensation, would become an international star only after she was shot to death one year later, and at that time was known only to Tejano music lovers and the sharp-eyed fans who'd spotted her tiny cameo as a singer in the film *Don Juan DeMarco*.

Gloria Trevi, meanwhile, was not only one of Latin America's top recording stars, but also a top-rated TV personality *and* Mexico's number-one box-office draw *and* Latin America's most popular pinup girl. Her first three albums (*¿Qué Hago Aquí?*, 1990; *Tu Ángel de la Guarda*, 1991; and *Me Siento Tan Sola*, 1992) shot to the top of the charts as soon as they appeared, selling more than five million copies, while the one she'd just released in 1994, *Mas Turbada que Nunca* (punningly translatable as either *Crazier Than Ever* or *Masturbating Like Crazy*) was on course to eclipse all previous sales. *Me Siento Tan Sola (I Feel So Alone)* had won her a *Billboard* Latin Music award nomination for the song "Con los ojos cerrados" ("With Closed Eyes") and made her a huge hit on Latin music video shows.

By the time *Me Siento Tan Sola* appeared in 1993, the U.S. press was taking notice. *Variety* called her "a one-woman revolution," and added, "No imitation, La Trevi is a genuine political and cultural phenomenon in her own right." *People* magazine published a gushing profile in 1993, noting that "the emergence of Gloria Trevi as probably the biggest pop star in Latin America is something of a miracle," and depicting her as more raw, witty, and authentic than Madonna. Mexico's wild child, *People* noted, performed a woman-of-the-people gesture it was impossible to imagine the Material Girl, for all her calculated naughtiness, ever making: Gloria presented a pair of her used panties to the 250,000th buyer of her album *Me Siento Tan Sola*. And just one month before Gloria met Karina, the *Chicago Tribune* was describing Gloria as more of a historical force than an entertainer:

> Gloria Trevi, who has often been called the "Madonna of Mexico," may well be the most important Spanish-language female singer of her generation. Not because of the Madonna comparison—which she rejects by saying that Madonna is the Gloria Trevi of North America—but because of her subversive, and very particular, mix of art and politics.

> Trevi's influence on Latin American popular culture is no passing fancy. Before Trevi, there were no real female rock singers in Latin America. Before Trevi, there were no rebellious, spit-in-your-eye female singers in any genre in the Spanish-speaking world. The boys in the audience may drool over her saucy image, but the girls feel empowered—and for young Latinas, that's a rare and extraordinary experience.

Already Gloria's trips to the United States were electifying U.S.-living Latinos. She'd sold out two concerts at Madison Square Garden, and just a few months before making her offer to Karina, Gloria drew an astounding forty thousand spectators to an outdoor concert at Los Angeles' Hollywood Park. She hadn't yet made the big crossover jump to the U.S. market, but she was brilliantly poised; Sergio had spread the word about Gloria through the serious-music grapevine by enlisting cutting-edge musicians for her third album, including Vinnie Colaiuta, Sting's drummer, and Jeamie Gleaser, ace guitarist for Jean Luc Ponte and Chick Corea. Collaborating with these legends gave Gloria international credibility.

Amazingly, she'd managed to maintain her fist-in-the-air feminist image while still making a fortune from her annual pinup calendars, which featured Gloria in near-nude poses: in one she parodied Pancho Villa with bullet bandoliers over her naked breasts; in another she giggled as the Coppertone dog pulled her bikini bottoms down to her knees. She explained the apparent contradiction between her advocacy of women as more than sex objects and her apparently demeaning calendar photos by arguing that as an empowered woman, sexuality was hers to give or deny—and she chose to give. "I'm not using my body to get famous," she said. "I showed off my body *after* I was famous. The calendars are a gift to those who love me. It's meant to put a smile on the lips of the mechanic working in a garage, the truck driver who spends his nights on the road." Her first "gift" in 1992 quickly sold out all three hundred thousand copies printed, while the '93 version sold more than a half-million *in the United States alone*. Even before they'd heard her voice, Americans were learning Gloria's name and having the image of her too-curvy-to-be-true body seared into their minds. (As Gloria once said, "God must have been in a naughty mood when he created my body.")

Despite the panty giveaways and the nudie photos, even Mexican academics and intellectuals loved her. It was around the time that Gloria met Karina that Carlos Monsiváis, one of Mexico's most celebrated cultural critics, had provided a stunningly unexpected tribute to the singer when he dedicated a chapter to her in his collection of essays *Los Rituales del Caos (The Rituals of Chaos)*. "Gloria transcends the limits of both record and radio industries," Carlos Monsiváis wrote. "She supports the decriminalization of abortion and, in her '94 calendar, she symbolizes her support for condom use." (Condoms, of course, were still taboo in staunchly Roman Catholic Mexico. In one photo, a topless Gloria is shown playing with condoms blown up like kids' balloons.) "In Gloria Trevi, provocation is the ingenious method she has found to unite her sincere effusions and the strategy of selling her image. This makes her unique—nothing is completely manufactured, neither is it entirely provocation." His fellow intellectual icon, Elena Poniatowska, joined Monsiváis in the Trevi fan club, calling her "one of our most authentic artists." Even Subcomandante Marcos, leader of the Zapatista movement, was an admirer; he is said to have promised, "If she comes here, the flowers of the jungle will embrace her."

Sergio's genius, it turned out, had been figuring out a way to turn his exile into triumph. Back in the mid-eighties, when his rumored scandal with an underage singer forced him undercover for the first time, he was cut off from the standard production route for Mexican pop stardom:

Pick a promising candidate from the Televisa stable, fashion her according to the three-B formula (Beautiful, Blonde, and Bland), and most important, equip her with a selection of wholesome songs that wouldn't offend the all-powerful Azcárraga family.

Keeping the Azcárragas happy was crucial, since they controlled not only the sole Mexican television network, but also a record company, Fonovisa, and countless magazines and radio stations. Launching a singer with The Tiger's blessing meant instant and guaranteed TV, radio, and press coverage. Going renegade meant . . . well, it was hard to say, because no one had ever really done it. The odds were too long—generating publicity would be nearly impossible, and no record store would carry an invisible singer whose song wasn't on the radio and whose face had no chance of appearing on a magazine cover or TV. As for going renegade with a *rock* album, forget it—until the mid-eighties, there wasn't a single radio station in the entire country devoted to rock. Even if a singer wanted to defy Televisa and record hard-edged music, there was no hard-edged station to play it.

Sergio knew the formula all too well; he'd helped shape it with Lucerito, and with Crystal, and with the smiling brother-sister cuteness of Grupo OkiDoki. But he also sensed the end was coming—despite state censorship of rock music, which the right-wing government banned as morally harmful, U.S. and European rock albums were filtering across the border. Small, grungy clubs were playing these clandestine tapes and staging acts modeled after foreign thrash bands, building a taste among young Mexicans for much harder fare than Televisa was offering. An eruption was coming—Sergio could feel it. There was too much pressure building between what the entertainment industry was offering and what Mexican teenagers wanted. It was a revolution that couldn't be contained, Sergio knew, because he'd seized on the future truth of a key demographic: By the late eighties, more than half the Mexican population was estimated to be fifteen years old or under. They wouldn't be spoon-fed *mariachi* music and *cumbias* anymore, not when there was so much black market rock music available. They wanted something new, something rebellious, something their parents hated.

Sergio positioned Gloria perfectly to ride the tide when the dam burst.

Being temporarily blacklisted by Televisa was a stroke of luck that only a master strategist like Sergio could have turned to Gloria's advantage. Such a visible attack by the Televisa establishment put Gloria squarely in the camp Sergio was trying to attract. That's why Sergio had made her perform in dive bars in the early days in the first place; he wanted her to absorb the culture and attitude of the underground rock movement and earn some street credibility at the same time. The Azcárraga banishment, subsequently, was like a field promotion to head of the rebel forces.

Yet Gloria's was always a deft revolt, and a deliberately commercial one. Sergio didn't want her operating on the fringes forever, and he certainly didn't plan to make a living by selling homemade Trevi cassettes outside rock clubs, like the other antiestablishment *rockeros*. Gloria would become a crossover star within her own country by fashioning herself into the first outsider to be accepted in mainstream entertainment. Her behavior, therefore, was wild enough to be attractive, without being dangerous. She wasn't tearing up photos of the Pope on live TV, as "girl rebel" Sinéad O'Connor did on *Saturday Night Live* in 1992, and she wasn't burning down her boyfriend's house, as Lisa "Left Eye" Lopez— "the poster child for female rage"—did in 1994. Gloria, in contrast, might make saber-rattling statements in favor of premarital sex that caused her own grandmother to write an open letter to a Monterrey newspaper begging her to stop shaming the family, but she would also announce, loudly and often, that she didn't drink, or do drugs, or stop working long enough for romance. Whenever she was asked about a man in her life, Gloria always responded that she hadn't had time for a boyfriend since she was eighteen years old. In other words, her hell-raising was what she *said*, not what she *did*—and that made her safe. Everyone was entitled to different views, as long as they behaved themselves; and as far as anyone outside the clan knew, Gloria behaved herself better than most parents.

It wasn't easy tiptoeing such a tight balance between sin and civility, but Sergio and Gloria took advantage of an extraordinarily effective tool to fine-tune their message and make it seem genuine: Gloria's movie scripts. The brainstorm was using her real name in make-believe stories: No matter how preposterous the plot, calling the lead character "Gloria Trevi" subtly blurred the line between fact and fiction, suggesting that while the events might not be real, the person was. And that person, that big-screen version of "Gloria Trevi," was always heroic and heart-warming—a hell-raiser, true, but always in the best, most mythologized Pancho Villa sort of way. Movie Gloria is a free spirit, but also generous, brave, industrious, playful and loyal; she's sassy but virtuous.

Seriously virtuous—in her first two films Gloria engages in nothing more steamy than a hug. That lack of even an onscreen kiss, in hindsight, is glaringly peculiar; how could two romantic comedies neglect to include any romance? And isn't it odd that a sex symbol would be portrayed as more sexless than Cinderella? One possible explanation, of course, leads back to Sergio: He may have been too possessive to permit it. To allow a good-looking leading man to take Gloria in his arms would have been a torment for short, homely Sergio; and since he had script approval for the first movie and directed the second, he easily could have stopped it. Per-haps, like her onstage belt-whipping routine, this was another clue about Gloria's secret life that was hidden in plain sight, right before the eyes of millions of popcorn-munching viewers. Only much later, of course, would anyone outside the clan realize that what all along seemed most ex-aggerated about Gloria was actually true, and what seemed true was pure disguise. Perhaps that's the reason she was so comfortable with a wanton image that embarrassed other Mexican performers—for Gloria, it was pure comedy, a farce that she enjoyed hamming up because it had nothing to do with her real life.

Yet despite their bizarrely artificial nature and lack of the usual cine-matic attraction of sex and romance, those first two films were Gloria's most astounding successes. With *Pelo Suelto* and *Zapatos Viejos*, Gloria accomplished something that very few other divas have managed, before or since. Whitney Houston couldn't make the switch to movies; neither could Mariah Carey, Britney Spears, or Madonna (though she insists on trying). Despite their beauty and charisma, not one of those singers could attract viewers in anything more than a small secondary role.

Pelo Suelto was only expected to bring in Gloria's teenage fans. In-stead, it broke the Mexican box office record for the highest-grossing film, bringing in more than thirty million viewers. And it wasn't as if 1991 was a slow year for movies and she didn't have much competition. That was a landmark year for cinema, with three of the all-time greatest box office draws coming out. Released at the same time as *Pelo Suelto* were *Terminator II* and *Home Alone* (two of the biggest box office hits of all time); *The Commitments* (aimed at rock music fans); *Beauty and the Beast* (aimed at kids and young teens); and *Thelma and Louise* (which targeted Gloria's feminist fans). All of those better produced, better acted, and better advertised movies should have decimated Gloria's audience share; but amid such weighty competition, *Pelo Suelto* had lines running around the block for weeks.

The story line could have been borrowed from one of Gloria's own comic strips: "Gloria Trevi" is a beautiful girl who works in a run-down gas station by day and sings in an even more run-down rock club by night, dreaming of the day she'll go to Mexico City and become a star, "the biggest star in the world." At the same time, a major record label is searching for a fresh new singing sensation to replace its spoiled, blond diva, and a cartoonish villain in black cape and eye patch is kidnapping children from a nearby orphanage. Mingled throughout the plot, however, are scenes that carefully duplicate events from Gloria's real life: "Gloria Trevi" is shown arguing with her mother by phone, begging for money on the Mexico City streets by singing in a public bus, and bunking down for the night in an alley. In the end, "Gloria Trevi" rescues the orphans, wins a record contract, and skips off laughing and triumphant in her skimpy bikini to splash in the ocean.

What isn't surprising is that Gloria, as a movie newcomer, is so good; what's surprising is that Gloria, as a graduate of Televisa's elite training program and a professional entertainer, is so *bad*. Her acting style seems to have been copied directly from Charo, the *cuchi-cuchi* queen of overblown Latin hysteria and bad seventies sitcoms. Gloria is mostly shown tottering around on high heels, or rapid-talking in mock panic, or trying to fight off immense villains with girly little pitty-pat slaps. Her scenes, and the way she handles them, are astonishingly predictable; it's hard to believe that any director in the 1990s, or any actress, would not have freshened up material that was already tired twenty years earlier. With just one exception, the whole movie could have been spliced together from *I Love Lucy* episodes and after-school specials: Here's Gloria chasing the kid who doesn't want to take a bath; there's Gloria outsmarting the huge villain by kicking him in the crotch; here's Gloria biting her little fingernail and frowning while thinking up a plan . . . and lunging for the kid and flopping in the mud . . . and arguing Lucille Ball–style without knowing she's already won while her boss patiently repeats "But Gloria . . . but Gloria." At one point, Gloria even comes out with Charo's actual tag line: "Ay, Chihuahua."

But there is one arresting element to the movie, and that's what made it a success. It first appears about ten minutes into the film: Gloria is sitting outside her pink Barbie camper, talking to her new foundling friend, and she's about to explain why she lives out here, alone, in the middle of nowhere. Suddenly, she somehow pops up on the roof of the camper; an invisible band breaks into "¿Que Voy Hacer?" and Gloria begins rocking out. Contextually, it's ridiculous; seconds earlier, she was having an intimate chat with a scared orphan, and now she's strutting ten feet above his head while belting out a rock tune in the middle of the woods. Yet the moment is utterly compelling; even though the poorly adjusted audio makes it clear she's lip-synching, Gloria's loneliness and doubt seem heartfelt and honest. For the first time, real emotion is on display, and it's both painful to watch and exhilarating.

X   X   X

The rest of *Pelo Suelto*'s dramatic narrative, such as it is, is little more than anticipation builder; while Gloria is mugging it up with the orphan and slapsticking with the villains, the only suspense is wondering when the music will kick in and she'll cut loose with another song. Romance, it turns out, isn't missing after all: "Gloria Trevi" does find her own true love, when she's dancing above the world on her camper roof or writhing alone on stage. Gloria is rapturous, giving herself unconditionally to . . . Gloria. She's on fire with her own words and feelings, with the image of the world at her feet. Gloria's self-absorption is never more apparent than in *Pelo Suelto,* where she can barely manage the slightest peck on the cheek of her handsome co-star, yet accompanies each song by hugging herself with a tight grip of true affection.

Mr. Midas always said he didn't repeat a mistake; the flip side to that motto is that he also never failed to repeat a success. The method he came up with for repeating *Pelo Suelto*'s success was essentially to make the same movie all over again. *Zapatos Viejos* came out the following year, blatantly duplicating not only *Pelo Suelto*'s basic story, but most of the key scenes. Once again, a solitary girl dreams of singing; she battles the establishment, exposes an evil plot, saves little kids, and becomes rich and famous. In doing so, she once again begs for change by singing on a public bus, camps out on the street with an orphan, kicks the bad guy in the crotch, and has precisely two scenes in a bursting bikini, even though none of the action is set anywhere near a beach.

Sergio wrote and directed *Zapatos Viejos* himself, which allowed him to indulge (whether consciously or not) his personal idiosyncrasies on camera. He situates Gloria in the most man-free environment imaginable—an all-girls orphanage run by nuns—and stages several creepily sensual scenes. In one, the now grown-up and buxom "Gloria Trevi" is urging some of the preteen girls in the orphanage to try on the skimpy little bras she's fashioned out of rags; in another, she and the same group of very young girls defy the nuns by sunbathing in the convent courtyard in barely-there bikinis. Strikingly, the film suddenly takes on a whole new focus after the secrets of the clan are revealed: The key premise is that a group of young girls is being imprisoned and tortured, with Gloria as their leader.

Because of the heavy borrowing from Gloria's previous film, which had, of course, borrowed from other old formula comedies, *Zapatos Viejos* seems as worn as any other copy of a copy. It's only when Gloria gets the chance to rip into a song that the movie comes to life, and the result is the same as it was with *Pelo Suelto:* Despite the cringeworthy plot and the fact that it was up against the latest hit movie in the *Batman* franchise, *Zapatos Viejos* set off a frenzy of fan worship. It set another Mexican box office record and started a nationwide craze for battered purple ten-eyed Dr. Martens boots with the thick lug sole, just like the ones Gloria wore. The style became so popular, and so associated with Gloria, that her fan club chose it as their identifying signature: They'd be known as Zapatos Viejos.

With fans in the millions and an unbroken string of hits to her credit, 1995 found Gloria with a choice of arenas for her next triumph. Televicine was clamoring for her next movie, record stores were eager for her next album, and talks had already begun with Hollywood producers to decide when and how she'd make her blockbuster debut. (A plan to co-star in Robert Rodriguez' 1992 movie *El Mariachi* had just been scuttled; Gloria would later say that on paper the sleeper hit made by a twenty-year-old director on a seven-thousand-dollar budget didn't seem nearly big enough for her.) Televisa, having repented for banishing Gloria in the past, now wanted exclusive rights for her TV appearances. With upstart network TV Azteca hot for Gloria as well, Sergio told Televisa that exclusivity would cost millions of dollars, more than for any other female performer in Latin America—take it or leave it. Televisa took it. The girl who'd offended the archbishop and ruined Emilio Azcárragas's dinner party was now his most highly paid celebrity.

Sergio, meanwhile, seemed to be settling rather uneasily into the life of a multimillionaire entertainment producer. Although Aline would try to seize half his assets during a divorce that would last more than two years, Sergio would manage to settle with her for a more modest alimony and retain his homes in Cuernavaca, Texas, Los Angeles, Spain, and Mexico City. He upgraded from the small sedans he'd been chauffeured in and adopted a black Lincoln sedan. He developed a taste for modern art and became a prominent patron of surrealist Sergio Bustamente, buying many of the artist's prized sculptures. Yet despite the affluence at his disposal, Sergio dressed terribly, usually in sweat clothes or rumpled jeans, and liked to sleep in a used mobile home. "That was so no one would know where he was," Aline said later. "He'd park the camper near his house so he could be close to home, but anyone passing by would see the lights off in the house and think he was out of town."

Gloria was also living much the way she had years earlier, when she'd bunked down with Mary Boquitas on the sofas in Sergio's studio. She'd celebrated her massive contract with Televisa by buying her own house in Mexico City, but by Gloria's own description, it functioned more like a sorority house than a superstar's mansion. Even though she'd furnished it with fine crystal, thick white carpets, and hand-painted porcelain vases,

Gloria had no domestic staff—there was no cook, no security guard, no cleaning woman. Instead, her mansion was always full of girls from the clan. Gloria treats this matter-of-factly: "Because I was traveling so much with Mary and Marlene, it was a relief to have people in the house," she explains in her memoir. That way, she continues, there was always someone stocking the refrigerator and keeping an eye on the garden. "We washed our clothes at the laundromat and took turns cleaning the house," Gloria says. "Whenever I was there, I took my turn washing the dishes, vacuuming, or dusting."

The *laundromat?* That made Gloria perhaps the only millionaire in the world who hauled her own sack of soiled laundry down to the public machines. If she really wanted to make sure there were snacks in the fridge and clean undies in her drawer, why wouldn't she just contract a housekeeper? Instead, the only ones in the house were Katia, Gaby, Andrea, Marlene and, until she ran off, Aline. Even Aline's mother, with her modest income, had a live-in housekeeper, but Gloria would rather split the chores with fellow members of Sergio's clan than hire someone. She provides an explanation, but it is a statement of fact, not a reason: "I didn't want any outsiders in my house." But it's *why* she didn't want outsiders in the house that's interesting, and left unexplained: With no domestic staff, no one outside the clan would ever know what was going on behind the door of Casa Trevi.

Gloria's house had another peculiar feature. Even though the only man in her life was married to one teenager and dating at least four others, Gloria equipped her house with a full nursery. "I bought a crib, a dresser, baby toys, nightlights, everything," Gloria notes in her memoir. "I was dreaming about having a baby of my own." She's as matter-of-fact about this admission as she was about her choice of twelve- and thirteen-year-old roommates instead of a housekeeper, apparently unaware that anyone would find it unusual that a part of her house was dedicated to her phantom baby and the relationship she'd never had.

Karina and her mother saw none of this when they arrived in Mexico City—not Sergio's secret camper, not Gloria's sorority house with the ghostly nursery. As Karina would later testify in court, they were met at the airport by Katia de la Cuesta, who had lately become one of Sergio's top lieutenants, and Mary Boquitas. The two girls escorted the Yapors to the luxurious Hotel del Bosque, near Chapultepec Park, and showed them to their suite. Mary said she'd be by to pick them up early the next morning for Karina's audition. As Karina unpacked her bags, she was sorry she hadn't brought some of her Barbies; it was going to be hard calming herself to sleep without them.

Her first impression of Sergio the following morning was, "He's very fat, and he's very serious." Karina and her mother had been chauffeured to another hotel, the grand Seville Palace, where they'd had breakfast. When it was time for the audition to begin, Karina's mother started to get up from the table, but Mary told her to sit down and stay comfortable: No parents allowed. Karina's audition was beginning just the way Aline had described hers, and it would continue to play out nearly identically. Karina was led upstairs to a master suite and left to stand uncomfortably alone, wondering what would happen next. Then Gloria entered and, as Karina recalls it, gave her a pep talk, which only made her more anxious. Here was her living daydream, her Barbie made real, urging her to give the audition all she had and not let her down. "Don't let anything stop you and do everything he asks," Gloria instructed. "Please, don't disappoint me."

That's when Sergio came through the door. Gloria had warned Karina that Sergio was very selective, and she felt she could see it in his forbidding face. Gloria presented Sergio, then left them alone—Mexico's most legendary star maker and a twelve-year-old girl who'd never left home before and slept with her Barbies. Sergio started in with an unexpected line of questioning: How close was Karina to her family? Was she religious? Did she have a boyfriend?

That last one made Karina crack up, just as Aline had years before, and she gave the same answer. *A boyfriend? I'm only twelve.* After she'd giggled a bit and said, "No," Sergio sent her to the bathroom to change clothes. Laid out for her was a short blouse, a miniskirt, and a pair of white boots. But the skirt was too small! Karina was struggling to make it work, to somehow pull it down far enough in back to cover her cheeks without exposing too much in front. She got more nervous and frantic when Gabriela Holguín came in and told her to hurry up. Everyone was waiting. Karina began to panic, but then recalled what Gloria had said:

"Don't let anything stop you." She gave the too-tiny skirt a final tug and walked back into the suite.

Sergio was stone-faced. He ordered her to profile right, profile left, turn around, dance a bit, then go back and change. When she emerged in her own clothes, Karina felt more comfortable, so she was more relaxed when Sergio asked her to improvise a bit. He wanted her to act sort of slutty, like a "fresh" girl. She gave it a try and won a laugh from Sergio. He thanked her, told her he'd make a decision very shortly, and prepared to leave. One of the girls would show her back downstairs, Sergio said, and he called for Katia. Immediately, a closet door popped open and Katia stepped out. Karina was startled—why was Katia hiding in there?—but she was too shy to ask and too nervous about saying anything that would ruin her chances.

Karina thought she'd have to wait days before someone would call with a decision, but before she and her mother had even left the Seville Palace Hotel, Sergio came down for a word with Mrs. Yapor. Karina had passed the audition, he said; but while Karina's heart was pounding with the news, Sergio went on to spell out a few points of business with her mother. Karina would have to move to Mexico City right away; she would need a passport, a U.S. visa, an original copy of her birth certificate, and a notarized letter from both parents granting legal guardianship to Sergio. All that was necessary, he explained to a bewildered Teresa Yapor, so her underage daughter could travel with the group on tour and to the recording studio in California. Once all Karina's documents were in order and she'd passed her three-month trial period, the Yapors would start receiving her monthly salary, just as Gloria had promised.

Karina's mother wept during the entire flight back to Chihuahua, Karina said later. Teresa Yapor seemed to accept the situation as decided and inevitable: Her only daughter was going to leave home, leave her family and her Barbies to travel the world with this rock group. She might not see Karina again for months; there would be no more family Christmas, no more birthday parties, no more bedtime chats in Karina's room. Her childhood was over.

Karina's father was equally troubled, but instead of coming out with a flat "No," he sought advice from the family's parish priest. Curiously, rather than confirming Miguel's doubts and reinforcing his opposition to the plan, something the priest said gave Miguel a whole new outlook. Keep in mind, the priest told him, good Christians have always been fearless missionaries. Karina might have a calling; it could very well be that her mission in life was to immerse herself in the world of these bawdy rock-and-rollers to evangelize and guide them. Perhaps, with the proper example living amongst them, Gloria and Sergio and all those young girls who lived with them could become devout Christians.

And so, with that rationale, Miguel Yapor sent his twelve-year-old daughter off to convert Mexico's most notorious pop star.

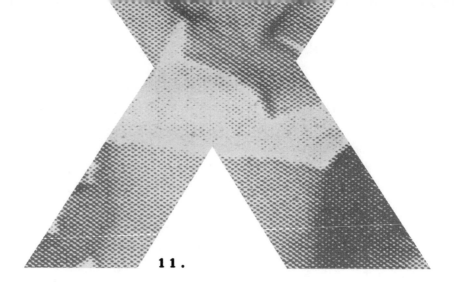

11.

Welcome to the White House

*W*hy were they always asking her about sex?

As soon as she arrived back in Mexico City to begin her classes, Karina would later testify, Mary and Katia again met her at the airport, but instead of bringing her to the star academy to meet her new classmates, they took her to a hotel near the airport. They'd be spending the night there, Mary said. She didn't explain why. Instead, the sexual interrogation began.

Right after they checked in, Karina says, Mary began asking questions about boys: Did Karina have a boyfriend? Did she like boys? What had she done with them? Hadn't she touched them, a little? Karina had nothing to say, but because Mary kept asking, she talked a little about a cute boy in her class whom she liked. That seemed to satisfy Mary for the present. Katia, meanwhile, listened in silence. Katia sort of creeped Karina out, the way she stared gloomily and never opened her mouth, like a robot. Maybe that's why Sergio stored her in the closet.

Early the next morning, the three girls caught a bus into the city and made their way to a small house on a side street. Mary took Karina's suitcase, saying she'd bring it to the residence for her, and then she left Karina alone with Katia. Karina was very excited . . . until she got inside. It was cold and barely furnished, and there was no one else there. Karina had been expecting classrooms alive with students and music, something like the studio where she'd taken jazz dance classes in Chihuahua. After all, Sergio had promised her she'd be given expert instruction in voice, dance, piano, languages, and choral arrangement. But where were the classes? Where were the instructors?

Right here, Katia told her; I'm your instructor. Katia handed her a pair of shorts and a T-shirt and told the girl to get changed. As soon as Karina returned, Katia began running her through calisthenics. Sit-ups, leg lifts, push-ups, squat thrusts . . . It went on for hours, until Karina was exhausted and ready to faint. Finally, after a full day of relentless exercise with no food and barely a break, Katia allowed Karina to stop. She opened a can of tuna for the girls to share; there was nothing else in the house to eat. Katia then pointed her toward a bed and told her to get some rest: The real work would begin the next morning.

For the next three days, Karina sweated, slept, and nibbled on tuna. Katia would rouse her early, exercise her all day, then open a can for her in the evening. She would have to lose weight, Katia told her, even though Karina was tall and slim for her age. She was told that only very fit, very slender girls could go onstage with Gloria or have any chance of landing a solo career. Karina continued following orders, even though she was sick with fatigue and ravenously hungry. Finally, on the fourth day, Mary showed up in an unmarked white van. Get in, Mary told her; it's time for the next part of your training.

Mary drove her to an address in Cuernavaca, to a place she called Casa Blanca. There she was given several outfits—two tiny bikinis, a pair of red high heels, a minidress, and a see-through dress—and told to model them, one after the other, for Sergio. Each time Karina tottered out of the room, awkward on the unfamiliar heels, Sergio would look on approvingly and snap Polaroids. Then he was gone, and Mary took over. She introduced Karina to the other clan girls in the house, calling them by names Sergio had made up for them. No one in the clan used their real names, Karina was told; they used "stage names" so they wouldn't be mobbed in public. As for lunch . . . well, Mary told her, most of the girls were starving down to get ready for Gloria's 1995 calendar shoot, so they wouldn't be eating that day.

Or the next, Karina discovered. By the third morning, she was woozy and feeling desperate. Even though the girls weren't being fed, there was no letup in their daily routine. Mary had added dance and voice lessons, so the group she was in—usually Karina, Wendy, and a Chilean girl, Edith Zuñiga—would spend ten hours working on dance routines, then singing scales, and always beginning and ending with the dreaded calisthenics. Also in the house at that time were Sonia Ríos, Gabriela Holguín, Marlene Calderón, and Katia and Karla de la Cuesta. Gloria was also a regular visitor whenever she was in town, and would occasionally spend the night. With ten young women at a time in residence, beds were scarce, so Karina usually found herself sharing a double bed with one, and sometimes two, other girls.

But by nightfall she didn't care how crammed the beds were; Karina was so worn out from hunger and her daily drills that she could barely stay on her feet. Before she fell asleep one of those first nights in Casa Blanca, however, she saw Wendy Castelo, then about fifteen, heading out the door. Wendy was going over to Casa Rosa, Sergio's private home, Mary told her: El Señor sometimes liked to talk with girls in private. It was a real privilege, Mary added, and a mark of esteem if El Señor showed that much interest in one of the girls. Sergio had so much esteem for Wendy, Karina noticed, that she didn't get back until the next morning.

That next evening, Sunday, it was Karina's turn. Sergio came by the house and said he was taking her out to eat. He drove her to a Burger King, where Karina devoured a hamburger. She began to feel better. Afterward, Sergio took her to the movies, which surprised Karina; she'd only just arrived and was only days into her test period, and already the head of this entire entertainment operation was taking her out to a movie. Until that night, he'd barely spoken to her, even when he was snapping Polaroids while she modeled in her bikinis and sheer dress. Karina recalls it was a Sylvester Stallone movie Sergio took her to see, because of the nude scene; when she saw the actors drop their clothes, she clamped her eyes shut. She wasn't used to seeing films with naked bodies, and it startled her.

That was a mistake.

After the movie, Sergio drove Karina back to the house and dropped her off. It was funny, she thought, how quiet he'd suddenly gotten after all his chattiness at Burger King. During the meal, he'd wanted to know all about her "values" and her "way of thinking," questions she hadn't understood at all until he translated them into a twelve-year-old's terms: What did she think about lying, and about people who told lies? He thought lies were just "the worst," Sergio told her. Karina agreed; lies were certainly very bad. He seemed happy with her answer.

But ever since the movie, Sergio had been silent. Karina found out why later that same night, when Wendy Castelo came back from another visit to Sergio's house. (Karina was already having trouble remembering Wendy's real name; Wendy was so devoted to Sergio and so fierce about maintaining his rules that Wendy always referred to herself as "Claudia," the code name Sergio had given her.) Wendy had bad news for Karina: Sergio was very upset, Wendy said, because Karina had acted like such a phony by pretending to be shocked by the movie. Sergio just hated hypocrites, Wendy told her. He didn't believe she was a virgin, so all this pretending to be shocked by some little nude scene really offended him. Sergio was so angry, he was seriously thinking about throwing Karina out of the group.

Karina was in a panic. But she *was* a virgin, she insisted.

Well, Wendy said, she'd have to prove it—otherwise Sergio was going to send her home.

Prove it? How could she prove it?

Marlene had an idea. All you have to do, she told Karina, is confess to Sergio that you're in love with him, and then when you have sex with him, he'll find out you're telling the truth about being a virgin. There—problem solved.

Karina's head was spinning. *What were these girls talking about?*

Mary showed up a little while later. She'd just come from Sergio's house, she said, and confirmed what Wendy had told Karina: Sergio was so upset, he'd ordered Mary to drive Karina to Mexico City first thing in the morning and put her on the next plane back to Chihuahua. Honesty was very important in an artist, Mary told Karina; there was no way Sergio could turn her into a true interpreter of passion and poetry if she wasn't going to be absolutely honest with him, to begin with, and then with her audience. If Sergio suspected a singer was a liar, he wouldn't waste his time on her.

Karina was desperate. Wasn't there *anything* she could do? Mary could only think of one possibility: Karina could go over to Sergio's house right away, try to talk to him, and see if she could convince him that she wasn't a liar. It was late, and he'd already made up his mind, but it might be worth a try. Karina hesitated—she'd never seen Sergio enraged before, but she'd heard frightening stories from the other girls. However, Mary was urging her and even volunteered to drive, so Karina mustered her nerve.

When they got to Sergio's house, as Karina would later testify, all the lights were out. Mary brought Karina inside, and led her through the darkened house to a door. She pushed it half open, nudged Karina inside, and shut the door behind her. Karina was nearly trembling; there were no lights on in this room, either. Then she heard Sergio's voice and saw the glow from his luminous watch. The faint blue blob began waving through the air; Sergio was calling her over. Karina approached and discovered he was lying in bed. She immediately began to cry and apologize, trying to explain that she really wasn't a liar, but as soon as she started, Sergio pulled her toward him, giving Karina a hug and a kiss on the forehead.

Being held in a hug made Karina even more nervous. She began talking uncontrollably, chattering out more explanations and apologies, until Sergio cut her short. "Will you please do me the favor," he requested, "of shutting up?" Still, he had to repeat it several times before Karina was able to control her nerves enough to obey. As soon as she stopped talking, Sergio kissed her again, this time on the lips. He started fumbling for her "intimate parts," as Karina would later say, forcing his hands into her blouse and down the front of her pants. Karina, shocked, twisted away and pulled his hands out of her clothes, but Sergio only used the momentum of her parry to draw her hand onto his penis.

Karina jerked back her hand. She sat there frozen with confusion. Sergio let her go. He yelled out for Mary, who appeared at the door within moments. Bring Karina back to the house, he ordered Mary. Karina got up to leave, feeling like she was about to faint. They would talk again later, Sergio told Karina as she was going. During the drive back to the house, Karina didn't say anything to Mary about what had just happened. There was no more talk, either, about her being thrown out of the group. Mary didn't mention it again, and Karina, stunned and brooding, had momentarily forgotten about it.

The next morning, Sergio breezed in to the girls' house. He had Karina summoned and began chatting with her as if nothing had happened—not the threat of dismissal, not his clumsy fumbling in her clothes the night before. Karina kept her eyes on his feet while he talked, unable to look him in the face. But Sergio was so warm and friendly that after a while, she began to relax and lift her gaze. The whole episode must have been some kind of . . . some kind of mistake. She didn't know what *kind* of a mistake, since no middle-aged man had ever groped her before, but she wanted it to be a mistake—she *wanted* to believe that Sergio was the benevolent genius who would make her a star—so she decided a misunderstanding had led to a blind impulse. It was over; she would forget it. Sergio took her out for lunch, and it was actually kind of fun: He seemed really interested in Karina and gave no hint of any discomfort between them.

Much later, after she'd ended her fugitive days with Sergio and Gloria and had been reunited with her family and the newborn son she'd abandoned on the run, Karina would be asked in court why, after that first night in Sergio's bedroom, she didn't call her parents and go home. Why would she remain in a house that was run more like a prison camp than a music school, where she was molested, criticized, tortured with endless exercise, and only fed an occasional can of tuna? It obviously wasn't the high-powered star academy she'd been led to expect, and the so-called classes, given by a pair of twenty-year-old backup singers, were even inferior to the dance classes she'd gotten in a no-name studio on a backstreet in Chihuahua. So why stay?

Years later, another young teen would struggle to answer the same question. Elizabeth Smart had just turned fourteen when, late on the night of June 5, 2002, a forty-nine-year-old religious zealot named Brian David Mitchell and his wife cut a hole in the screen of her suburban Utah bedroom window and led her out at knifepoint. When the trio was finally located nine months later, the young teen was disguised under a wig, veil, and dark glasses, and at first denied her identity. Even when police separated her from her two abductors, Elizabeth insisted that her name was Augustine and responded to the officers' questions with tears in her eyes and the biblical denial, "Thou sayest." Later, after her identity had been confirmed and she'd been reunited with her family, Elizabeth would try to explain how she'd become so mysteriously attached to her two captors: For months, she said, she'd been held in a remote campsite by the two zealots, who proclaimed, "We are messengers of the Lord, Jesus Christ." So assertive was their authority that Elizabeth, instead of trying to flee, began to believe her captors' constant refrain that her true role in life was to become Mitchell's second wife and bear him children.

While it seems awful and unthinkable to anyone outside the situation, abduction experts understand that to a girl whose identity is in a state of psychosexual flux, an outside force that suddenly appears and offers answers to her secret questions can be very hard to resist. As a new fourteen-year-old, Elizabeth was very likely in the midst of a struggle to make sense of a budding sexuality, which can be confusing and, in a religiously oppressive environment like Salt Lake City, frightening and shameful. So when a powerful man took control of her life and told her what she should be doing with these new feelings, Elizabeth may have felt relief. As one psychiatrist who'd analyzed the Smart case put it, "What he may have set up in her mind is that everyone and everything outside their family group [the abductors and Elizabeth] was evil and threatening, and even her future, her salvation and safety depended on him for safety and guidance." There was another key similarity between Elizabeth Smart and the girls in Sergio's clan: even though Elizabeth's family requested privacy on her behalf after she'd been liberated, Elizabeth reportedly wanted to play herself in a TV movie about the abduction. The allure of fame and of an identity outside the family was still powerful, even after an experience as traumatic as hers.

When Karina had to answer the same question about why she never fled when she had the chance, she struggled in both the courtroom and her own written account of her clan years, called *Revelaciones: Mis amargas experiencias con Gloria Trevi, Sergio Andrade y Mary Boquitas,* to come up with something better than "I honestly don't know." She talked about how much she wanted to be a star, and how afraid she was of blowing this opportunity and disappointing her parents. But also, more significantly, she talked about how she was afraid of disappointing Gloria. The transference of authority, in mental coercion terms, had already taken place; and judging by Karina's description of her first few days in the Trevi-Andrade mansion, it had been executed in textbook fashion: She had been selected at the most vulnerable age; she'd been physically weakened through hard exercise, poor food, and interrupted sleep; her belief systems had been pecked at and challenged by the more conditioned girls, a peer group she naturally identified with; and finally, just as her anxiety level was reaching its peak, a proxy was provided who would take the place of her parents. Gloria became the "substitute friend" referred to by Denise Winn in *The Manipulated Mind: Brainwashing, Conditioning, and Indoctrination;* when Karina needed someone to clear her confusion and help her decide what to do, the person she reached out to was Gloria.

And Gloria was there, Karina says.

By the end of that week, Karina was back in Sergio's bed. A few days after her friendly lunch with Sergio, she says, Mary brought her back to Sergio's house for another "talk." Sergio closed the door behind them, as Karina would later testify, and began caressing her. There's no indication that the twelve-year-old put up any kind of fight this time. "I don't remember how it happened," Karina says, "but I woke up the following morning in his bed, naked and covered with a sheet." During the night, Sergio told her, Gloria had peeked in on them; she was very happy to see them together, Sergio said. After they'd gotten up and dressed for breakfast, Karina adds, Gloria was there, and in a celebratory mood. "She said she was very happy for us, and would congratulate me by putting me on 'the pill,' and was very pleased because she hadn't seen Sergio so content in a long time."

Karina's response to all this? According to her, none. She wasn't upset, or frightened, or resigned. She felt . . . nothing. It's as if her mind had shut down and she was being led along in a stupor. "I felt absolutely confused," she says. "I didn't understand what was going on." She had no reaction to Gloria's gleeful promise to help continue whatever had just happened to Karina by arranging for birth control, and had no reaction when Gloria went into a rant about hymens. What's the big deal about virginity? Karina recalls Gloria asking. Don't we have the same rights as men? Then why should women be judged by whether a certain membrane had been penetrated? Most men are such mediocrities, Gloria went on, and that's why Karina was so lucky to have been deemed worthy by Sergio. He was the most tender and marvelous man imaginable, Gloria told her, and that's why it was so perfect that he would have a young girl like Karina to take care of him, because she had so much to give. Sergio, Gloria concluded, was *lo maximo.*

Once Karina's resistance was broken, Sergio's demands for sex became more voracious, varied, and abusive. Within days, Karina says, she was immersed in sadomasochism, group sex, and bisexuality. And as he had from the beginning, Sergio's technique for nudging Karina past her final resistance to each new taboo was to attack her for not being a loving and honest enough person. Essentially, he was preempting her reluctance to do something indecent by saying she already *had* done something indecent—*she had lied, the worst sin of all! she had been heartless!*—so the sex wasn't a sin, but an act of atonement. He'd make her feel guilty, then demand a punishment, and the first step of each new punishment required her to strip off her clothes. She could show that she was a loving, sincere, and giving person—*an artist!*—by making Sergio happy.

Soon Karina had gone beyond doing things she'd thought were wrong to doing things she'd never imagined. One evening, Sergio got angry when he learned Karina hadn't managed to memorize the melody and lyrics of "If" by the end of the day, as he'd ordered. He raised his hand to slap her; when Karina cringed from the blow, he stormed out of the house in a rage. Later that night, Karina says, Gloria and Mary brought her over to Sergio's house to make amends. She was told to wait outside Sergio's room in silence until she was summoned. Finally, she was called in. "If you love me or care for me, you have to learn what it really means to love," Sergio scolded her. "You can't keep acting like a little girl." He paced back and forth, Karina says, while continuing to berate her.

She had to grow up, Sergio shouted, and learn what real love meant. The other girls all got it; why were they so much more mature than she? He could give her the perfect example, Sergio said. There was another person who loved him, he told Karina, and even though that girl knew he was involved with Karina, she could accept it. *She loved him just the same!* Now that, Sergio said, is a girl who understands honesty and human emotion. That is a girl who will become a great artist. If Karina truly loved him, it wouldn't matter to her if he were involved with other women— she would accept it. Didn't she understand that making people happy was the most heartfelt way of showing how much she cared?

Again Karina felt like she was in a fog. She couldn't really make sense of what he was saying anymore, and found herself simply repeating, "Yes, sir. . . . Yes, Sergio. . . . Yes, sir." At some point, Karina says, in the midst of Sergio's rant and her mumbled acquiesence, Sergio shouted for Marlene. The other girl appeared quickly. Marlene was already naked, Karina says, and seemed to know exactly what Sergio wanted her to do, as if it had been prearranged. Marlene came over to Sergio and began caressing him. Karina stood there, not shocked so much as uncertain. Was this Sergio's way of dismissing her? No, he was beckoning her closer. She went. He wanted her to please both of them, Sergio said. She did. Afterward, he reminded her that she was still in trouble; her punishment wasn't over yet.

On another occasion, Sergio announced he was displeased with Marlene, Wendy, and Karina. The three girls were assembled outside Sergio's room. Marlene was summoned inside first, while the other two waited by the door. They could hear an electric cord whistling through the air, the sound of it cracking into Marlene's flesh, her whimpers. Ten blows. Wendy was called in next. Again Karina heard ten sharp cracks and Wendy's choked-off cries. Then it was her turn. Marlene and Wendy were no longer in the room. Sergio showed Karina where to kneel next to the bed. Karina buried her face in a pillow; she knew that screaming would only make Sergio angrier. But Sergio made her throw it aside. *You're acting like an infant,* he told her; could she please do him the favor of taking her punishment like a real woman?

When he was finished, when Karina was left with throbbing welts across her back and bottom, Marlene and Wendy came back into the room. "We all began to have sexual relations with him," Karina wrote later. "Sergio sat down, while one girl took his penis and masturbated him, introducing his penis into the other girl's mouth. First he penetrated one, then the other, and me last, kissing the other girls at the same time while they caressed him." The scene was repeated often, Karina says, with only the severity of the punishment and the combination of girls changing. To distinguish one punishment orgy from another, she had to situate them in her memory by cast and location, and even the confusion of bodies left her vague about who was doing what, when, and to whom. The girls become so interchangeable that Karina ends up referring to them, and occasionally even to herself, as either "the other girl" or just a number. "The first time I had sex when Wendy and Edith were present was in the Casa Rosa," begins one typical description. "He was seated in a big living-room chair. He put his fingers of his left hand into the vagina of one girl, his right hand on my breasts, while penetrating the third girl at the same time."

Sergio was somewhat concerned about birth control, but consistent with his apparently unrestrained self-indulgence, he took only adolescent precautions. If he wasn't able to withdraw before ejaculating, he ordered the girls to resort to a home prophylactic that largely went out of style with American teenagers in the 1950s. "Suddenly, he pushed two of us away and began pushing hard against the third girl, I thought because he was really excited. Afterward, he was irritated because she hadn't satisfied him the way he'd wanted. Apparently, she'd done something wrong, I don't know if she'd gone rigid or what. Anyway, he made me run into the kitchen. Wendy came in right afterward to get two Coca-Colas out of the case. I didn't understand what she was doing at first, but then I found out they were using them for vaginal douches, so they would avoid getting pregnant." Once the girls had finished washing each other with cola, Karina was allowed back into the room.

Within a few weeks, Karina was accepting clan life as her routine. Hunger, punishment, pleasing Sergio—that was the new center of her universe, and she accepted it without protest or complaint. Sergio had succeeded almost too well at taming the girls—for the few outsiders who had contact with the clan, the girls' mute obedience seemed uncomfortably strange. Even Gloria, Sergio's apparently devoted accomplice, was now knuckling under completely to Sergio's daily discipline. In private she suffered his rages and commands; in public she remained silent until Sergio indicated she could speak.

"I often heard or saw them arguing," Karina would recount in her *Revelaciones*. "Gloria only cried without saying anything, while he screamed the entire time. He would scold her for being rebellious, for disobeying his orders, and then he would send the rest of us upstairs to wait in one of the bedrooms. They would stay downstairs, and we could hear the shouts from him and the sobbing from her." This would sometimes go on all day or through the night, Karina says; the girls wouldn't be allowed to leave the bedroom for six or seven hours, sometimes until the next morning. Sergio's obsession with dominating and humiliating the woman who'd made him successful could have destroyed both their careers, but perversely, it turned out to be a huge benefit. Sergio's abuse touched off an odd circular reaction: The more Sergio abused Gloria in private, the more outrageous Gloria behaved in public; the greater her outrages, the greater her popularity; the greater her popularity, the greater Sergio's compulsion to break her. And the cycle began again.

Gloria endured more than just tongue-lashings, Karina adds; even though Sergio's fortune was largely based on Gloria's face and ability to look sensational in a bikini, he would occasionally beat Gloria savagely enough to leave bruises. One time, Karina says, when she was having sex with Sergio, Gloria, and Liliana, she found it strange that Sergio wouldn't let Gloria take her shirt off. Even when Sergio was penetrating Gloria "in a nontraditional position," Karina says, Sergio held on to Gloria's shirt so it wouldn't fly up. She believes it was to hide the marks of a beating.

"There were times when I thought even she was unhappy," Karina recounts. "One day, for instance, I saw her coming out of Sergio's room in tears. She came up to me, weeping, and asked me to promise her that I would never do what she had done. Since I was being punished then by not being allowed to speak to anyone, I couldn't ask her what she had done and could only nod in agreement. Later, though, once I got to know Sergio better, I figured out that she must have told him that she wanted to leave, that she couldn't take it anymore." Yet even though Gloria might have gone into the room to tell Sergio she was leaving, she came out not only committed to staying, but tearfully urging Karina not to act as foolishly as she had. Somehow Sergio only needed a single conversation to quell a rebellion and turn it to his advantage—even a rebellion by his wealthiest and most willful disciple.

For those who'd known Gloria from her first *Siempre en Domingo* days, this change in her was new and unsettling, but most people didn't have a chance to see enough of Gloria or the girls to notice a difference. Offstage, Gloria was very rarely in public, and when she was, it was usually the brief, controlled, stage-crafted setting of a press interview or promotional appearance. She wasn't known to attend parties or to socialize with anyone apart from Sergio. The only people who seemed to see much of Gloria anymore were the fans beneath the footlights and the stage assistants behind them. Once the curtain dropped, Gloria was gone.

Maritza López, however, had a chance to catch up with Gloria every year. Maritza had been photographing Gloria ever since her breakthrough, first for her album covers, and then every year after for Gloria's pinup calendars. The two women got along beautifully; Gloria loved the attention of a photo shoot, and Maritza loved a model who looked spectacular on film and was willing to do anything. But by the time Maritza met up with Gloria and the girls to shoot the 1995 calendar, their relationship had suddenly changed. "Strange things were happening," Maritza López would later tell the Mexico City newspaper *La Jornada*. Previously, Gloria and Maritza would joke around and brainstorm ideas; but by 1995, Sergio would no longer allow even Maritza to speak to Gloria in private. Gloria would be just as fun and nutty as ever during the shoot—but the instant the arc lights were extinguished, Maritza said, "she would turn into someone else." Gloria talked to no one but Sergio, Maritza recalled, "and it was all 'Yes sir, No sir,' with her eyes down."

The girls in her entourage were no different. The backdrop of one set of photos was supposed to be a pool party, with the girls laughing and splashing together in tiny bikinis, then setting off for bed in panties and micronighties. But when Gloria and the clan girls arrived at the luxury home being used for the shoot, Maritza was surprised to find them grimy and unwashed, with filthy clothes and greasy hair. Even after they'd been spruced up for the camera, the girls were cowed and quiet—and starving, Maritza added. Sergio allowed them nothing to eat, so the girls all sat in stomach-rumbling silence until Gloria managed to sneak out and come back with some potato chips and snack cakes, which they devoured. When it came time to hop into the pool and prance around in their nighties, the girls lit up; when the flashbulbs stopped, they shut down like Gloria.

Karina took it all in numbly. From a brainwashing perspective, that is exactly the reaction to be expected. One of the underlying theories of mental coercion comes from the conditioning experiments Russian scientist Ivan Pavlov conducted with dogs in the 1920s, and an accidental discovery he made after the dogs nearly drowned. When a flood swept through Leningrad in 1924, Pavlov's dogs were trapped in their cages and slowly submerged. Only their muzzles were still reaching air when a lab assistant managed to make his way into the lab to free them. After the intense anxiety of that trauma, Pavlov found, the dogs fell into depression: They were listless and much less responsive. However, they were also much more malleable: mentally exhausted from the stress, the dogs followed instructions with much less resistance. Their adherence to normal habits had been broken. They didn't have the will or inclination anymore to follow their own instincts. Instead, they did as Pavlov wanted.

Pavlov called this effect "cortical inhibition of the higher cerebral function." On a more acute level, it's commonly known as a "mental breakdown." Essentially, cortical inhibition occurs when the stress is so great that the mind surrenders; it goes into a protective shutdown mode, much like a circuit breaker cutting off energy flow when the surge is too intense for the machinery to handle. Something similiar happens with mental circuitry. When stress is so intense that it threatens to permanently harm a person's sanity, the mind can go into a "sleep" mode. This deadened responsiveness helps insulate the mind from further stress, but as a corollary, it also makes the individual more receptive to controlling influences. Since the mind is abdicating the decision-making process, the door is open for an outside authority to take over.

It doesn't take a life-threatening experience to reach that level of stress; through further experimentation, Pavlov found he could prompt cortical inhibition through the use of four techniques. According to a CIA study of brainwashing, interrogators in Asian prisoner-of-war camps adapted Pavlov's findings almost point for point, and used them to brainwash resistant prisoners. The fours steps are: exhaustion, brought about by forced labor or exercise and poor food; chronic physical pain, which is not the acute pain of electroshock or whipping, but the dull discomfort of cold and hunger; confusion, created by asking difficult and artfully crafted questions that cause the subject to question what he really knows; and finally, emotional tension, the escalating self-doubt that causes the brainwashing victim to be desperate for someone to tell him what to do—he can no longer tell if resistance is noble or foolish, and is ripe for anyone to make the decision for him. At that point the brainwasher suddenly transforms from tormentor to savior, because he can make the suffering go away.

In Karina's case, exhaustion was induced from the moment she was put into Sergio's care; she slept in crowded beds and was roused early to struggle through grueling workouts. "Deprivation of sleep," the CIA study points out, "results in more intense psychological debilitation than does any other method of engendering fatigue." Karina also endured the chronic pain of constant, gnawing hunger, and the accompanying mental weakening caused by poor nutrition. According to the CIA study, "Studies of controlled starvation indicate that the whole value-system of the subjects underwent a change." The technique, typically, was for brainwashing subjects to be starved for several days, then treated to a meal. Without any explicit offer being stated, they are quickly conditioned to understand that if they cooperate, they are fed. Similarly, Karina learned that if she was pleasant to Sergio, she went to Burger King. If not, Mary might give her a can of tuna, like feeding a cat. Even the meal Sergio treated Karina to after he groped her worked to his strategic advantage:

"Friendliness of the interrogator, when least expected, upsets the prisoner's ability to maintain a critical attitude," the CIA study found.

One unexpected discovery in brainwashing research is that strong willpower can actually work *against* the subject. By trying to resist, the subject makes himself even more vulnerable to coercion. One common technique in the camps was to force prisoners to stand in place for long periods of time, much like the famous parade formation scene in the World War II movie *Bridge on the River Kwai*. Those prisoners determined to grit it out and show no weakness would eventually be attacked by self-doubt—the longer they stood, the more their pain; the more their pain, the more they had to consider whether they were making the right choice. Once the prisoner started doubting his own judgment, his mind automatically started looking for guidance: Who could solve his dilemma and show him what he should do? As pain increases, so does doubt; as doubt increases, so does the longing for relief and the instinctive search for guidance. That's why, by their very resistance, the stronger prisoners inadvertently played into the hands of their brainwashers—they planted the seeds of doubt in their own minds, making themselves ripe for an outside authority to tell them what to do. By Karina's description, her dilemma was present from the first day: Should she stick out the long hours of exercise or give up and go home?

For help she turned to the other girls in the clan. That's when the confusion stage was launched. Karina's confusion was both situational—she didn't know what was expected of her, or what would happen next in this strange star academy, or why Sergio was always angry with her, or even where she was—and also conversational, in the head-spinning exchanges she had with Gloria and the other girls. The goal of confusion in mental-coercion efforts is to throw the subject's sense of reality off balance; the question itself can be based on false notion, but because the subject is so intent on finding an answer, he doesn't realize that he's unwittingly accepting a perspective he wouldn't ordinarily agree with. Karina faced that very scenario after she'd clamped her eyes shut during the movie with Sergio. As she struggled to understand what she'd done wrong, Wendy and Marlene engaged her in this disorienting syllogism: Artists can't be liars; if you're a virgin, you have to prove you're not lying; you can prove you're not lying by surrendering your virginity, thereby making you an artist.

The combination of those four forces left Karina in a weakened state for dealing with her ultimate dilemma: Should she have sex with Sergio? If she did, it would violate her sense of right and wrong; if she didn't, she would have to leave Sergio's star school and go home. The anxiety of that predicament was yet another stress for her to deal with: In addition to hunger, exhaustion, self-doubt, and confusion, she also had to fend off Sergio's groping. And of all those woes, sex was the only one Karina had any control over. She couldn't get more food on her own, or opt out of the workouts, or find mental clarity—but she could submit and have sex with Sergio. As soon as she did, she would be relieved of one of her stresses. And that, in the end, is the final stage of brainwashing: to offer the subject a single choice he can make to bring some relief to his life. It's not an automatic decision, however; the subject has to find a way to accept this submission, and that is done by changing his values. Once it dawns on the brainwashing subject that all he has to do is reconsider his opinion on one moral point, suddenly the path to relief is clear.

"The realization that there is an acceptable solution to his problem is the first stage of reducing the individual's conflict," the CIA study concludes. "It is characteristically reported by victims of brainwashing that this discovery led to an overwhelming feeling of relief.... It is at this point that they are prepared to make major changes in their value-system. This is an automatic rather than voluntary choice. They have lost their ability to be critical."

Karina didn't need to search for her rationale for relief; it was provided for her by Gloria, when Gloria launched into dismissive rants about the value of virginity. Suddenly, Karina had a way out: If she changed her mind about the morality of having sex with Sergio, she could both stay in school *and* avoid doing something wrong. Sex would instantly be the right thing to do.

Why? Simple—because Karina had decided it was no longer wrong.

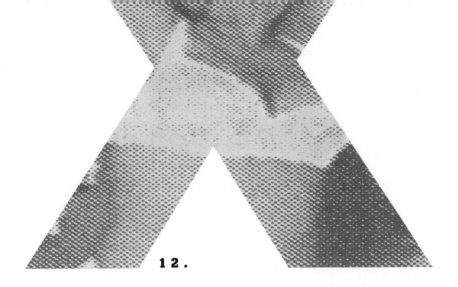

The Mennonites

This had to be some kind of trick.

What else could explain what was going on with Gloria? Patricia Chapoy couldn't figure it out. The three of them—Sergio, Gloria, and Paty Chapoy—were spending hours a day in her office at TV Azteca, working through the terms of a blockbuster contract, and Gloria just sat there in a stupor. This was complicated and important business they were working on, and it was more important for Gloria than anyone. Yet hour after hour, she just stared down at the table and wouldn't say a word.

The outside world saw no hint that anything was wrong with Gloria. To her millions of fans, the politicians begging for her endorsement, and the intellectual elite who'd come to respect her, the only commotion visible was the approach of the next Trevi-Andrade entertainment juggernaut. That year, 1996, was shaping into the greatest of Gloria's career. She and Sergio had just finished filming her third movie, *Una Papa Sin Catsup (A French Fry Without Ketchup)*, which Sergio had written, cast, and directed; their latest album, *Si Mi Llevas Contigo (If You Take Me*

With You) had just come out; Gloria had just been voted "Mexico's Favorite Star" by *TVyNovelas* magazine; and another of her wildly popular pinup calendars was on the stands.

And to top it all, a furious bidding war had broken out for her between the two television networks. TV Azteca had just been launched the year before and was already ferocious in its pursuit of viewers, airing shows as wild and titillating as the government would allow. TV Azteca was targeting teenagers: Teenage fashion set the entertainment agenda for the nation, and advertisers always poured their money into the network that could attract them. Almost anything TV Azteca could do to brand itself right from the start as the hip choice would be worth the cost of investment.

Televisa was now facing competition for the first time. The Tiger knew how buzz worked, and unless he quelled this upstart very quickly, the media angle on the story for the coming years would focus relentlessly on how the underdog was chipping away at the tired giant. Those kinds of stories would be brutal for Televisa and the best kind of free promotion for TV Azteca, because the more TV Azteca was seen as an up-and-comer, the more it would be identified with freshness, rebellion, and youth—the very market it was trying to capture. The Tiger needed to make a powerful statement, once and for all, to show that only Televisa could provide the very best in Mexican entertainment. TV Azteca, on the other hand, had to associate itself with the coolest acts around.

The answer to both their predicaments was Gloria.

That's how Paty Chapoy, TV Azteca's production director, found herself locked in secret talks with Sergio and Gloria. She was on the verge of pulling a tremendous coup; she was about to steal Mexican TV's biggest attraction away from Mexico's biggest TV network. In just a matter of days, if everything worked out as planned, she'd be getting Gloria Trevi to abandon Televisa and sign an exclusive contract with TV Azteca. It was tricky work: The contract could deal with hundreds of contingencies and tens of millions of dollars, and a mistake could damage all of their careers. Yet throughout each of the meetings, Gloria sat slumped in a chair, silent.

This had to be a tactic, Paty thought; it just wasn't possible that Latin

America's most famous firebrand was this . . . *lifeless*. Sergio had to be up to something. Paty may not have known Gloria very well, but she had seen Sergio in action for a long time, and she knew exactly what he was capable of. That's why, when they were vying back and forth over contract conditions and payment, she had to suspect he was somehow orchestrating this strange silence by his star to get an edge. "He's been a liar all his life," Paty says. "[The singer] César Costa once told me that when Sergio was making his album, they met at the Mexico City airport to fly to L.A. where they were going to record. After they boarded the plane, Sergio said he was going to get off and grab a newspaper. He never came back. The plane took off, and César Costa never saw him again. That's Sergio Andrade."

Paty had also known for some time now that there was something odd about Sergio's star school. "Once I went to Sergio's office, where he worked with these youngsters. He said he was preparing to launch their musical careers, but to me they looked very young. All I saw were thirteen-year-old girls there," Paty would later recall. When asked if any music producers besides Sergio surrounded themselves with teenage girls, Paty shook her head. "No," she replied. "I never saw anything like that anywhere else. Other producers came to me with a boy or a girl, but not with a singular group of girls like Sergio's."

And no doubt about it, Sergio's girl gang was peculiar-looking. For glamorous calendar girls and aspiring celebrities, they looked awful; as Maritza López had remarked, the girls went around dressed in stained, rumpled clothes, with their long hair stringy and unwashed and dirt crusted in their fingernails. What made their poor hygiene so noticeable was their numbers: None of the girls, it seemed—not even Gloria—ever traveled alone. Instead, where one went, they all went. "Whenever they came to my office, Gloria was never by herself, and she never looked anything like what you see on stage," says Paty Chapoy. "She was always escorted by Sergio and a bunch of the girls, about fifteen of them at a time. Gloria never had bodyguards, only these young girls who looked after her. They were ten-, eleven-, twelve-year-old girls, all of them dressed in old jeans and hats."

Still, despite these unmistakable signs that something was not quite right about Sergio's organization, Paty never thought of backing out of the contract they were negotiating. No matter how strangely Gloria was acting or how suspicious Paty already was of Sergio's scruples, this deal was too big for her fledgling network and her personally for Paty to quash. Azteca's owner, Ricardo Salinas Pliego, didn't have a fraction of Televisa's money; he didn't even have television experience. Yet he was already on his way to grabbing 40 percent of the Mexican viewing market—an astounding amount for such a raw, tiny network—and he hadn't gotten there by avoiding risk.

Salinas had made his money selling furniture and electrical appliances, and only got into entertainment as a long-shot investment when the government decided to grant a second TV license. Salinas didn't know anything about show business, but he knew how to run a business, and one of the first things he did was to sniff around and find out who was behind the scenes making the stars look good at Televisa. He knew that ultimately, on-air talent was replaceable—what made the TV anchors and talk show hosts and game show presenters seem so special was the work of a few key people in production and management who knew how to prep and package them. Get the right backstage people, Salinas figured, and creating on-air stars shouldn't be a problem. He needed to steal a great TV mind from Televisa, and he got one: Paty Chapoy.

Pretty and petite in a Sally Field sort of way, Paty Chapoy has always looked a good decade younger than her age. Perhaps that's why, in an industry devoted to flamboyance, she had always cut back against the grain and dressed and styled herself in prim, First Lady–like fashion. Her pink suits with shoulder-shawls and nail polish to match evoked a look Jaqueline Kennedy had popularized thirty years earlier, and her lush brown hair was always tamed into a matronly bob. If Gloria Trevi had an astral opposite, it was Paty Chapoy.

But there was nothing matronly or conservative about Paty Chapoy when it came time to work—and she was always working. Paty Chapoy was one major reason, perhaps *the* major reason, for Raúl Velasco's perpetual, continent-wide success on *Siempre en Domingo*. During her years as the show's talent coordinator, Paty's job description was simple: Know everything about Mexican entertainment before anyone else. The show had to constantly appear fresh and authoritative, which meant Paty had to be the first to know which raw band was on the verge of pulling its sound together and needed to be scheduled at once and which revered veteran was sounding flat in the studio and shouldn't be scheduled again.

So keeping on top of music world intrigue became her driving obsession, as it had to be; unlike writers or actors, who develop over time and have a predetermined debut date, musicians can set the country on fire in a random, unforeseeable instant. Everyone knows when a novel or movie will be launched; but no one can predict when a certain melody, a quirky voice, an innovative image will suddenly jangle the national nerve. No one could know in advance when that kind of lightning would strike— but Paty *had* to know. She worked at it all the time, tapping Sergio and other top producers, like "El Güero" Gil and Hector Meneses, for constant updates about the talent they had in development. Paty Chapoy was her own industry-wide central intelligence agency.

Eventually, her nose for news led her from gathering it to dispensing it. Whether it was the natural talent for reporting that made her a great talent coordinator or the work of sniffing out undiscovered talent that made her a great reporter, Paty transformed herself into the director of top TV news programs. After she was hired away by TV Azteca in 1994, she became one of the very rare executives in the business who starred on both sides of the camera. Even though she was the network's director of TV production, she continued hosting her own news and interview program, *Ventaneando*. She'd become too much of a newshound to direct from the wings; like Barbara Walters, Paty Chapoy could command nearly any position she wanted at the network, but what she wanted most of all was to be in the middle of the latest, biggest story.

One more thing: Paty Chapoy didn't want to just read news from a TelePrompTer—she wanted to *make* it. Later, when Sergio was on the run, only TV Azteca's director of television productions would land that interview with Sergio's mortified brother, Senator Eduardo "Lalo" Andrade. Only Paty Chapoy would manage to track down and interview Gloria's mysterious Texan cousin, Mariana, despite the fact that Mariana had no listed phone number or address and was by then going by the name Brandy. And when she thought there was a chance of interviewing Sergio himself, Paty didn't dispatch one of her reporters: She dropped everything and got on a flight deep into Brazil, to Papuda prison. By that point, both Sergio and Gloria were blaming Paty for their imprisonment and accusing her of slander and adultery. But Paty went anyway. She had to—it was great TV.

But all that would come later. During their contract talks, Paty tried hard to make Gloria and Sergio feel warm and at home. Gloria had to leave Televisa, Sergio told Paty, because of a peculiar artistic difference: somehow Televisa was both too high- and too lowbrow for them. On the one hand, Televisa couldn't come up with any program for Gloria except a remake of some stupid old game show. On the other, the network refused to air the special video Sergio had made during the shooting of Gloria's 1995 calendar. Televisa executives said the video was "shocking" and "in bad taste," Sergio complained, but didn't they realize that in the United States *Sports Illustrated* made a fortune every year by airing the back-scene footage of its famous swimsuit issue? Of course, Paty Chapoy could have pointed out that *Sports Illustrated* only photographed mature, professional models, while Sergio's girls were young enough and nearly naked enough to classify his video as child porn.

Nevertheless, Paty agreed to do her best to get the '95 calendar video on the air, as one of the perks if Gloria signed an exclusive contract with TV Azteca. And what else did Gloria want to do, Paty asked—were there any other projects she was dying to try? She would have the creative manpower of an entire network at her disposal, Paty told her. In response, Gloria said . . . nothing.

"When I met Gloria, she didn't talk," Paty Chapoy says. "She was a girl that didn't say a word unless Sergio said so. In a two-hour period, she was silent. If I asked Gloria something directly, if I said, 'What do you think about this, Gloria?' Sergio would say to her, 'Gloria, Mrs. Chapoy is asking you something, answer her.' Only then would Gloria lift her face and answer me. Otherwise she was always staring at the floor, silent."

In private Paty pulled Sergio aside to ask him what was wrong. Was Gloria angry at her or something? "Sergio only smiled," Paty recounts. "He just said Gloria was very shy. I would have them over to my house for dinner, and she'd be exactly the same. Sergio would bring Gloria and

Mary Boquitas, and the two girls wouldn't talk the entire evening. Sometimes they whispered a little bit to each other, but otherwise they didn't say a word. The never offered any opinion in the conversation."

Sergio, on the other hand, had plenty to say. He talked so much, it was impossible to get the contract signed. As a sign of good faith, Sergio and Azteca had partnered to air Gloria's latest concert in the National Auditorium. After that, the plan was to star Gloria in her own soap opera. "But Sergio kept changing his mind every day," Paty says. "He'd call me one day and say he was going to write; then the next day, he decided he was going to produce; the day after that, he's going to direct and cast the entire soap himself." For some reason, Sergio's fickleness reminded Paty of the time he'd gotten off a plane for a newspaper and never come back, using a lie to buy time and abandon his client. It didn't take Paty too long to figure out that Sergio was the one who was acting, not Gloria.

"I started to realize that Sergio was waffling like that to buy time," Paty says. "He was manipulating the situation. Time kept passing, and the only thing Sergio was doing was talking. Sergio told us all the camera equipment was bought, the scripts were ready, the casting was complete, but he wouldn't give me any of the scripts or even show me photos of the actors he'd supposedly selected. So I sat down with the TV executives and told them that I thought he was using us as a bargaining chip while he secretly negotiated with Televisa. He wasn't serious about signing with TV Azteca—he was using us so he could gain more leverage."

Paty was right. But the way she found out was doubly infuriating: in an attempt to blame her, she says, Sergio and Gloria went around Paty's back and told network owner Ricardo Salinas that talks had broken down because of Paty. They'd tried their best to work something out with Paty, they told Salinas, but frankly, she was impossible to work with. "Gloria told Ricardo that under the circumstances she couldn't work for TV Azteca and was going to sign a contract with Televisa," Paty Chapoy says. "It happened exactly as I'd warned. That same day, Gloria signed a deal with Televisa to host a TV show named *XETU Remix*."

Sergio would soon learn he'd made two big mistakes. The first one was making an enemy out of Paty Chapoy; now that Gloria and Sergio were not going to be members of the TV Azteca family, there was nothing to stop a determined newshound like Paty Chapoy from taking a deep, hard look into the suspicions she had about Sergio's clan. Sergio's second mistake was abandoning Aline's career when she abandoned their marriage. It would have been awkward, of course, and it violated Sergio's basic operating principle of trading fame for obedience, but it would have gained him something very valuable: It would have prevented Aline from looking for work elsewhere. Despite all she'd been through, Aline was still hungry for stardom; even hungrier than before, in fact, because she'd paid her dues in beatings and starvation and misery, and now she wanted the payoff. Aline was looking for another show business break.

It wasn't long before she landed in Paty Chapoy's office. The two women had a chat—a very long chat. "She came and started telling me her story, and I almost fainted, because I'd never heard anything like it before," Paty Chapoy says. Aline was so distressed by the memories, Paty says, that Aline's face, neck, and arms began breaking out in red and purple hives. "Just by remembering what she had been through, her whole body reacted," Paty says. "It took three hours for her to tell me the whole story, and by the end, I frankly didn't believe it. It was just too shocking."

Aline came back a few days later with her mother. She told the story all over again, this time with her mother to corroborate, and she answered all of Paty's questions. "Aline's information gave me the chance to start investigating this case," Paty says, "and I got right on it and stayed with it." Her first step was a phone call; there was only one other person she knew who'd had an inside look at Sergio's operation, and it just turned out that he was a writer at TV Azteca. Aline knew him, too: it was Rubén Aviña.

Soon after that, Aline and Rubén were sitting down in front of a tape recorder. And then Aline really began to talk.

X   X   X

Meanwhile, during that same autumn of 1996, TV producers and stagehands at Televisa studios on the far side of Mexico City were watching in amazement each morning as Gloria came trooping in for work with a dozen or so silent, filthy teenage girls trailing behind her.

"We called them 'The Mennonites,' since they all lived together and dressed alike and didn't talk to anyone except each other," says a female producer who worked closely with Gloria. "It was the strangest sight, to see these young girls come marching in, all of them silent, wearing each other's clothes and never doing anything unless Sergio told them to."

That September, Gloria made her triumphant return to Televisa. After the scare of losing her to TV Azteca, Televisa was thrilled to have Gloria back and basically gave her a blank check: The Tiger paid Gloria a reported $8 million, and allowed Sergio to order virtually anything he wanted in the way of guest stars, stage settings, and production materials. So powerful had Sergio become, in fact, that The Tiger only reined him in when it came to those buckets of human feces: According to producers on the show, Sergio came up with the idea of dumping actual shit and urine on game show contestants. The fact that the question would even come up at a network where, barely five years before, Gloria had been banned for ripping her dance tights was a sign of how much power she and Sergio had, and how far they had personally advanced the tolerance threshold.

Gloria's new show was going to be a blockbuster. Televisa had decided to revive one of the country's most popular variety game shows, *XETU Remix*. It was a great idea—it meant Mexico's top show would now be hosted by Mexico's top star. And every Monday, the show would feature a special game that had beautiful girls suspended on swings, inching their way closer to a vat of liquid gunk as they incorrectly answered questions. So excited was Televisa, it spent millions on a state-of-the-art set, flying in designers from New York and Los Angeles to devise high-concept backdrops sketched to Sergio's specifications.

"We knew it was going to be a big hit," says the producer. "We had Gloria at her peak, and that's all the newspapers could talk about, how Gloria had come back to Televisa, so people were all very interested in seeing her." It wasn't just Gloria, but Gloria *live*—who could resist tuning in to see what part of her body might pop out of her artfully ripped outfits or what jaw-dropping comment would come ripping out of her unrestrained mouth? "She was as crazy as Sergio," the producer says. "On one show, Gloria brought in this homeless boy named Marcelo.

She'd found him living on the streets, and right there on national TV she adopted him. She said, 'You're going to be my kid, and let the entire country bear witness. I'll take care of you from now on like my son. You are now Marcelo Trevi.' That's the kind of thing that could happen—you never knew what she might do."

What a combination—drama, suspense, Gloria, gorgeous sets, degraded women in soaking wet T-shirts—*the ratings would be through the roof!*

But the anticipatory glee of a hit show was soon overwhelmed by intrigue. From Gloria's first day on set, the cast and crew of *XETU Remix* were buzzing about the clan's strange behavior. "You knew they were staying at the most expensive hotels in Mexico City, but they always wore cheap, dirty clothes and shared them—even Gloria," says the Televisa producer. "One day one of the girls would be wearing a pair of shoes, and the next day Gloria would have them on. Do you know any other boss who wears her employees' clothes?"

Whenever they weren't needed in the studio, Sergio made the girls wait outside in his big black Lincoln. Once, when Sergio and all the girls were busy consulting with the makeup artists, the Televisa producer and several crew members snuck outside to take a peek inside. "It was a *mess!*" exclaims the producer. "I swear, it looked like they must have been living out of that car. They had clothes and underwear and hairbrushes all over the place. I don't how *he* could stand even riding in there with all the girls cluttering up the seats and the floor." Sergio caught the Televisa crew peering into the car, but laughed off their amazed questions. No, no, they weren't living out of the car, he said; they were just moving between hotels and hadn't checked in yet. "None of us knew what was going on, but none of us believed him," says the producer. "His clothes were filthy, too."

Gloria's dressing room was just as strange, but in exactly the opposite way. "Gloria was a weird girl," says the producer. "I've been working at Televisa for a long time, and I can tell you in the dressing room of every other star, they have perfume, antiperspirant, a picture of a loved one because they spent the whole day there. Gloria didn't have any of that. You didn't even see a toothbrush." And even though the dressing room was as stark as a prison cell, Gloria spent all of her downtime closed up inside, never fraternizing with the crew like other cast members. The clan opened its ranks so rarely, the producer recalls one of those moments precisely: "One day we hired some models," she says. "One was from Argentina and looked a lot like Sergio's girls, with a great body, curly black hair, in her early twenties, pretty. Karla and Katia never talked with anyone, but when they saw that girl, they became very friendly. As soon as we finished taping, they told her Gloria and Sergio wanted to meet her. They took her to the dressing room. I never knew what happened with her. I don't know if she joined them or not."

Whenever she wasn't on camera, Gloria was always and immediately flanked by her two Amazonian escorts, the sisters de la Cuesta, even when she went to the bathroom. "Gloria was never alone," the producer marvels. "She was always escorted by these two girls, short girls but very strong. Gloria walked in the front, with those two always behind her. When we did the show, the two girls were always on the set and watching everything Gloria did. I'm telling you, it was very weird. When Sergio wasn't with them, the girls seemed relaxed, they whispered to each other and even laughed," the Televisa producer continues. "I'm one of the only ones who saw this, though, because I was the only one allowed to talk to them. Sergio wouldn't let Gloria speak directly with Bernardo López Valdés, the director of the show. Instead, everything had to go through me."

Bizarre as it might have seemed that the director was not permitted to speak to the star of his own show, after a while it didn't seem out of the ordinary to the Televisa crew because Gloria wasn't allowed to speak to *any* man besides Sergio. "All the technicians are men, but Sergio had his own girls do their job for them. For example, when Gloria had to wear a microphone, Karla de la Cuesta was the one who put it on her. They didn't let any man touch her."

It wasn't long before the Televisa crew's disbelief at Sergio's treatment of the girls had turned to disgust. "One of the very young ones, Karola de la Cuesta, asked Sergio for permission to go to the bathroom," the producer recalls. "He got angry because she interrupted him and shouted, 'No!' Then he went back to talking. The poor girl stood there, waiting for Sergio to finish, until she couldn't hold it anymore and peed her pants. I felt horrible for her." When sandwiches were brought in, the girls were forbidden to touch one until—and unless—Sergio gave them permission. Until he did, the filthy young women would stand by the food table like characters from a Dickens tale, waiting and watching miserably while Sergio helped himself.

"Diets," Sergio would tell the murmuring Televisa crew. "Girls blow up at that age." If he did give the go-ahead, the girls devoured everything they could and stuffed all the leftovers into their pockets and handbags. They didn't just scavenge food, the producer adds. "They took everything that wasn't locked up. The toilet paper from the bathrooms, coffee from the lunchroom, creamers, sugar packs—they were like a pack of starving mice." Gloria, curiously, seemed just as poor; whenever she had her period, she begged sanitary napkins every day from the female crew members. "We never knew why she didn't have any," the producer says. "At first I thought it was because she was such a big star, so she was used to people giving her everything—but after seeing her so much in those dirty old clothes, I started wondering what Sergio was doing with her money. She was a millionaire, but she acted like a beggar.

"We always felt there were two Glorias, and we started calling them by different names," the producer continues. "If it had to do with the show, she was 'Gloria Trevi.' If it was offstage, she was 'Gloria Treviño.' Even for an interview, she had to transform her self. She started talking and moving in a different way, and as soon as the reporter leaves, she went back to being Gloria Treviño again, taking all Sergio's orders. If we asked her what she wanted for lunch, Sergio answered. If someone wanted an autograph, she looked at Sergio first."

Yet no one did anything. The Televisa crew watched Sergio dominate and humiliate both the hungry teenage girls and the show's multimillion-dollar franchise performer, but no one said anything. "Fear," the producer explains. "We knew what Sergio and Gloria could do. Sergio was laughing all the time about how he'd stood up the executives at TV Azteca, so we were really afraid he'd do the same thing and we'd get blamed." Who would risk their job by infuriating Sergio and having him yank Gloria off the *XETU Remix* set? No one wanted the blame for that, not after The Tiger had poured millions into this project. So everyone kept quiet—even as Sergio helped ruin the program.

Right from the start there were problems, and it wasn't just due to Sergio's feces-dumping suggestions. "He argued with everyone, all the time, about everything," says the producer, who feared consequences from Televisa if she were identified. "He tried to control the program, the same way he controlled all those girls he had around him, and it caused big trouble with the director." But of course, there was no way Sergio could take a subordinate role—not in front of his girls. In their eyes he was the master of every situation, the man whose commands were respected and immediately obeyed. Unlike most managers, who restrict their direct intervention to contract negotiations and project selection, Sergio had taken over nearly all Gloria's creative decisions: She was still writing her own songs, but he was deciding which would be recorded, how they'd be arranged, what she'd wear, and how she would pose in her calendar photos. He had no film experience, but after her first movie, he'd stepped in and written and directed the last two. Subordinating himself to another professional, no matter how much more skilled, was out of the question.

"Even though he wasn't the director, things had to be the way he wanted or else he got very mad," says another Televisa executive, who worked with Gloria and Sergio on a separate TV special that same year. "He was very dominating. With just a look he said everything. When he stared at you, it meant you did something wrong, or said anything he didn't like. He manipulated you with his stare." The more the director and Sergio disagreed, the more decisions were delayed and scripts were scrawled over with confusing changes. As an hour-long, daily program, *XETU Remix* was demanding enough, but with the cast caught in a clash for creative control, the final minutes before airtime were constant chaos.

The Televisa executive was so unnerved by Sergio that she did her best to avoid him. "I always tried not to talk to Sergio," she says. "But Sergio tried to look into my eyes to dominate me. He was always looking for your eyes. Once you looked into his eyes, you were in his hands. Gloria always had her head down when he was around, especially after that one time she tried to speak up about something. She tried to make a suggestion for the program and Sergio just snapped at her. 'I'm the one who makes the decisions,' he told her. 'So please shut up.' "

The Televisa exec has seen a lot of damaged women in her years in show business, especially through the specials she did with beauty pageants, and as time passed, she began to understand something about Gloria's remarkably varied behavior. "You could tell she didn't love herself," she explains. "A lot of stars are very powerful but have very low confidence, and when you saw Gloria behind the scenes, you could see it so clearly. From a very young age, she didn't have family support. She was a young girl on her own, and in Sergio she had family. He was her father, her lover, her brother—everything she didn't have at home."

Sergio gave Gloria the confidence she needed to break out from the back row of Boquitas Pintadas and take the mike herself. During those lost years when she was living in Sergio's studio and largely cut off from the outside world, she developed tremendously quickly as a singer, but it came at a price. "He developed Gloria into 'The Star,' but he didn't allow her to evolve as a woman," the Televisa exec believes. "He kept her doubting herself, stunted, so she only felt that she knew what she was doing when she was following his instructions. She was like a tree—you prune it, tie it, and it only grows in one direction. Gloria had no other way to open her mouth except on stage, so it turned her into a sensational performer, but a stunted human being."

During the planning stages of the TV special, though, not even Gloria's performer side was visible. "In our planning meetings, everyone has to give their opinion, but she never did and she was the MC of the show," the exec says. Everything was done through Sergio; no one could talk to Gloria. If she said anything, it was just about how she agreed with Sergio." The exec and her staff were getting extremely nervous. "Was she going to ruin the show by being so flat? At the end of every meeting, everyone said, 'Where's the explosive Gloria? Where's that strong woman?' She wasn't that tough and sexy girl."

But when it was time for the first live rehearsal, Gloria wowed them. "My God, you couldn't believe it was the same person," the Televisa exec thrills. "We were amazed! Even next to beauty queens, she looked magnificent, and she was so smart and funny!" Gloria's incandescence, however, didn't last any longer than the rehearsal: The instant rehearsal ended, and before the production crew could even come up to congratulate her, Gloria's escorts hustled her back to the dressing room. "They locked the door and stayed outside guarding," the Televisa executive recalls. "If you wanted to talk to Gloria or Sergio, you had to get through them. I'd never seen anything like it."

Looking back, after the secret life of Sergio's clan was exposed, the Televisa exec realized something else. "When Gloria was talking about women's rights, perhaps that was her way of saying, 'Help me.' She was always making noise about the rights of women when secretly she was as abused as the worst of them. Maybe when she was whipping boys in the audience and throwing herself on the floor and all that crazy stuff, she was trying to be the strong woman she talked about. She never was the woman she wanted to be, the strong one. The girl with power. The one that could lead rallies for abused women. It was only onstage that Gloria could be the woman she wanted to be. She was only powerful onstage. After that, you saw a quiet and lonely girl."

XETU Remix, meanwhile, debuted to great ratings—then quickly plummeted. The show was so rough and disorganized, it appeared as awkward at times as an amateur home movie. Critics complained that Gloria was too much; she was too aggressive, and overwhelmed her guests with rat-a-tat-tat questions and explosive laughter. The girls brought in as contestants for the dunk-in-gunk game were almost stunned into silence; they'd be so cowed by Gloria, it would take forever for one of them to answer enough questions to finally make her way into the vat.

In a desperate bid to tighten up the show, Televisa cut it from one hour to thirty minutes. But the ratings continued to drop, and Sergio became more intrusive and demanding, mortified by the possibility that Gloria would suffer the humiliation of cancellation after only a few months. One night Gloria declared that if more people didn't tune in and watch, she would kill herself. The next show, she pulled out a knife and slashed at her wrists. Blood gushed from her arms as she collapsed to the floor in a mob of frenzied stagehands. "She had faked the whole thing," the producer says. "It was a dummy knife and fake blood, but she hadn't told anyone she was going to do it. That kind of thing is forbidden on TV, and the government threatened to ban the program."

The director freaked out. *Were these people crazy?* He hadn't been told Gloria was going to pull that fake suicide stunt, and he knew Sergio had to be behind it. This time he let Sergio have it. It was one thing to be pushed around about whether Gloria was going to sing or which of the clan girls should get a minute or two on camera; it was another thing when careers were at stake. Bernardo López Valdés dressed him down so thoroughly that Sergio walked off the set, vowing never to return.

After that, Gloria and the girls were impossible. "When I would go to her dressing room to tell her she had ten minutes to go on stage, they would shut the door in my face," the Televisa producer says. "She said she was mad because we had insulted the man she loves the most, and she would never forgive us." One day, Gloria just didn't show up. Emilio Azcárraga personally tried calling Sergio, but couldn't find him. "With minutes to go before airtime, Gloria came breezing in and walked straight on stage, like a diva," the producer complaints. "You can't run a show like that."

The Tiger wasn't going to. Halfway into the season, he cancelled *XETU Remix*.

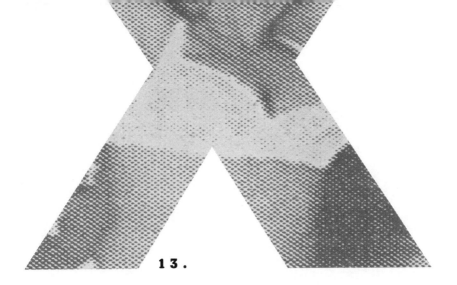

"Pack Your Bags, and Keep Your Mouth Shut"

*H*ad Mr. Midas lost his touch? Sergio had stutter-stepped before, but he'd always corrected his mistake and come back stronger than ever. By 1997, however, one flop had followed hard on another. First, there was his doomed attempt in 1994 to turn meagerly talented Aline into a star, followed by the *XETU Remix* debacle in 1996 and the worst-selling Gloria calendar ever in 1997. Worst of all, though, was Gloria's final movie, *Una Papa Sin Catsup (A French Fry Without Ketchup)*.

He could blame all kinds of factors outside his control for the failure of the TV show—the director, the time slot, the format—and as for Aline, well, he would concede that he might have received poor counsel from his groin on that one. But the calendar—that was 100 percent Sergio, and he'd made it the hottest one yet. He'd given the guys everything he thought they wanted: More girls, more nudity, more voyeuristic poses. Flipping through the calendar was like peeping through the keyhole of a cute girl's bedroom. So why weren't they buying it?

If Sergio knew the answer to that, he'd have the solution to all his recent disasters. The calendar was a Rosetta Stone that could clarify everything that was going wrong—if only Sergio knew how to interpret it. But he couldn't see the problem himself, and there was no longer anyone who could tell him; he'd intimidated or infuriated nearly all his professional colleagues, and he had no friends outside the clan. Sergio had no one who could point out that his own hankerings had taken over his professional judgment: He'd been immersed for so long in his lust for barely adolescent girls by then that he'd come to believe it was universal. During the past five years, he'd gradually lowered the age of his calendar models and backup singers while simultaneously increasing the rawness of their eroticism until he'd crossed the barrier between titillating and disturbing. The calendars still might have been appealing to certain men, but they certainly weren't marketable; those men might share Sergio's aberration, but they didn't want it hanging on their office wall.

Una Papa Sin Catsup, Gloria's third movie and the second to be written and directed by Sergio, was like the calendar turned into a flip-page cartoon. In 1995, Sergio had won complete creative control of the film from Televisa as a lure toward bringing Gloria back to the network, so when he drafted the script, it was with the full confidence that whatever he dreamed up would go unchallenged. Given that kind of freedom and the closed informational feedback loop that had become Sergio's life, the result reels out across the screen like Sergio's own private fantasies come to life. In retrospect, it actually makes sense that after nearly a decade of indulging himself like an omnipotent adolescent, Sergio would have begun thinking like one; but what's still surprising is that Televisa would allow its top star to be so degraded—and that Gloria would go along with it.

In the movie Gloria once again plays a thirteen-year-old schoolgirl in a too-short skirt. This time, though, she plays a second role as an evil criminal genius, Las Greñas. The two characters seem to perfectly sum up Sergio's view of women, especially of Gloria: on the one hand, she's a little girl who needs to be taught and punished; on the other, she's a wicked temptress who can never be trusted and deserves what she gets. Although Gloria gets to wear tiny miniskirts and breast-bulging bodices as Las Greñas, Sergio's camera lingers longest on her when she's playing the schoolgirl, especially during the gratuitous shots when she's slipping into her panties and bra to get dressed for school and crossing her bare legs beneath her desk.

It's embarrassing enough to watch the then twenty-six-year-old Gloria playing a girl half her age, but it only gets worse: In a scene that's remarkably humiliating for an established star and international sex symbol, Sergio has schoolgirl Gloria sent to plunge out a toilet overflowing with diarrhea. She prepares herself with snorkel and goggles, which is for the best because she somehow plunges into the toilet. Then, in a scene that goes on for nearly five minutes of the ninety-minute film, Sergio depicts Gloria swimming through a thick brown sea of diarrhea and floating chunks of urine, feces, and shit-stained toilet paper. As the pipes begin to leak, dribbles of diarrhea leak onto the heads of the children and into the sandwich that the school's principal is eating. The message is complete and unmistakable: Sergio is shitting on everyone he controls and everyone who tries to control him—and Gloria is suspended in his ordure like a fly in amber.

Variety, Hollywood's last word in cinema news, was as much mystified by the film as repulsed. The highlight of Gloria's previous films was her singing, so why was she barely given a song in this one? And once again, where was her love interest?

> *Third time definitely is not the charm for Mexico pop idol Gloria Trevi's big-screen acting career. After scoring big with "Pelo Suelto" and "Zapatos Viejos," singer saw her fans desert her with this outing, a big box-office disappointment locally.*

> *Trevi plays a double role as "Las Greñas," leader of a drug-running gang who cheats some U.S. gangsters out of $2 million; and as Gloria, a rebellious schoolgirl who is, of course, a dead ringer for "Las Greñas" and is coerced into substituting for her in a fake funeral.*

> *By the end, Gloria is chased through the Mexico City streets by criminals, police and a crowd of marathon runners. Conceived as a*

*vehicle for Trevi's bizarre personality—half spoiled brat, half
sexpot—the pic allows her to sing only the popular theme song (while
three of her other hits are heard as background music). Strangely,
despite the strong sexual innuendoes in Trevi's songs, there are no
romantic subplots in her films and no leading men to speak of.*

*Bad taste is the highlight here, and maybe the main reason it alienated
its audience. In a sequence in which Trevi is punished by the school
principal with latrine duty, the singer is seen handling excremental
material with a childish delight, resulting in the most literal form of
toilet humor. Bit doesn't score many laughs, but its barf potential is
quite high.*

While Sergio was writing the script, Karina said later, she heard
shrieks and slaps coming from the bedroom where he'd holed himself up
with a few of the clan girls. Gloria said they were just trying out some
scenes and dialogue; Karina knew better, and dreaded the moment when
she would be summoned to take dictation and act out her role. Luckily,
she says, Sergio still didn't have faith in her ability to collaborate on the
script or take down his words accurately; after all, Karina still wasn't old
enough for high school.

But Sergio granted her a role anyway, casting Karina as the young
daughter of a suburban family, and her few minutes on camera serve as
inadvertent documentary footage. Viewing the film today, knowing that
by the time it had been shown Karina had been with the clan for nearly six
months and was already deeply sexually involved with Sergio and her fellow clan members, Karina's appearance is shocking. She is thin, awkward, and pimply, looking more boy than woman.

Later on, Karina would put on a good amount of weight, however,
and see her complexion clear up. In photos from that period, taken along
an aqueduct in central Spain, fourteen-year-old Karina is smiling and radiant.

She's also pregnant.

X   X   X

Sergio hadn't been seen in a while—months, actually. Gloria broke into tears at the end of a concert and announced that Sergio had prostate cancer. She was retiring from singing to nurse him, she declared, and hoped her sacrifice would convince the Virgin of Guadalupe to heal him. "He helped me," she said. "Now I must stand by him."

Then Gloria was gone, too. So were Karina, Marlene, Wendy, Mary Boquitas, the three de la Cuesta sisters, and the rest of the girls in the clan.

Aline was one of the first to publicly doubt the cancer story. She had seen Sergio not long before he'd dropped out of sight, she said on Paty Chapoy's show, *Ventaneando,* and he was still very fat. "That's not consistent with a person who's wasting away from cancer, as far as I know," Aline said. But word had spread that Aline was working on a tell-all book about her life with Sergio, so her allegations were dismissed as the self-interested rant of a gold digger trying to cash in on her ex-husband's fame by villainizing him. She couldn't get attention as a singer, the entertainment press sniped, so she was trying as a gossip. Aline was ignored.

Much later, after Karina's parents had been shocked by a phone call from Spain informing them their fourteen-year-old daughter had abandoned a newborn baby in a Madrid orphanage and vanished, everyone would assume that Karina's pregnancy was the solution to the greatest mystery of the Gloria Trevi case: Why did Sergio take the clan on the run? Once Karina's baby was revealed, the answer seemed obvious: Clearly, it was assumed, Sergio had panicked when he found out Karina was pregnant and ran off with his girls to duck the scandal.

But if Sergio hadn't gone on the run, there wouldn't have *been* a scandal, and there certainly wouldn't have been any criminal charges. Kidnapping, corruption of a minor, rape—all those accusations were a *result* of Sergio's disappearance, not the cause. If he had stayed put in Mexico, he might have suffered some embarrassment, but nothing much different than the scares he had weathered and survived in the past. Sergio had been dealing with these kinds of close calls for more than ten years; he'd always managed to quell them without even leaving the city, let alone the continent. In fact, the furthest he'd ever run in the past was to Crystal's house. So why flee now?

Karina, incidentally, only discovered she was pregnant *after* the clan arrived in Spain, and even that was no real cause for alarm: By 1997, pregnancy was no longer any big deal in the clan. Since Sergio was having sex with several of the girls nearly every day and relying on Coca-Cola douches for birth control, frequent inseminations were inevitable. At least half the girls in the clan had either miscarried or flown to Houston for secret abortions, Karina would later report: Gloria had, Karina was told, and Wendy, and Karla de la Cuesta, as well as Marlene at thirteen years old, and Karola de le Cuesta at fifteen.

Even if abortion wasn't an option, Sergio had another well-practiced method for handling the consequences of his teen entanglements: marriage. He'd already used a wedding license as protection from angry parents and possible prosecution after it was discovered he was sleeping with Mary Boquitas and Aline Hernández. Now that he was divorced from Aline, nothing prevented him from making Karina the fifth Mrs. Sergio Andrade. All it would have taken was another small ceremony in a Mexico City restaurant, and Sergio would have saved a fortune in airfare. Marrying Karina would also have shielded Sergio from any sticky allegations after Aline's book came out, since Karina was the youngest girl in the clan and might have been having sex with Sergio since the illegal age of twelve.

So what made Sergio run? Curiously, the explanation he gave from behind bars might actually have been the truth: "I wanted some time away to work on a novel and to prepare Gloria's next record," Sergio would claim. "I wasn't running away, because there was nothing to run away from. What I wanted to do was refresh my creativity." What drove Sergio out of Mexico wasn't scandal, but failure. Ever since his obese, unhappy childhood under the eye of a demanding father, Sergio had prided himself on being the infallible boy genius, and he'd maintained that in his professional life. Starting from the time he'd broken into the business, Sergio had always been "the best," "the youngest," "Mr. Midas." His self-worth was based on his ability to turn out hits, which shouldn't be surprising: His only romantic relationships as an adult had been with young women who'd been awestruck by his fame.

Sergio's Midas touch, in fact, was the only reason the clan existed in the first place; once he lost it, he'd no longer have any way of attracting the young, controllable women he craved. Already he must have known that his authority was in jeopardy; the clan girls had to be wondering why the man who claimed to be so brilliant was suffering an unbroken string of flops. It's likely that as much as Sergio wanted to get away to repair his ego and search for fresh ideas for Gloria's next album, he also wanted to get his girls outside the range of doubters, away from Mexican newspapers and especially Mexican television, where Paty Chapoy had been ridiculing *XETU Remix* relentlessly on *Ventaneando*. If Sergio was going to keep the illusion of stardom alive in his girls' minds, he had to get them out of town.

Of course, vanishing for a bit when there was trouble and reemerging later, as if nothing had happened, was a familiar tactic for Sergio. He'd done it every time he'd run into a career hitch or budding scandal in the past. In fact, he was chronologically overdue for a quick exit, judging by his cycle to date: over the previous twenty years, he had dropped out of sight for an extended period just about every five to six years. This time, of course, it was more complicated—with 10, 12, 15 girls at a time to move around with him, not to mention Mexico's most popular movie star, he couldn't just sneak into the spare bedroom of a friend's house or expect to remain invisible anywhere in Mexico. If he was going to follow the tactic that had always worked so well for him before, Sergio was going to have to find someplace where a Spanish-speaking retinue could feel at home but remain unrecognized.

Before leaving, Sergio sent Karina home to visit her parents, in May 1997, with an armful of gifts and rehearsed stories about how much she loved star school and how bitter and unfair Aline was being to poor Sergio. Of course, she wasn't alone: Sergio sent one of his most trusted lieutenants, Marlene Calderón, to stay by Karina's side. "I was supposed to tell them that a book was coming out by Aline and they shouldn't believe anything in it, that Aline was a liar and part of a defamation campaign orchestrated by TV Azteca," Karina says. "After that, we traveled to Los Mochis so Marlene could see her family and carry out the same mission."

Karina's parents were startled by her appearance; their baby had lost so much weight, her eyes looked haggard, her skin was a mess, and her stringy hair was hanging down over one side of her face. Karina was unusually cold to them, she never smiled, and she barely said a word to her brother. Karina's mother tried to find out what was wrong, but she felt intimidated by her gruff and scornful daughter, the protégée of celebrities. Don't worry about it, Karina told them as Marlene listened carefully, I'm just a little tired from all our rehearsals and concert tours. But Sergio is taking us on a long vacation, Karina continued; he's selected the best girls in the school for a special training seminar in Spain, at the Manuel de Falla Academy. We'll be gone for a few months, Karina said, but I'll write every week. I promise.

Later, when the Yapors were blinking timidly into the glare of TV news cameras, they were asked, "Why did you let her go?" They'd heard bits of what was coming out in Aline's book, they'd said themselves how terrible Karina looked—so why didn't they stop her from leaving the country with Sergio? Miguel Yapor, looking withered and defenseless in his wheelchair, struggled to explain. Yes, he admitted he was "offended by those songs about abortion and everything that was against the ethics of the Bible." He was also unhappy with the seminude photographs of his daughter in Gloria's calendar and her appearance in that horrible movie, *Una Papa Sin Catsup.*

"We began to have doubts, but we still had to give a vote of confidence to Gloria and Sergio," Miguel told one newspaper. "We thought that Aline was a jealous woman, a mediocrity. Besides, she was unknown, and not a very good singer." There, succinctly, he summed up what he considered the currency of credibility: To Miguel Yapor, famous people were just more believable. Their word was *worth* more. Perhaps the Yapors could survive without Sergio's two thousand dollars a month, but it seemed what they were striving for was that extra regard that fame would bring: Karina was making them into people to be listened to.

Once the girls had assembled back in Mexico City, they were told to pack two small bags. They obeyed, even though by that point they should have been suffering serious doubts about whether Sergio really had them on a course to stardom. Logically, it seemed less and less plausible that Sergio would turn any of them into stars, and certainly not *all* of them. At no time in his career had Sergio ever managed more than two top performers at a time, so how could anyone believe he would launch a dozen?

Especially a dozen girls of varying ages who all looked alike and dressed identically? But if there was no sign that Sergio would make them wealthy and famous, why would the girls continue to follow and obey him—especially when it meant traveling even further from the place where their careers could be launched and leaving behind their families and any hope of a normal love life?

x   x   x

To answer that question, Karina could tell her story about bath time. Karina had become so indoctrinated, she would later testify, that she had stopped considering whether something was right, or even if it was something she wanted to do, and only weighed whether it was something Sergio wanted. She was not only obeying his wishes, but anticipating his expectations. When Sergio ordered her to take a bath, she obeyed without question: "That meant he was going to punish me, and we'd have sexual relations afterward." Karina didn't ask anymore what she'd done wrong, or plead for mercy: she just bathed and presented herself to Sergio wrapped in a towel.

She was so quick to anticipate his demands, in fact, that she once got herself in even more trouble: "In the room next to the bathroom was Tamara Zuñiga, who'd recently joined the group, so when I came out wrapped in a towel and headed toward the recording studio for my beating, Sergio got really angry, since Tamara wasn't supposed to know what was going on." Sergio threatened her so viciously, Karina says, that she almost fainted in dread; Katia de la Cuesta had to run for some alcohol to revive her. When she came around, Karina hoped Sergio would beat her right away, since she couldn't stand thinking about it. He did, holding her down on the sound board and whipping her with four power cords. Afterward, he had sex with the terrified, weeping girl and Katia. "Sexual relations and punishments took place almost every day," Karina would say. "That was our way of life."

There were some defections, however. Despite Sergio's attempts to break her in slowly, Tamara Zuñiga soon learned about the punishments and began looking for a way to get away—even though her big sister,

Edith, was urging her to keep quiet and do as Sergio said. The two girls were recruited from Chile, where Gloria had gone to perform. Edith was fourteen when she met Gloria after the Viña del Mar festival and went off to join the clan; two years later, Edith told Sergio about her pretty thirteen-year-old sister, so Mary Boquitas flew back to Santiago, Chile, with Edith and spoke to the Zuñigas.

Spotting Karina heading toward the recording studio in a towel might have made Tamara suspicious, but confirmation only came a few days later, when she was wearing a pair of Karina's pants and discovered a note mentioning sex and beatings that Karina had meant for one of the other girls. Still, she was exempt from the same treatment herself until several months later, when Gloria suddenly began telling her about Sergio's "sadness." As Tamara would later testify, Gloria said Sergio had never recovered from the broken heart he'd suffered from a thwarted romance with Lucerito. If only Tamara would join him in the Jacuzzi and make him feel like a man, Gloria told her, that would do wonders for lifting Sergio's spirits. By then Tamara knew what would happen if she resisted; she had seen Sergio smack Gloria and slash at her with power cords, just as he did with the other girls. If he treated his star that way, what would he do to a rebellious thirteen-year-old?

But Tamara was so horrified, she still refused to join Sergio in the hot tub. She was desperate to flee that night, but she was a thirteen-year-old girl in a foreign country, with no money and no certainty where she was. Sergio moved the girls from house to house every week or so, usually in a van with the windows blacked out, ostensibly for Gloria's safety, but it also prevented the girls from spotting landmarks. Later that night, Tamara says, Sergio came into her room, tore off her clothes, and raped her. He continued to visit her room at night for months, Tamara says, and kept her locked in most days, until she began to act more passively. Only then would he let Tamara and Edith travel back to Santiago to visit their parents—accompanied, of course, by the ever-vigilant Mary Boquitas. While they were in Chile, however, Mary was suddenly called away by Sergio on urgent business, and Tamara poured out everything she and Edith had been through to her parents.

Guadalupe Carrasco also escaped. She was a beauty pageant winner from Chiapas who'd come to Mexico City in 1995 to tape a TV special emceed by Gloria. One of the clan girls pulled Guadalupe aside to meet Sergio. He asked her strip down to panties and bra, and when she did, he offered her a scholarship to his star school. When she arrived to begin classes, Guadalupe would later testify, at least seventeen girls were living in Sergio's house. Sergio started her on music and exercise classes, but soon she was spending more and more of her time working alongside Karina and the other girls, doing back-breaking yard work in the hot sun with no food and little water; Sergio had them hauling stones, repaving the driveway, and hacking through overgrown weeds in the garden.

At night, Guadalupe said, exhaustion left her collapsed on the bed, and that's when the midnight visits began: Sergio would come to her room, slide into her bed, and climb on top of her while the other girls in the room watched. "I don't know how he does it, but he makes you admire him," Guadalupe would later say in a magazine interview. "You really think he is a good person, and you admire him so much that you start thinking he has the right to possess you sexually. Nonetheless, when he forced me to have sex, I was in shock." For more than a year, the nineteen-year-old beauty queen blistered her hands by day and endured Sergio by night, but like Aline before her, she managed to maintain some flicker of independence: After fourteen months, Guadalupe made up a story about her mother suffering a heart attack and managed to convince Sergio to let her go home for a visit. Once outside the clan, she never went back.

Amazingly, these girls weren't believed at first, and their stories weren't publicized. "My parents thought I was making it up," Tamara Zuñiga told the judge when she came back to Chihuahua to testify. "The police didn't buy our story either." And while these parents and the police were scoffing, Sergio was herding his remaining girls onto a plane bound for Madrid.

14.

Vanished

*O*nce Aline's book hit the stands on April 15, 1998, rumors began bubbling, then boiled over.

"La Atrevida: Desaparacida?" the headlines of the celebrity gossip magazines began wondering ("The Bold Girl: Vanished?"). For the first time in years there was no sign of the most photographed woman in the country. Not only wasn't she popping up at music festivals, movie premieres, or talk shows, as usual, but in a far more significant development, there was no big Trevi project in the pipeline. There was no new movie under contract, no concert appearances were announced, and there had been no 1998 Gloria Trevi calendar. Ever since she'd burst onto the international stage in 1989, the Gloria Trevi entertainment machine had not stopped steaming along: magazine covers followed TV specials followed comic books followed movies. Every year, there was a new Gloria Trevi album and concert tour.

But now, for more than half a year, there had been nothing.

Gloria had been kidnapped, TV gossip shows began saying. Gloria is secretly a drug addict and is hiding away somewhere in rehab. . . . That's why she's so wild on stage. . . . Gloria is having Sergio's baby. . . . Maybe Aline is telling the truth, after all: Sergio was in love with Gloria all this time, and finally grabbed her and ran off. . . . Isn't it strange that no one has ever seen her with a boyfriend? . . . Gloria's mother tried to smother the frenzied speculation, taking her daughter's place in the media glare and pooh-poohing the book and all the Sergio kidnapping speculation as pure insanity. "It's just because of wild talk like this that Gloria decided to go on an artistic retreat," Gloria Ruiz declared, looking glamorously platinum under the TV lights. "She wants to concentrate on her next album and a new movie." In fact, she had just spoken to her daughter, Gloria Ruiz said; she was in Europe, having fun and working hard. Sergio, she added, was writing a novel.

TV Azteca had put the word out to its affiliated networks in the United States and Europe: If you hear of any Gloria Trevi sightings, track them down and get her on camera. Mexican newspaper reporters began sniffing around McAllen, Texas, the border town north of Monterrey where Gloria Ruiz lived, and Sergio had a home, to see if anyone had spotted the superstar recently. Yes, in fact, she had been there, a few locals recalled . . . but they'd seen her briefly, and that had been months ago, sometime in the winter of 1998.

Since then, nothing—and in the unfamiliar vacuum of Gloria's absence the talk show speculation grew darker. *It's quite possible Sergio murdered her,* gossip hosts mused authoritatively, *and then killed himself.* They began referring more and more to *Star 80,* the Bob Fosse film about the murder of Dorothy Stratten, the 1979 Playboy Playmate of the Year who was shot to death by her domineering boyfriend when her stardom outgrew his control. *It looks like the same story all over again,* the talk show hosts said. *The warning signs were there, but we never noticed them. . . .*

Then suddenly, on April 27, 1998, here was Gloria herself, as gorgeous and bouncy as ever, turning up on Margarita Grill's Televisa program *Hoy Mismo.* Grill's producers had gotten a call the day before from Sergio, who'd stunned them with an offer: Gloria was alive, she was fine, and she would give *Hoy Mismo* an exclusive, but there had to be no press and no advance publicity. Sergio was serious—if there was a single re- porter in sight when Gloria's car arrived, if they got the slightest hint that word of her appearance had leaked, she'd be gone.

"Absolutely, absolutely," the *Hoy Mismo* team hastily agreed to all Sergio's conditions. And as Sergio promised, Gloria arrived at the secret location looking as beautiful and radiant as ever.

So, Margarita Grill asked, once the cameras had gone live, about the orgies . . . ?

"Por favor!" Gloria Trevi laughed in stunned amazement, shaking her hair and throwing herself back in her chair. "I've heard some crazy ones before," Gloria said, "but nothing like *this*. If I'm lying, let lightning strike me right now."

Before she'd even begun rebutting the rumors, her appearance alone dealt Aline's story quite a blow. It wasn't that Gloria looked normal—in front of a camera, she never looked anything that could be described as "normal." Her iridescent brown hair was wild and loose, showing those glints of gold that caught the gold in her brown eyes, and her body, look- ing slimmer and curvier than ever in her loose shirt and slacks, seemed coiled with dormant energy. She was the usual fun, mischievous, unpre- dictable Gloria, seeming far too lovely and serene to have ever been a vic- tim or a villain.

"I have not been kidnapped—far from it," Gloria declared. "I am sane, I do not belong to any Satanic cult, I am a Roman Catholic, Apos- tolic Christian. The whole thing about poisoning strikes me as crazy, but . . ." OK, she'd done her best to be solemn, but she couldn't keep it serious anymore. "Especially since I don't think I've eaten any bad shrimp lately."

From that point on, as she always did, Gloria took control by losing control. She joked, she ranted, she was witty and angry and goofily digressive. Her tone was unpredictable and erratic, swerving from self- righteous indignation to self-mocking humor. She was great TV, in other words, and thoroughly convincing.

She'd been busy in Italy, Gloria explained, working in seclusion on her next record and movie script. She was also, believe it or not, studying politics; she was seriously planning for the political career she'd only joked about before, back when she talked about running for president of Mexico. She wouldn't have even bothered coming back for this nonsense except out of loyalty to Sergio and concern for her fans and family.

"Can you imagine how my mother must feel to come home and hear that Gloria Trevi has committed suicide?" she exclaimed. "Thank God she didn't have a heart attack!"

And now people were searching her songs for clues, claiming to find subversive messages in her lyrics. They were even contorting her 1991 anti-abuse anthem "Ya no," into a *celebration* of abuse, because it contained the line "Being a woman, I have to obey." Play the song backwards, one magazine reported, and you could just—sort of—make out male and female voices growling, *"¡Por eso deben obedecer!"* ("That's why you should obey!") and *"¡Castigando!"* ("Punishing!") and *"¡Lo hiciste mal!"* ("You did it badly!").

Okay, that's a little nuts, Margarita agreed. But how about Aline's book?

I don't know much about it, Gloria responded. I hear it's all lies and nonsense.

Aline says that Sergio beats you.

Por favor!

Well, Margarita asked, do you have any welts on your body?

Immediately, Gloria yanked up her shirt. It looked like she was going to pull it right over her head, giving Mexican viewers a taste of prime-time celebrity nudity. Even in the midst of a crisis, Gloria couldn't help being sexy and entertaining. She halted her hand, however, just below her breasts. Her skin was unblemished.

"You've all seen me in much shorter shorts, in my calendars and during my shows," Gloria retorted. "But here, take a good look—there are no bruises on my body."

How about the slave girl incident? Margarita asked.

Rubén Aviña, the author of Aline's as-told-to memoir, said he knew Aline was telling the truth because of something he'd personally witnessed. Previously a respected reporter and music industry publicist, Rubén said he'd once stopped by Sergio's studios, long before Aline came forward, and found Aline being punished by being forced to remain underneath Sergio's desk while she wrote "I will not lie to Sergio Andrade" one million times.

Gloria went slack-jawed as Margarita summed up the incident. "Anyone with a scrap of brains in their heads should be able to tell that's not true," Gloria stormed. Sergio is *not* a monster. "He's a fine, tender, caring man. On the other hand, I think the person who wrote *this* is a monster." And let's not ignore TV Azteca's sinister hand in all this, Gloria warned; let's keep in mind that Aline's ghostwriter worked for TV Azteca.

"And Paty Chapoy even wrote the introduction," Gloria added in stunned outrage. According to Gloria, this whole slanderous mess was a revenge plot cooked up by Chapoy, TV Azteca's powerful production director. Paty Chapoy had been one of Sergio's lovers, Gloria said. She'd been so in love with Sergio that she'd cheated with him behind her husband's back, and was still so in love with Sergio that she'd rather see him destroyed than in love with anyone else. Paty was a jilted and vicious ex-lover, Gloria went on, who was now using TV Azteca to whip up a witch hunt of greedy, lying teenagers willing to tell phony stories of sex and sadomasochism in exchange for TV time and book deals. That's right, Gloria stormed: Paty Chapoy, with her perfect salmon suits and prim shoulder shawls, was a sneaking cheat who was jealous of Gloria and hell-bent on destroying Sergio.

"See where this attack is coming from?" Gloria said. "Ask yourself who the writer is, and who wrote the prologue? Answer that, and you'll see that all this nonsense is just a war between television networks; it's a way of stirring up trouble when nothing much is going on." This is what happens when girls go crazy for fame, Gloria said with a sniff, turning Aline's rationale back against her. Since Aline couldn't make it as a performer, Gloria said, she was trying to make a name for herself by pulling down those who could.

"I want to tell everyone, if you really like being hooked like that, you must really like science fiction. In that case," Gloria continued, scootching back comfortably in her seat, knowing instinctively that she'd won her public relations battle and could now settle back and entertain, "I'd strongly recommend you buy something by Stephen King, who writes extraordinary science fiction and is a person with a great deal of talent."

One more thing, Gloria added: Sergio Andrade has "a heart of gold. I've seen him help the poor, I've seen him help people in need, and if he's guilty of *anything*, it's of being overprotective. After news spread of fans killing artists, he got nervous if anyone came near me. That's why I don't understand how anyone can say he hit me." But despite all the nonsense, Gloria added, she was happy to be back in Mexico—she was sick of Italian food. "Ravioli here, ravioli there . . . I couldn't wait to get home and eat *tortillas* and *chile*."

Ravioli? Italy? Miguel Yapor, watching the program from his wheelchair in the living room of his small house in Chihuahua, wondered what Gloria was talking about. Karina told him they'd spent the entire time in *Spain,* not Italy. Well, Miguel reflected, maybe there were still things he had to learn about about stardom; maybe stars had to fib a little about their whereabouts to protect themselves from mobs of fans. And what was all this talk about no one being able to find Sergio and Gloria? A few weeks after Gloria's appearance on the show, Miguel saw them himself, right there in his own house.

In May 1998, less than a month after Aline's book was released, Gloria and Sergio had brought Karina back home for a surprise visit. They also wanted to pay the Yapors the courtesy, Sergio said, of personally explaining what that whole Aline mess was about. It was a pity, Sergio said, and rather embarrassing, but the truth of the matter was, Aline was trying to destroy Sergio to punish him for her own failure. Gloria nodded in agreement; Karina, oddly, remained silent. But Gloria had been so affectionate during that visit, she distracted everyone's attention. She doted so lovingly on Miguel, he got a little bashful; when it came time for a group photo, Gloria made sure to cuddle up next to Miguel, making him duck his head a little and blush. Even Sergio had been especially charming, though a little jumpy—he didn't want anyone to photograph him and edged out of the frame whenever the family video camera swung in his direction.

A few months later, in September 1998, Karina was back again. Two visits in six months! Her parents were thrilled—this was the most they'd seen her in the past two years. Usually, she just phoned about one or twice a month, and the past year, they'd only seen her once. This time, though,

Karina and Gloria had come with a purpose: Things were getting a little sticky for Sergio because of this whole Aline business, Gloria explained, so they needed the Yapors to do them a little favor—they needed a little note that said that the Yapors had no objection to the way Sergio supervised Karina. Well, more than a little note, actually: Gloria wanted a notarized letter.

And she got one. Gloria took all the Yapors out to dinner—to celebrate Karina's birthday, she said—and while they were eating, Gloria talked on and on about how wonderfully Karina was progressing, how well she was doing at the Manuel de Falla music school in Madrid, how fantastic a success she would be once Sergio launched her as a soloist. Gloria was a little worried, she said—once Karina hit the stage, everyone would forget about her! Teresa Yapor wanted to talk to Karina about this in private—something was troubling her about the way her daughter stared down at the table and barely answered questions—but Gloria seemed to be all over the place, all the time.

"We never managed to talk to her alone, but I felt okay because she assured us they were taking good care of her," Teresa Yapor would later testify. "Gloria asked us for a letter they could use to defend themselves against the defamation that she said Aline was publishing about them." Incredibly, even though her daughter was in the care of a man who was publicly being called a sadistic pedophile, Teresa wasn't even sure what Aline had written: "None of us had read the book yet," Teresa would recall. So on September 17, 1998, Teresa and Miguel Yapor sat down before a notary public and signed a document swearing that as parents of Karina Yapor, they were pleased with the professional and ethical manner in which Sergio Andrade was overseeing their daughter. Then Gloria said that she and Karina were returning to Spain.

Three weeks later, Miguel would receive an astounding phone call that would make him bitterly regret signing that letter. The Mexican Foreign Ministry was on the phone. Was he the father of Karina Yapor? Well, then, it was requested that he fly to Spain and pick up his grandson. An infant boy, registered under Karina's name, had been left at La Paz Hospital in Spain. The boy was several months old, the Mexican consul continued, and badly malnourished. It appeared that a fourteen-year-old Mexican citizen by the name of Karina Yapor Gómez had given birth to a male baby last December 12, 1997. The baby had come close to death and was delivered to the hospital. The woman who brought the baby in had then disappeared.

But that's impossible, Miguel protested. I just saw my daughter a few weeks ago, right here in Chihuahua! She doesn't even have a boyfriend! She is in the care of Gloria Trevi, studying under very strict conditions at the Manuel de Falla Music Academy.

Sir, the Mexican consul responded. There is no such thing as the "Manuel de Falla" music school. The police in Spain believe your daughter is involved in a prostitution ring.

X   X   X

"On the first day we arrived in Spain, something incredible happened to me," Karina would later recount in the kind of breathless tumbling out of words that gives a good indication of how her mind was spinning. "While I was having group sex with Sergio, Wendy, and Marlene, Sergio felt something strange in my abdomen, and he told me to get a pregnancy test that he himself would administer. The result was positive. I was pregnant!"

And so within days of arriving, before she was even to have begun her classes at the "Manuel de Falla Academy," Karina was back on a plane, this time headed toward an abortion clinic in Houston, Texas, with Mary Boquitas. (It was during that time, Karina adds in an aside, that Sergio first forced her to clean up her vomit by eating it. Because she was suffering morning sickness, Karina woke up one morning in their room at the Holiday Inn and vomited on the floor, "something that looked like a raw egg." Sergio, she says, made her get a spoon and eat the runny, yellowish stomach heavings off the tile floor; when she could get no more with the spoon, she had to clean the tiles with her tongue.)

When Karina and Mary arrived at the Houston clinic, Karina was told she was too far advanced to abort the fetus. She would have to carry the baby to term. Mary advised Sergio of the situation by phone, then put Karina on a flight back to Spain. (Mary had other business to take care of in Mexico; so no one could trace their location by overseas bank with-drawals, Sergio had the girls acting as his bagwomen, carrying thousands of dollars in cash from Mexico to him in their suitcases.) Karina was met at Barajas Airport in Madrid by Sergio, Gloria, and two of the de la Cuesta sisters, Karola and Katia. At least there was a silver lining to the situation, Sergio told Karina as they left the airport: Maybe it will be a girl.

It wasn't. Karina would later be convinced that as soon as the sono-gram revealed that the child she was carrying was a boy, Sergio began scheming of a way to get rid of "that" (which is the word he used to refer to the growing bulge in Karina's midsection: "As soon as *that* is born," Karina recalls Sergio saying, "we'll have to make some changes"). First, though, to make sure Karina's parents were mollified back in Chihuahua, Sergio took advantage of the time before Karina began showing to take the girls on a photo-op sightseeing tour. He snapped photos of Karina posing with a big smile on her face outside the Prado Museum in Madrid, in Retiro Park, and next to the ancient Roman aqueduct in nearby Segovia. Stuffed into the envelope with her photos would be long letters from Karina, raving to her parents about how wonderfully she was doing at the "Manuel de Falla Music Academy." The letters were written in Karina's breathless, typically adolescent tone, but the phrases sounded like they'd been dictated to her by Sergio in a jumble of pseudophiloso-phizing and make-believe music appreciation lingo.

"This is the best thing that could have happened to me and I am very happy despite the sacrifices that sometimes don't even leave me room to breathe, but this is still very satisfactory for me." Karina wrote to her par-ents in September 1997, when she was nearly eight months pregnant.

> *I have learned the secret of life, something very few people ever master, and that it is, "Patience above all things," one has to be calm because no matter how difficult things appear, those things that make you suffer will make you king of the heavens. . . . You can't imagine how much work they give me in school, right now I have, besides everything else, to transcribe songs from one tone to another, for example from G major to C major, which means from "sol" major to*

"do" major, and first, I also have to write from memory the songs that I am playing. This scholarship is really a great opportunity to increase my knowledge and for that reason, I am really happy.

In reality, Karina was living in a bare house, often being punished by having to sit on a straightbacked chair for hours in an empty room. Whenever she wasn't in trouble, she was busy at a typewriter, working as Sergio's stenographer. Sergio had moved the girls to Toledo, in the outskirts of Madrid, where he'd bought a house and set himself up as sort of a combination pasha and poet-in-residence. For the next few months, Sergio lived the life of a country *auteur,* sort of a perverse variation of Wordsworth's life at the Lakes with his attentive, cheerfully secretarial sister. By day, Sergio would dictate or scrawl out poems and chapters of a novel for the girls to transcribe on the typewriter; by night, he climbed into bed with several of the girls, including an increasingly anxious and ever-more-pregnant Karina.

On the night of December 12, 1997, Karina was awakened by fierce contractions. She stumbled from room to room in the darkened house, looking for Sergio and finally finding him in one of the back bedrooms, busy scolding Liliana Regueiro, a young Argentinian woman who had joined the clan shortly before it decamped to Spain. Doubled over in pain, Karina supported herself against the door frame and first begged Sergio's pardon before saying she was in horrible pain and felt the baby coming. "Okay," Sergio replied. "I'll be with you in a moment." He then continued berating Liliana. Once he finished with Liliana, he packed Karina and the ever-present Katia de la Cuesta into the car and began the two-hour drive to Madrid. Karina barely made it—minutes after being rushed through the door of the emergency room, she gave birth to a tiny five-pound baby boy. Sergio chose the name: "Francisco Ariel." But he wouldn't touch him.

Sergio gave Karina a few weeks to recover in Toledo, then he ordered the girls to pack up again for another move. This time, he took them several hundred miles south, to the tourist-dense seaside town of Málaga, where a pack of young women would be unnoticeable among the tour groups, and even a rare beauty like Gloria could be easily and convincingly disguised by dressing her in the same sunglasses and floppy hats many of the northern European tourists were wearing against the burning sun of the Costa del Sol. Gloria had also put on a tremendous amount of weight, Karina recalls; free for the first time in decades from the demands of stardom, Gloria began indulging her sweet tooth voraciously, stuffing herself with holiday *turrón*.

The clan wasn't long in Málaga; after barely two months, they were headed back to Madrid. Not all the girls went at once, Karina would later point out: "His usual tactic was to separate me from my son, leaving him in the care of the girls who remained behind so I wouldn't attempt to escape." Karina, however, never mentions any time when she actually did try to escape, or call her parents, or mail them a note telling them the truth and asking for help. With all the typing paper at hand, with all the time she spent at the typewriter working over Sergio's scrawlings, it would seem simple for her to quickly tap out a short SOS message to her family and covertly mail it with a 50-peseta stamp or even slip it into one of the photo-crammed envelopes Sergio insisted she send home every few weeks. And when Karina claims that Sergio insisted she leave her three-month-old son behind with the other girls, Karina gives no indication that she ever protested.

When Spanish police would later retrace the clan's movements and try to determine how Karina's infant could end up in a Madrid hospital, alone and on the verge of death, they came to the conclusion that Sergio must have been forcing his girls to prostitute themselves. The theory matched a number of known facts about their behavior: the clan moved quickly from house to house, rarely staying in any one house for more than a few weeks and never resting in the same town for more than a few months; small packs of filthy, demanding girls who matched the clan's description had been spotted soliciting strangers at truck stops along the Spanish highways and along the Gran Vía in Madrid, which is just a few blocks from back alleys of the city's red-light district. Most convincingly, there was no record that Sergio had made any wire transfers or had shuttled any of his girls back to Mexico to hand carry cash. So where was he getting his money?

Karina goes to great lengths in her book to rebut the prostitution theory. The truth would turn out to be equally seedy, albeit nonsexual. As they headed back north, Sergio would stop the car at rest stops and in small roadside towns and order the girls out to beg for gas money. He was having a temporary problem with "liquidity," Sergio explained; basically, he was pouring all his available cash into acquiring real estate in his name. This was a prudent and far-seeing maneuver: Why put money into the gas tank or his girls' stomachs when a time could come when he would need convertible assets that couldn't be found or seized by Mexican police?

Even in Madrid, where the girls should have been most worried about keeping a low profile and passing unnoticed, Sergio would occasionally send them out onto the main shopping thoroughfare, the Gran Vía, to beg together a little pot of money. What's amazing is that Gloria, with her millions in the bank, the incredible risk she ran of being recognized, and the career-ruining humiliation she would suffer if exposed, was right out there with them, begging for fistfuls of pesetas. What's not so surprising, however, is that when it came to hustling coins from strangers, Gloria was the best. She sweet-talked old ladies outside supermarkets, telling them that she and her friends were Latin American students who'd run out of money and were saving for a flight home.

Gloria would also set out with a sketch pad and crayons and, relying on those simple, round-eyed cartoon figures she always drew, she would offer to draw caricatures of Gran Vía shoppers. In a ten-year cycle, Gloria had risen to the top of the entertainment business and fallen right back to where she'd started—humbling herself for Sergio and scrapping for food money at bus stops. That's why today, without their knowing it, certain charitable Spaniards may be in possession of original art by Latin America's greatest rock star of the 1990s and its most notorious Mexican prisoner—unsigned, of course.

Sergio had hoped that Aline's book would be disregarded as tabloid trash and disappear quickly, but instead, it began pushing its way up the sales charts, thanks to a serious miscalculation on Sergio's part. In the past, his disappearances in times of trouble had helped quell his problems, but this time it made them far worse. Sergio had forgotten that going undercover as a single man is very different from going undercover with a superstar entertainer and her retinue of teenage girls. The entertainment press had been fed for years on a steady diet of Gloria photos, announcements, and intrigue, and now, without warning, they were cut off. Into the void stepped Aline. If Gloria had been on hand to soak print pages with some harmless new outrage of her own, she could have quickly overshadowed Aline's allegations and helped snuff interest in her book. As it was, Gloria's invisibility began to lend credence to Aline: Why else would Gloria be silent during the very time in her life when she should have been on the attack?

But by the time Sergio realized his mistake and mobilized to do damage control, things were rapidly spinning beyond his control. Now that Sergio knew what was actually in the book, it was much worse than he'd expected. He had most likely counted on being shielded from the worst allegations by Aline's pride; how many eighteen-year-old girls, especially in a Roman Catholic country like Mexico, would have been bold enough to reveal intimate secrets of their sex lives? So Sergio wouldn't have expected Aline to produce anything more damaging than a whining diatribe about his failures as a manager and husband; it's unlikely he anticipated a detailed account of beatings, orgies, and mind control.

But if Aline had learned one thing from her time with Gloria and Sergio, it was Sergio's key tenet: You must be prepared to do anything—*anything!*—for stardom. Aline had learned from the best: If Gloria was willing to run laps around the Chihuahua cathedral in front of unbelieving fans, then Aline could tighten her resolve and pour everything into her book that would make it sell. To Sergio's alarm and amazement, she held nothing back. And then, emboldened by the unexpected public response to her story, Aline followed it up by filing corruption-of-minors charges. Aline wasn't just willing to expose Sergio and Gloria to the gossip columnists; she was willing to turn them over to the police and swear by everything she'd said in a court of law. This was getting serious.

That's when Sergio must have realized his temporary exile could become permanent. At any moment, he realized, other girls could step forward with stories of their own. How long till Mariana spoke up? And Tamara Zuñiga, and Edith Zuñiga, and Guadalupe Carrasco? What prevented the girls from his past, now grown up and more confident, from stepping forward with long-suppressed stories from years ago, stories that even Sergio himself could no longer keep track of? And then, just when he was trying to think up a strategy, Sergio received another jolt: Sonia Ríos and Karla de la Cuesta were pregnant.

Sergio had to act, and act fast. He needed to get back to Mexico immediately, before an arrest warrant was filed against him. Once back home, he had a tight schedule: He needed to get Karina back for a quick visit to her parents, to prevent them from becoming alarmed by Aline's book and asking questions that could reveal the existence of their secret grandson; he needed to get to his houses in Mexico and tear through them for evidence, burning anything that could be used against him, before the police were issued a search warrant; he then needed to transfer huge amounts of cash out of Mexico. And finally, he needed to deploy his greatest media weapon: Gloria. Maybe, just maybe, a bravura performance on national TV could reverse public opinion. Gloria had always done it in the past; ever since her all-or-nothing appearance on *Siempre en Domingo* years ago, Gloria had never failed to score big when the pressure was highest.

So Sergio mobilized, launching what would become a frenzied crossing/recrossing of the Atlantic in an attempt to quell suspicions at home and relocate the clan in small groups that wouldn't attract attention. By now Sergio had realized that fleeing with the clan had been a huge strategic mistake. With such a potent spokeswoman as Gloria on his side, he would have been much better off if he'd attacked the Aline problem in advance instead of watching it develop from afar. His first step toward repairing the damage, he decided, would be to slip back into Mexico and see how bad it really was. So in April 1998, Sergio left the rest of the clan behind in Spain and quietly returned to Mexico with Gloria and Mary.

"Thank God!" Karina later said she exclaimed once the three clan leaders were gone. "I wasn't alone, since Sergio had left behind the others and they were instructed to keep an eye on me, but I felt a lot more at ease. At least I wasn't being beaten anymore. . . ." True; but there was also no one who could prevent her from simply swaddling her child and walking out the door. As sullen and gloweringly obedient as Katia de la Cuesta was reputed to be, there was no hint that she would have gotten in Karina's way if Karina ever decided to go. And yet she stayed. For all her retrospective claims of fear and coercion, Karina easily could have done exactly what Aline had done years before, and Guadalupe and Tamara more recently still; she could have waited till the de la Cuesta sisters were asleep, pilfered a bit of cash from their handbags, and caught a taxi to the nearest police station. The fact that she didn't, and could later come up with no reasonable explanation why not, suggests that Karina herself did not understand what had happened to her. It was illogical for her to stay in such a miserable situation, but logic no longer applied: the normal, human instincts of self-preservation and self-reliance had been replaced by a strongly conditioned instinct to do what Sergio wanted.

A few days later, Sergio called—from Argentina. The situation in Mexico was much worse than he'd thought, he told them. The police were taking Aline's corruption-of-minors accusation seriously. There was no warrant out for his arrest yet, but an investigation was under way and a detention order could be issued at any time. So shortly after arriving in Mexico, Sergio fled again, this time to Argentina. It was too risky for him to try returning to Spain; Mexican relations with Spain were so strong and Spanish passport control was so rigid that if an arrest warrant were issued while Sergio was in transit, he would surely be caught and immediately extradited. Sergio came up with a new plan: Instead of returning to the girls in Spain, they would close up the house and join him in Argentina until he figured a way out of his legal mess. But there was one hitch: Karina would have to abandon her baby.

In her memoir, Karina gives the reason for leaving her newborn behind. "Because he was a minor, they wouldn't give me a passport for him," she first explained in her memoir. "When I told Sergio, he said, 'Ah, what a pity. Looks like you'll have to travel without your little boy.' " This broke her heart, Karina would write, but she acquiesced. Of course, she could have easily gotten a passport for Francisco Ariel by going to the Mexican Embassy, but because she was a minor herself, the embassy would certainly have contacted her parents directly. The dilemma ultimately wasn't whether Karina could get a passport for her son; the dilemma was whether she could get it without her parents finding out and forcing her to return home. Given that risk, Karina must have agreed to leave her son until she could find some way to retrieve him.

The girls split into small groups. In May 1998, Karina flew to Argentina with Liliana, Wendy, and Marlene, while the de la Cuesta sisters stayed behind to take care of Francisco Ariel. Once the group arrived in Mexico, Sergio risked returning to Chihuahua with Karina and Gloria for a quick, placating visit to the Yapors, and then he quickly returned to Buenos Aires. Karina remained an extra few days with her parents, accompanied the entire time by Wendy. When she left, she told her parents she was returning to Madrid for summer music classes. From Chihuahua, however, she secretly traveled to Mexico City, where she holed up in Sergio's mother's house. Once again, just as she was when the Hernández clan was hunting for Sergio and fifteen-year-old Aline, the long-suffering Doña Justina was thrust between her middle-aged son and the families of his teenage girlfriends.

For more than a month, Karina remained undercover in Mexico City. Sergio, meanwhile, was back in Argentina, organizing the clan's next move. His only option seemed to be first gathering the girls in Buenos Aires, then choosing a country where he could avoid extradition. From there he might be able to make contact with Aline and somehow convince her to drop the charges. Maybe with the promise of another record deal . . . ? There was always hope.

So in June 1998, Sergio sent Mary *back* to Madrid to close up the house, withdraw the last of Sergio's and Gloria's money from their Spanish bank accounts, and take care of Francisco Ariel until Karina arrived. The de la Cuesta girls flew from Madrid to Argentina, and Karina flew from Mexico City to Madrid, although she still had no clear idea how she would manage to get her son a passport. It turned out she'd never get a chance to try anyway: As soon as Karina arrived, she was stopped at immigration control because her tourist visa had expired and was deported back to Mexico. Mary was forced to stay on in Spain while Sergio decided what to do about Karina's baby.

In the meantime, there was plenty to keep Karina busy back in Mexico. Gloria was still making occasional TV appearances by night to protest Sergio's innocence, but by day she was busy clearing evidence out of his houses. With all the girls who had been in his homes over the years, there was no telling what the police would find should Aline's accusations turn into criminal charges and a search warrant. After all, one of Sergio's punishments had been making the girls write long, adoring, apologetic letters to him; piles and piles of them were still in the houses.

Karina even recalled seeing the fabled sheets of paper with Aline's punishments, the ones Rubén Aviña had talked about when he described finding Aline under Sergio's desk; the one million repetitions of "I will never lie to Sergio Andrade" still existed. The desk drawers were also stuffed with photographs, Karina says, including nude Polaroids of Gloria and Mary taken years ago, when they were barely teenagers, as members of Boquitas Pintadas. Sergio didn't attract the neighbors' attention by igniting all the compromising documents and pictures in a backyard bonfire; instead, Karina alleges, Gloria got one of her brothers to come down from Monterrey and help her secretly cart everything away in bulging trash bags.

Gloria then went to BMG Records, Karina says, in a long-shot attempt to get money for the clan, as well as papers that would allow Karina to work in Spain. Rather than try to apply for a new tourist visa, which would have required consent from Karina's parents, who thought their daughter already *was* in Spain, Gloria asked BMG to provide Karina with phony documents that would claim she was a member of a BMG recording team. Karina recalls Gloria also turned in a recording of the first single for her new album—and could she have some payment in advance, Karina recalls her requesting, about a hundred thousand dollars or so? By that point, however, Aline's allegations were making BMG uncomfortable. They agreed to pay Gloria the money she'd requested—after all, her albums unfailingly made millions—but as for phony papers, forget it. BMG became even more intractable when Gloria brought back the check and requested a different currency. Perhaps suspecting they were being asked to aid a possible fugitive from justice, BMG refused. Nevertheless, when the scandal erupted several months later, BMG would still release the new single, "No Soy Monedita de Oro" ("I'm Not a Little Gold Coin"). When asked how BMG happened to find itself with a recording from a woman not even the police could find, a BMG spokesman would shrug his shoulders and claim that a "plain white envelope appeared at the reception desk."

Sergio read a dire message in BMG's response: Gloria's attempts to gather transportable cash and to get Karina out of the country were attracting far too much attention. Any day now, the net could close as tightly around Gloria as it had around him. Sergio knew that he had to get Gloria and Karina out of Mexico, get Mary out of Spain, and move everyone, as soon as possible, to a safe haven. But what would they do about the baby? Sergio came up with one last idea—the legal guardianship and testimonial letters from Karina's parents. In September, Gloria and Karina made their return trip to the Yapors in Chihuahua. Once the notarized documents were secured, everything seemed ready for the clan to gather and, once again, disappear.

All Sergio needed now was a trusty person who could handle his real estate and finances in Mexico while he was on the run, someone whose fortunes would be legally bound to his. He felt he could trust Sonia Ríos, so he decided to leave her behind in Mexico to have his child and be his bagwoman when he needed money. Quietly, Sergio slipped back into Mexico for the last time. Even though he'd just had one infant with Karina and had another one on the way with Karla de la Cuesta, and not long ago finalized his divorce from Aline, he married Sonia and flew back to Argentina with Gloria and Karina.

Sergio had picked the ideal country for their escape. The girls had each carried as much cash as they could on their departure from Mexico, and the clan was ready to go. All they were waiting for now was Mary.

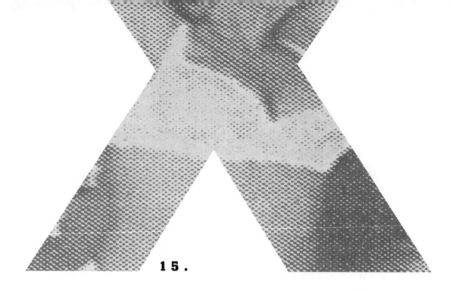

15.

"What Should We Do with the Corpse?"

For thirty-five years, Britain's most wanted criminal had lived a happy and public life in Brazil, dating a showgirl and strolling the beaches of Rio. That's because Brazilian law had a special stipulation: No parent of a Brazilian child could be extradited on criminal charges. And so Ronnie Biggs, the great British train robber who'd escaped from prison and run off to Rio, found himself untouchable when Scotland Yard tracked him down and tried to bring him home.

Ronnie Biggs had arrived in Brazil with enough of a head start to father a son by his Brazilian girlfriend. The British detectives went home, empty-handed and furious, while Ronnie Biggs went on to become a folk hero. And not just Ronnie: Thanks to Brazil's soft spot for outlaws, the son who'd prevented his capture, Mikey, was given a starring spot on a kids' TV show.

No wonder Sergio thought Brazil was the perfect destination for him and his clan on the run. Since Karla's child would be born on Brazilian soil, he could not only be free from any legal threat back home in Mexico, but perfectly positioned to relaunch Gloria's career in Rio de Janeiro. If the Brazilians loved Mikey Biggs and Xuxa, the bubbly blond bombshell, just wait till they got a load of Gloria and her clan of beautiful backup singers.

So as Karla's pregnancy advanced, and perhaps in anticipation of the day she would deliver his living defense against Mexican prosecution, Sergio moved the clan to Brazil, continuing his tried-and-true method of keeping his girls in motion, moving them from house to house and city to city, always leaving whenever he suspected the neighbors were beginning to wonder about the fat little man and the obedient crowd of Spanish-speaking girls who were always around him. After the clan arrived in Rio de Janeiro, Sergio quickly shuttled them to São Paulo, and then to a remote house outside of town before transporting them, once again, back toward Rio.

However, if escaping the law through childbirth was truly his intention, Sergio had been inadvertently misled by the Ronnie Biggs legend; it was specifically *because* of the British outcry over Biggs that Brazil had decided, in the early 1990s, to repeal that controversial statute. The parent of a Brazilian child could still be spared extradition, but only at the mercy of the court. It was no longer a guarantee, and by now, it seemed, Sergio would need one: The criminal charges he'd been dreading had just been filed against him by Karina's parents. A surprise phone call from Spain had suddenly let them know exactly where Sergio and their daughter had been, and at least partly what they had been up to.

It seemed Mary Boquitas had been severely lacking in her duties to feed Karina's baby, and she watched as his weight dropped and his color worsened. Finally, fearing the infant was about to die, she brought it to the hospital in Madrid. Mary must have intended to retrieve Francisco once he had recovered; otherwise why would she have given the child's real name at registration and her own? But a complication arose when she returned to visit: Since she wasn't the child's mother and didn't have written authorization from a parent, Mary wasn't permitted into the baby's room.

Sergio and the girls were already out of Mexico by that point, traveling through Argentina en route to Brazil, so Mary had no way of knowing that Karina had secured notarized guardianship papers from her parents and was about to depart for Madrid. By the time Sergio called Mary to check in, it was too late; the Mexican consulate had already received notice of an abandoned Mexican child and had tracked down the nearest next of kin. Realizing there was nothing more she could do, Mary Boquitas quietly left Spain and flew off to join the group. She reassured Karina that Francisco would be fine, that the Mexican authorities would make sure that he was delivered safely to Karina's family. She would later swear devotion to her son, but Karina didn't pick up the phone at that point to check with her parents and make sure they truly had agreed to care for Francisco. According to her memoir, the first time she called was months later.

It took the Yapors a long time to respond. Although they first received word of their grandson in October 1998, it would take them months to take action. Instead of immediately flying to Madrid to recover Francisco, they remained at home and waited until the Mexican consulate flew their grandson to Chihuahua instead. Then, for another six months, they did nothing about finding Karina.

The Yapors could never fully explain why it took so long. In their stammering responses to the press, the simple truth seemed to emerge that they were simply too confused and intimidated, both by Gloria's fame and the Chihuahua police department's notoriety. The Yapors were working-class people who'd never dealt with lawyers and police before. In Chihuahua, with its history of police corruption, men with guns and badges were to be avoided at all cost, regardless of which side of the law you were on. For months, Miguel and Teresa Yapor seemed to hope that this nightmare would suddenly just end and Karina would come home, as unreasonably optimistic a hope as Miguel's earlier belief that at age twelve Karina could convert Sergio and Gloria to a life of virtue.

Finally, though, after hearing nothing from Karina for months and fearing she might be dead, the Yapors decided they had to go to the police. In March 1999, they accused Sergio and Gloria of rape, kidnapping, and corruption of minors, and a warrant was issued for their arrest. The national manhunt that Sergio had feared for months was now under way.

Sergio's lawyer was quick to answer the Yapors' charges. Far from being a child molester, the attorney said, Sergio was a selfless and courageous patron of the arts who had spent his own money to develop young musicians, even though he was in the middle of a personal fight against cancer. The attorney said he had just been in touch with Sergio; Karina was fine, Sergio had told him, and the three of them—Sergio, Gloria, and Karina—were flying home right away to clear up this sad misunderstanding and have the charges dismissed.

On the appointed day, police and reporters turned out in force at Chihuahua's airport. They watched as one plane after another arrived. Sergio never appeared.

Soon after, an international manhunt was launched. Mexican police began collaborating with Interpol, and a search for Gloria and Sergio, as well as an undetermined number of young women from an unknown number of countries, was deployed in full force. Suddenly, Gloria was no longer someone police just wanted to talk with; she was now a suspect in a criminal case and a fugitive from international authorities. The sudden escalation of events was nearly mind-boggling—just six months after she'd appeared for the last time, giggling, scornful, and defiant, on nationwide TV, Gloria's smiling face was next to Sergio's on "Most Wanted" posters plastered across the country.

This was a complication Sergio couldn't have foreseen—all his plans till now, apparently, were designed to shield him from extradition, but Karla's baby wouldn't do anything to protect Gloria. Gloria would need some form of Brazilian parentage of her own. What could she do? Easy—Gloria got pregnant, too.

She wouldn't be alone—in fact, it seemed Sergio was trying to personally guarantee every girl in his clan the right to remain in Brazil for the rest of their lives, because he began impregnating the girls at an astounding rate. Sonia was pregnant, and Gloria, and Karla de la Cuesta. When Karla suffered a miscarriage, Sergio impregnated her again, as well as her fifteen-year-old sister, Karola. Under their misapprehension of Brazilian law, Gloria and Sergio could assume that once the girls had their babies, they'd all be protected, too.

Or perhaps another instinct was at work in Sergio; perhaps his obsessed reproduction was pure reflex, an unconscious reaction to the sense that time was running out and his captors were closing in. Before he was cornered, perhaps something inside Sergio told him to spread as many of his offspring throughout the world as he could with the time he had left. With four pregnant girls in the house, according to Karina's recollection of those days in Brazil, Sergio still seemed intent on adding a fifth. "Sergio was punishing me," Karina later noted, "and having sexual relations with me incessantly."

Sergio's only explanation for his manic procreation was an astoundingly juvenile smirk. "What man would resist?" he'd ask in prison, spreading his manacled hands in a gesture of mischievous innocence. "So many beautiful, talented young women who followed me wherever I went, can anyone blame me if accidents occurred? Believe me, I was trying to get *away* from the girls, but they followed me wherever I went." His excuse is easily dismissable on one level—it's clearly a lie, for instance, that a group of penniless girls could independently locate Sergio and follow him from country to country while the police couldn't—but important on another: Like Gloria, Sergio seems to have lost cognitive contact with the people he was lying *to*. While Gloria seemed to believe that it was permissable for thirty-something Sergio to have an affair with a teenybopper, Sergio seems convinced that any red-blooded guy would accept his rationale that impregating fourteen-year-olds is okay if they really seem to want sex.

But for all his retrospective glamorizing of his life on the run, the truth was, keeping the clan together was turning into a nonstop headache. Sergio had buried a lot of his cash in real estate in Spain and Mexico, and left a good portion in banks in Argentina, where it could be retrieved by Liliana, so all he had in Brazil was the money he'd carried in with him. To conserve his funds, he sent the girls out to sell sandwiches and beg along the beaches, and he crammed all of them into tiny apartments.

It wasn't so bad during the few months the clan spent in São Paulo; there Sergio found an unfurnished house in the suburbs. It was remote, and for most other people it would have been depressingly spartan, with its vast, empty living room and its mattresses jammed side by side on the bedroom floors. But after years of bouncing around from house to house in Mexico, Spain, and, briefly, Argentina, the clan girls were well used to the harshness of urban camping. What they weren't used to was a choking lack of space, which is what Sergio forced them to deal with once he moved them back to Rio de Janeiro. For reasons he kept to himself, Sergio decided the clan would be better off in Rio, so he made everyone pack once again and leave São Paulo.

This time he squeezed them all—ten young women, four of them pregnant, and one obese, middle-aged man—into a tiny two-bedroom apartment. Space was so tight, Karina would recall, that there wasn't enough room for the girls to roll over in their sleep. In one of the cramped bedrooms, Karina slept with Marlene, Liliana, Mary Boquitas, and two of the de la Cuesta sisters, Katia and Karla. Gloria and Sergio slept in the smaller bedroom; Sonia Rios and the youngest de la Cuesta sister, Karola, slept on the floor in the kitchenette, while Wendy bunked out in the living room.

The constant close contact caused the girls to squabble like never before, to the point where even several of the most obedient occasionally erupted in rebellion. A very pregnant Karla ran off, and for the next few days, Sergio and the girls searched the city for her, staking out the airport and the entrance to the Mexican embassy. Finally, after a scary three days, Karla was tracked down by Liliana and dour Katia. Karina never did find out where Karla had been. A few weeks later, it was Karola's turn; after she'd been screamed at by Sergio, the pregnant teenager climbed out one of the windows and startled the next-door neighbors by climbing in through one of their windows. The neighbors called the police, but before they arrived, Sergio hustled all the remaining girls off to the mall, while he and Gloria cowered in the back bedroom and waited for the police to stop pounding on the door and leave. Karola apparently had a change of heart, because she didn't tell the police the names of the people she'd run off from. With no official complaint and no one answering the apartment door, the police eventually left, and a repentant Karola rejoined the clan.

Sergio immediately packed up the girls and checked them into a hotel, but they'd no sooner arrived than Marlene disappeared. She was only gone a day, however; she, too, refused to tell the police who she was living with, and when they wouldn't pay for her ticket back to Mexico, Marlene returned to the hotel.

In the midst of this chaos, the babies began coming. First, Sonia had a daughter, whom Sergio named Antonia; then Karola de la Cuesta had a son, Milton, and her sister, Karla, had a daughter who was named Valentina. With ten women and three infants to take care of plus a fourth baby on the way, Sergio had to rent a second apartment. As for Gloria, she was happily swelling; it had been a decade since she'd first furnished a nursery, and even though her child would have to share space with a dozen other people and would spend hours a day separated from her mother while Gloria begged for centavos on the beaches of Rio, Gloria was delighted that she would finally have the baby she'd craved. In October 1999, she gave birth to a little girl, Ana Dalay.

One month later, on November 13, 1999, Sergio and Gloria were having dinner in the kitchen when Katia de la Cuesta came in holding baby Ana. According to Karina, Katia was giggling and gesturing toward the silent baby. "Look, how cute," Katia said. "She's sleeping so quietly, it's like she's dead." Gloria erupted from the table with a shriek and lunged for Ana. Sergio pulled her away and held tight to Gloria while Katia, who finally realized from Gloria's hysteria that something was wrong, dropped to the floor and clumsily tried to revive the infant. Liliana came running in when she heard Gloria's screams, and she joined Katia on the floor. None of them knew infant CPR or mouth-to-mouth resuscitation, however, so they fumbled around desperately with no idea what to do. At one point they even grabbed a can of Coca-Cola Lite from the fridge and dumped it on the motionless infant's face, hoping it would somehow revive her.

Nothing worked, however, and the girls eventually gave up. While Sergio tried to quiet Gloria's shrieking and sobbing, Mary Boquitas and Liliana began wondering what they should do with the tiny corpse. Karina, stunned and horrified, stood in the kitchen while the older girls discussed their options, none of which involved calling paramedics or a funeral parlor. The dead infant remained in the apartment for a full day, according to Karina, and then another, until something strange happened: on that third evening, Mary went into the kitchen and closed the door, saying she was going to prepare dinner. No one else was allowed to enter. Karina said she heard the sound of chopping and hacking, and much later, Mary left with a small suitcase. Karina found the kitchen had been freshly cleaned and mopped, and the corpse of Ana Dalay had disappeared.

Gloria was inconsolable. She wept and moaned, telling the girls over and over that she had dreamed that her daughter was going to die before it happened, and that it was a punishment from God for not having baptized Ana Dalay within the first month she was born. Karina had her own superstitious explanation: By her recollection, Ana Dalay had died on the exact anniversary of the first time she'd had sex with Sergio, five years before. "It seemed God was punishing them," she said later.

But at the time Karina entertained no such recriminatory thoughts. Perhaps that is why Sergio decided to risk one last great gamble to put an end to the trouble that continued to grow back in Mexico. His thinking might also have been addled by Gloria's keening grief or the stress of realizing that his avenues for escape were closing fast. Whatever his logic, he was about to make the mistake that would end his run forever: He decided to send Karina home to personally beg on his behalf with her parents.

On the face of it, trusting Karina was not all that crazy a notion. Unlike several of the other girls. Karina had never tried to run away, despite all the clear chances she'd had. Although she would later claim that she'd considered escaping, she had not taken advantage of several perfect opportunities: For example, nothing could have been easier than for her to alert the hospital staff to her situation when she was giving birth to Francisco Ariel in Madrid and request that her parents be notified and plane fare be wired for her to go home.

But unlike Karola de la Cuesta, who even climbed out an upper-floor apartment window while pregnant, Karina had apparently become as docile and worry-free to Sergio as Mary Boquitas. Sergio got further affirmation of Karina's loyalty when he first let her venture a phone call home. Miguel and Teresa were ecstatic to hear Karina's voice for the first time in nearly a year, but they hardened as soon as Karina began pleading with them to drop the criminal charges against Sergio and Gloria. We won't even talk about it, a newly resolved Miguel responded, until you come home. Karina argued and cried; Miguel and Teresa argued and cried along with her. They put her brother on the phone to try to lure her home, and when that didn't work, they even put Francisco Ariel to the receiver to gurgle. "Just tell the police that Gloria and Sergio didn't do anything wrong, and I'll fly right home," Karina promised. "The baby isn't even his—Francisco's father was my boyfriend in Spain." But as much as they feared that this could be the last time they ever heard from Karina, Miguel and Teresa dug in their heels: Until they had Karina in their house, they would not talk about clearing Sergio.

So ten days before Christmas of 1999, less than one month after Gloria's baby had died and disappeared, Karina Yapor emerged. Sergio bought tickets back to Mexico for her and Marlene Calderón, with pre-arranged stories: They were studying samba in Brazil, they needed Karina's parents to care for Francisco Ariel just a little while longer, and soon Sergio would launch her career and make them all millionaires, just as he had with Gloria. Karina didn't tell her parents what time she was arriving; the plan also called for her to try slipping in and out of the country anonymously, and Sergio even considered booking her a ticket with Liliana's passport. Ultimately, he figured that would be too tacit an admission of guilt, so Karina and Marlene flew back to Chihuahua under their own names.

As soon as they arrived, nineteen-year-old Marlene was arrested for kidnapping. The press had been alerted, and a mob of TV cameras awaited Karina outside her house. Karina, however, was unperturbed. She had spent nearly every day of the past half-decade by the side of one of the greatest entertainers Mexico had ever known, and she had learned very well how to handle herself under pressure. Karina looked waiflike and frail under the crush of reporters, but she calmly looked up at the cameras and did exactly what Gloria would have done: She lied. "Mr. Sergio Andrade and Gloria Trevi are wonderful people who have never harmed me in the slightest," Karina swore. "This is all an outrage against two very fine people. I was never raped, I was never kidnapped. I have nothing but respect for Mr. Sergio Andrade."

Despite her disavowal of her parents' criminal complaint and her refusal to say anything about Gloria's and Sergio's whereabouts, Karina had inadvertently given the police an important tip. Previously, they'd believed that Sergio was hidden away in a remote corner of Central America, perhaps in Guatemala, Panama, or El Salvador. With Karina's flight information, however, Interpol began zeroing in on Brazil, and the investigators soon discovered Sergio had dropped another clue: In order to be able to enter and exit Brazil as often as he wanted, he hadn't let his tourist visa expire. Rather than just keeping quiet, like any other foreigner going underground, Sergio decided to take precautions. He'd already had run-ins with the police, and judging by the difficulties he'd already had as various girls ran off and returned, he was likely to have more. The last thing he wanted was to try talking his way out of trouble with an expired tourist visa, so Sergio had decided to take the risky step of renewing his and Gloria's documents. Granted, he'd given an old address in Copacabana, but their new apartments weren't very far away.

Police began scouring the beach community, and it wasn't long before a sharp-eyed officer, on a January morning in 2000, noticed a beautiful young woman walking down the street who reminded him a lot of an album cover he'd seen. The woman had her thick, golden-brown curls shoved into a baseball cap, and her eyes were masked by glasses, but as the office approached, he felt his certainty grow.

Gloria and Mary were walking to the store when the police officers stopped them and asked to see identification. They smiled and flirted a bit and gave false names, but the officers were grimly serious: Unless they produced identification, they were going to jail. Trapped, Gloria could only think of one thing to do: Maybe Sergio could figure a way out of this. She offered to bring the officers back to their apartment to look for her identification. Sergio would think of something; he always did. But when Sergio opened the apartment door and saw Gloria and Mary flanked by two unsmiling police officers, he sagged. It was over. He'd known ever since Karina failed to return the previous month from her trip home to Chihuahua that the net was closing. He simply surrendered and allowed the officers to come inside. The police pushed their way into the apartment and were amazed by what they found: Instead of a plush suite with an ocean view, the famed and wealthy Gloria Trevi and her manager were living in squalor, in a filthy apartment filled with diapers, unbathed teenage girls, and squalling infants.

The officers radioed in their incredible luck—They'd done it! They'd captured Latin America's Most Wanted!—and soon TV news vans were zooming to the scene. Sergio was led down first, his hands cuffed tightly behind his back, and then Mary Boquitas. The rest of the clan—the de la Cuesta sisters, and Sonia Ríos, and Liliana and Wendy, and all their infants—were escorted down to a waiting police van so they could be brought in for questioning.

And then it was Gloria's turn. She could see the clamor down below from the apartment window, and as she looked down in the final moments before being driven off to jail, something seemed to come over her. The scene was so frightening and horrible, and yet so familiar—a pack of reporters, the glare of TV lights, a crush of eager onlookers and a thicket of police holding them back, all for her. The crowd on the street was growing larger and larger, all of them dying for a glimpse at her, the Mexican Madonna, Gloria Trevi. Gloria had never been in this situation before, but she knew exactly what to do. In private she might feel like a scared Gloria de los Ángeles Treviño Ruiz, but in public she only knew how to be Gloria Trevi—*La Atrevida!*—The Fearless One!—and Gloria Trevi could only be one way. Before the handcuffs were cinched around her wrists, before she was pushed into the back of a squad car and taken off to be booked and fingerprinted, before she was forced to take a disinfectant shower for lice and have her anus and vagina searched with rubber-gloved fingers for drugs and weapons, she made one final request.

"May I take a few minutes," she asked the officers, "to comb my hair and freshen my makeup?" Surprised, the officers agreed. Gloria pulled off her cap and yanked a brush though her lush mane until the gold highlights shone. She swiftly darkened her eyes and brightened her cheeks. And then, with that same glorious smile that had won the hearts of millions, Gloria Trevi went downstairs to meet her public.

*E*veryone assumed Gloria, Sergio, and Mary Boquitas were guilty, but Mexican prosecutors had a major problem: The only evidence they had to work with was a sensationalist book by an angry ex-wife and four girls who swore Sergio had never raped, molested, or kidnapped them.

"My parents are pressuring me to testify what they want," Karina Yapor told a Mexican newspaper, and claimed she was still in love with Sergio. "I feel like a prisoner," Karina wept. From behind bars, Katia de la Cuesta told another newspaper, "I never saw any abnormal behavior on the part of Sergio, Gloria, or any member of the group."

Even prison couldn't make Sergio's girls change their minds. The two youngest de la Cuesta sisters were allowed to go home to their parents, since they had been minors during their years with the clan, but the eldest sister, Katia, was taken off to Chihuahua prison to join Marlene Calderón. There Katia was greeted with a surprise: Marlene was pregnant, too. Sergio had managed to father one last child before everything came crashing down. When Katia and Marlene were processed before being locked up, Judge Hector Talamantes made their situation very clear: They could protect Sergio and go to jail or they could speak up and go free. The girls chose jail. Six months later, in June 2000, they burst into agonized tears when Sergio's attorney came to visit them in prison with news about Sergio: He'd been struck by some kind of neuromuscular ailment and was lying in a prison hospital, temporarily paralyzed. Karina Yapor was just as upset: "I'm really sad and depressed that Sergio Andrade is sick," she told a reporter. Secretly, according to Silvia Beeg, she was also placing long-distance calls to Brasilia; Silvia says that for a time Karina was calling at least once a week to pass hopeful messages along to Gloria, Mary, and Sergio.

Privately, prosecutors were relieved that the three leaders of the clan were fighting their extradition from Brazil; unless something changed, they faced the very real possibility that Mexico's most famous and notorious fugitives would finally come home, only to be turned free. Unless something changed, there would be no case against them. And then, bit by bit, the change started to come: The more time that passed, the more Sergio's hold over the girls began to fade. Just as Sergio had feared, it began with the girls who'd left the clan first. Guadalupe Carrasco came forward with her story about how Sergio had raped her while the other girls watched. Tamara Zuñiga went to police in Chile and described Sergio ripping her clothes off and lashing her with an electrical cord. TV Azteca located Gloria's cousin, Mariana (who was then going by the name Brandy) in McAllen, Texas, and flew her to Mexico to tell her story about being raped in Los Angeles. Then, after nearly a year in prison, Katia de la Cuesta had a conversion. "God has opened my eyes," she said, and she accused Sergio of inflicting her with "punishments, humiliation and torture."

The big breakthrough came when Karina Yapor also had a change of heart. In 2001, after months of living at home and seeing a psychologist, Karina finally changed her story and agreed to testify against Sergio, Gloria, and Mary. Her testimony before Judge Talamantes went on for two full days and reads like the tale of a concentration camp. Also, after denying it for nearly two years, Karina bowed to the evidence in her son's distinctive face and admitted that Sergio had fathered him. She began work on a tell-all book, *Revelaciones,* which would describe Sergio as a sadistic cult overlord who could only get sexually aroused through violence and humiliation.

With the evidence mounting against them, Gloria and Sergio appealed to the Brazilian government to grant them political asylum as refugees. It was a request, since Gloria's activism had been confined to little more than the occasional shouted slogan during a concert and there was no indication that Sergio or Mary had ever been involved in politics of any kind, but the Brazilian Supreme Court granted them a hearing anyway. For three hours, Gloria talked about how her life would be in jeopardy if she set foot back in Mexico. "Before the Virgin of Guadalupe, I'm telling you I am a dead woman as soon as they get their hands on me," Gloria said, beating her chest with her fist. She knew secrets about the government that could get her killed, Gloria swore.

But why? the justices asked. What are those secrets? Sergio would raise the specter of political skullduggery, with his brother as target and Sergio and Gloria as innocents caught in the middle, but not even his brother would attempt to pursue that defense. Gloria revealed only one secret; she said that Ricardo Salinas Pliego, the owner of TV Azteca, had tried to hire her and dodge tax laws by offering to put one million dollars in her name in an offshore account in the Cayman Islands. But if true, why hadn't Gloria's life been in danger *before,* when she was actually in Mexico? Why would Salinas suddenly be worried about her now, when she was scandal stained and discredited, and not before, when she had her own live nightly show and could have exposed him then, without censorship? Her asylum petition was denied, and plans were made for the trio's imminent extradition.

That's when Gloria, in a career devoted to shock and outrage, unveiled her greatest surprise: Somehow, without conjugal visits, after nearly two years in an all-female wing of a maximum security prison, she had gotten pregnant. Quickly, word spread that the father of her child was Fernandinho Beira Mar, Brazil's most notorious drug trafficker, who had recently been captured in Colombia during a raid on the jungle camp of his left-wing guerrilla protectors. No sooner had he arrived in Papuda prison than Beira Mar made a public offer to Gloria of ten thousand dollars for a single, private performance Gloria says she politely declined.

She refused to say anything more about her mystery pregnancy, but her attorneys immediately launched a media blitz. Gloria had been serially raped behind bars, her attorneys said; prison officials would routinely open her cell, tie her down, and rape her. The police, however, launched an investigation and returned with another theory: they insisted that Trevi had impregnated herself with the sperm of Marcelo Borelli, a despised Brazilian gangster in the men's cell block. According to the police report, Trevi chose Borelli because he was marked for death, sure to be shanked in prison for having tortured and raped a rival's three-year-old daughter. With Borelli out of the way, Trevi would never have to worry about him turning up as a free man and pressing a claim on the family fortune.

The police report claimed that plastic Baggies of Borelli's sperm were smuggled to Trevi inside glasses of warm milk, thereby keeping it roughly at body temperature. Trevi then inseminated herself with a syringe she had constructed from a ballpoint pen. Borelli himself told *ISTOE,* a respected Brazilian newsmagazine, that he was the mystery child's father. He said he sent Trevi at least five bags of sperm.

"Gloria has an interest in remaining in Brazil and not being deported to Mexico," said Francisco de Assis Guimaraes, the police official in charge of the investigation. "A Brazilian child would help her." Although the law no longer automatically guarantees residency to the foreign parent of a Brazilian child, the minister of justice, José Gregori, had to admit that Gloria's pregnancy could become a factor "from the emotional point of view."

The Supreme Tribunal conducted a special hearing, but Trevi said she was in too much danger to reveal the father's identity. She refused even to confirm her lawyers' account that she had been raped. The reason for her secrecy? Wealth and vulnerability, she said. As long as she remained in prison, she was at the mercy of the guards; once she was released, the child's father could claim the sex was consensual and argue for partial custody. If she died, he would then have a claim to her money. So she wasn't talking.

The Brazilian police, however, tried another means of testing her story. Just days before her delivery date, Gloria's attorney, Geraldo Magela, stopped by to visit Gloria in the maternity ward of a local hospital, where she was under guard and a week from giving birth. As Magela paused to chat with the hospital director, three men suddenly appeared in the doorway. One flipped open a police I.D., then squared his hands on his hips, pushing back his suit jacket to reveal the pistol holstered on his waist.

"We need an extraction of amniotic fluid from Trevi," the officer said, apparently assuming the lawyer was a hospital staffer. "Don't tell her what it's for. We want to perform verifiable DNA testing on the child before it's born."

"Ay ya!" Magela exclaimed as he hauled his bulk off the sofa. "Ay ya! Absolutely not! That's unconstitutional! It's an invasion of her privacy."

"You want an invasion?" the officer said. "I've got a van full of cops outside. We'll take this hospital by force, if we have to." Cell phones materialized and everyone started dialing. Magela hit the Supreme Tribunal on his speed dial; the hospital director, shaken, called the minister of health. Soon Magela cried out—"Ha!"—and handed his cell phone to one of the cops. The Supreme Tribunal had granted a stay. The cop slapped the cell phone into Magela's hand and led his partners out.

"Oh my God," Magela moaned, then repeated himself victoriously: "O! Deus! Meu!"

But the victory was short-lived: One week later, on February 18, Ángel Gabriel Trevi was born. Brazilian police seized the placenta, and seventy-five prison guards and police officers offered their DNA for paternity testing. Only one blood sample was necessary, though, and it was volunteered: The father, investigators say, is Sergio Andrade. Rather than acknowledge scientific evidence, Gloria continued to fight back, even going so far as to finally come forward with the rape story herself, in her memoir *Gloria, por Gloria Trevi*. She was the victim of human rights abuses, Gloria claimed, and her son was another victim, forced to live with her in a filthy Brazilian prison. She would continue to fight for asylum, she vowed, and no longer for herself: Now it was for her son. Mary Boquitas, on the other hand, was settling in peacefully to prison life: After years of acting as drill instructor for Sergio's teenage charges, she began teaching dance and aerobics classes to her fellow prisoners. She soon became very popular.

Sergio, meanwhile, was busy making another crucial mistake in his attempt to avoid a long jail sentence in Mexico. After steadfastly refusing any interviews with TV Azteca, he did agree to go on NBC's *Dateline*—not realizing that NBC is one of TV Azteca's financial backers. TV Azteca put *Dateline* in touch with Mariana/Brandy, Gloria's beautiful cousin. The *Dateline* episode was damning; it was built around Brandy's tearful recollections of rapes and beatings, interspersed with sound bites from Sergio trying to explain the difference between a pedophile and a guy who just likes young girls. It was great TV, but a terrible public relations blow for Sergio; TV Azteca was able to air excerpts, leaving little doubt in any Mexican's mind that Sergio was a monster. The image of that devastating news program lingered even after a very curious twist of events: Mariana suddenly dropped her charges against Sergio and disappeared. Police in McAllen, Texas, couldn't find her anymore; neither could the TV Azteca lawyers who'd represented her.

"There!" Sergio would exclaim. "That is proof of what I have been talking about all along! What more evidence do you need that this is just a deliberate campaign by TV Azteca to fabricate evidence, simply to destroy the careers of two people who would not work for them?" He explained his point thoroughly and impressively in a few newspaper interviews—but no one seemed to be listening to Mr. Midas anymore.

And then, just when it seemed the trio was settling in for a long court fight, Gloria suddenly dropped her plea for asylum. Behind the scenes, it seemed that a secret strategy by Gloria's and Sergio's lawyers was starting to work. Privately, they realized that Sergio had little or no hope of avoiding serious jail time. "He's a goner," one of Sergio's own attorneys confided. "He's kind of a shit, too, I have to be honest." But for Gloria and Mary—there was still hope. All along, her attorneys believed that

Gloria just needed to separate herself from Sergio, proclaim herself another victim of his mental manipulation, and she would go free.

Gloria had flat-out refused to do so, however; in every interview, in every appearance she referred to herself as "Sergio's maximum defender." But eventually her attorneys realized that to win they would have to take a lesson from the opposition. Over the course of the previous years, they'd seen how all Sergio's girls, once they'd been cut off from him for a few months, gradually lost interest in him. One by one, nearly all of them had renounced Sergio after they had been back in Mexico for five or six months. It was almost like a magic spell wearing off, they told each other. So what if they convinced Gloria to go back to Chihuahua . . .

The argument they used on Gloria was one they knew she'd listen to: Do it for Ángel Gabriel. Her cell in Chihuahua would have heating and air conditioning, and her family could visit more often. Ángel Gabriel could even go live with his grandmother and come visit Gloria often. What her lawyers told each other, however, was that if they could keep Gloria away from Sergio for the same amount of time as the other girls, she just might come around. So on December 22, 2002, Gloria dropped her plea for asylum and agreed to go home to Chihuahua. "It will be better in Mexico than in Brazil," Gloria said, as she exited Papuda en route to the airport. "I have faith in God, in my lawyers, in my family, and in justice."

"The soap opera is finally over," sighed Justice Nilson Naves, president of Brazil's Supreme Tribunal. A few months later, Mary Boquitas also voluntarily returned to Chihuahua. Sergio, however, remained in Brazil and continued to fight his extradition—on the advice of his attorneys, who were the same ones who'd advised Gloria and Mary to return home without Sergio.

Gloria's attorneys, however, turned out to be wrong. She did not change her mind about Sergio after six months of separation—instead, it took ten months. The first hint came in early October 2003, when a reporter for the Mexican newspaper *El Diario* scored the first behind-bars interview with the extradited star. As her son frolicked behind her in the visiting room, Gloria protested her innocence and, just like old times, cut loose with one of her immensely quotable eruptions, this time comparing wild stories about her impregnation by ballpoint pen to the murder of civil rights activist Digna Ochoa.

"The other day, I saw the results of the investigation into the death of Digna Ochoa, and I suppose that many Mexicans are feeling the same thing I feel: indignation. Because we're not stupid," Gloria said. "Because this version is like the story they invented that I impregnated myself with a pen, or whatever. Bics can't talk! All this is outrageous."

But the most revealing moment occurred when the reporter abruptly asked Gloria about Sergio. Gloria must have known the question was coming, but it seemed to catch her off guard. Gloria is used to using her rants and jokes to control the pace and timing of interviews; she's not accustomed to reporters sticking doggedly to a line of questioning in the face of her outrageous claims and bursts of bawdy humor, so she seemed surprised when, just as she'd finished answering a puff ball question about how she was feeling these days, the reporter zeroed in on Sergio. Previously, Gloria had answered glibly and self-confidently, even using rather regal language to respond to a query about her well-being.

"In Brazil, I was a weaker Gloria," she'd said. "My eyes are not the same anymore, and why? Because God has given me proof of his love."

"You say you've grown," the reporter immediately followed up. "So how do you now feel about Sergio Andrade?"

Uncharacteristically, Gloria had to think before answering. After a long pause, she said, "What I feel is what I'd feel for anyone in his situation."

"Wait, so he's not someone special for you?" the reporter persisted. "Because three years ago, you yourself told me that he was the one person you truly loved. And now you're saying he's the same to you as anyone else."

By this time Gloria had regained her footing. "Look," she began. "For starters, Sergio is in Brazil. He's not here. He's living his life. He has his fiancée, he has his wife, I don't know who he's going to stay with, I don't know if he's going to break up with his wife or fiancée, or what he's going to do. I've got no idea! I haven't spoken to him." It seemed Gloria was finally getting a little tired of Sergio spreading his love around.

Then, in October 2003, Gloria was back in the place she loved most, on the cover of a magazine. This time it was the Spanish version of *People*, the magazine that first gave her international credibility. As usual, she looked magnificent: On the cover, she's shown frolicking with Ángel Gabriel; her smile is joyful, her figure is as sexy and runway ready as ever, and her son is the exact image of Sergio Andrade.

Inside the magazine, Gloria is shown in shorts and a belly-baring T-shirt, showing off her body and announcing her hopes of launching another calendar. She also has dozens of songs she's written in prison, and an idea for a movie, and—oh!—the big news! Televisa wants her to star in a soap opera based on her own life. There might be complications, of course—Gloria, Sergio, and Mary were still facing trial in Chihuahua on charges of rape, statutory rape, kidnapping, and corruption of minors, and the prosecutor in Mexico City was still deciding whether to pursue a case based on Aline's charges from years ago. But that's okay, Gloria says; Televisa has figured out a very clever way for her to phone in her lines from prison. Just imagine—the ratings will be huge!

Could her radiance have anything to do with the news that had just come from Brazil? Earlier that week, the Brazilian court had made its final decision: Sergio's last appeal had been denied, and he'd be extradited to Mexico within sixty days. By Christmas he'd be back in Chihuahua, close to Gloria once again.

But when the *People* reporter asked Gloria how she felt about seeing Sergio again, Gloria's glow suddenly faded. Yes, she admitted, Sergio probably was the father of her child. As if blind to the fact that her accusations of rape had cost two prison officials their jobs and created a furor of suspicion, she now admitted that she had voluntarily traded sex with one of the guards in exchange for time alone with Sergio in one of the attorney-client conference rooms.

So she must be excited, the reporter asked, now that Sergio was coming back to Mexico and they'd soon be reunited?

"No," Gloria said simply. "Sergio is not the same man I fell in love with."

*O*n Tuesday, September 21, 2004, after four years, eight months, and eight days behind bars, Gloria Trevi was finally back in front of an audience.

This time she sat in a cage in the front of Judge Javier Pineda's court-room in Chihuahua, Mexico. Beside her was Mary Boquitas. For the few dozen fans who were lucky enough to be admitted to the stiflingly crowded courtoom, this was their first live look at Gloria in years. As always, she looked magnificent, as if she'd somehow stopped into a day spa on her way to court from prison. She wore a sedate red blouse to match her freshly tinted reddish hair, and a simple strand of pearls. A pair of brilliantly glimmering earrings set off the subtle makeup and serene expression. Only Gloria's hands revealed what she was feeling; as she waited for Judge Pineda to appear, she restlessly fingered a rosary.

In a few moments Gloria and Mary would learn how many years they would serve in prison for rape, kidnapping, and the corruption of minors. Also seated in the courtroom was Marlene Calderón, waiting to hear her sentence for abetting a felony. Marlene had been arrested and sent to prison after she'd accompanied Karina back to Chihuahua. But unlike the de la Cuesta sisters, Marlene steadfastly refused to say a word against Gloria or Sergio, and shespent a year behind bars before she was finally freed on bail. When she left prison, it was with a baby in her arms; the father is believed to be Sergio. Soon after her release, Marlene married Juan Medina Flores, a Chihuahua entrepreneur, and vanished into silence. To this day she has never breathed a word about the clan, their strange stay in Brazil, or the disappearance of Gloria's first child, Ana Dalay.

Seated not far from Marlene was Armando Gómez Martínez, Gloria's new lawyer and, it had recently been announced, her fiancé. Earlier that summer, Gloria had fired her previous team of lawyers, and Gómez had taken over her case. He took swift action: After years of delaying the process, Gloria dropped all her challenges and asked to be brought to trial immediately—and separately from Sergio. Her request was granted, and Karina Yapor was sworn in to tell her story once more. The trial was surprisingly swift and uneventful; when it was Gloria's turn to testify, she denied all the charges without elaboration. The one surprise came at the very end of the proceedings. "Your honor," Gloria said, "with great humility, I ask that these charges be dropped." *Great humility* . . . that was a dramatically different note from the one Gloria had sounded seven months before, when she had railed about the corruption in the court and said she'd never get a fair trial.

Despite Gloria's newfound humility, however, the prosecutors made their position clear: They asked the court to sentence Gloria and Mary to at least thirty years in prison.

At 6:00 P.M., Judge Pineda arrived and arranged himself at the bench. He opened a file folder and began to read. He had barely finished his opening remarks when Karina Yapor felt a sharp nudge. Her mother handed her a note. "Leave now," the note said. Apparently someone had been tipped off about the sentence; the first few phrases from the judge confirmed the rumor. "You don't want to be here," the note told Karina. Outside, hundreds of Gloria's diehard fans were waiting under a torrential downpour, and the mob could turn ugly toward Karina after it heard what Judge Pineda was about to say.

Karina and her mother quickly got up and slipped out the door. They were in their car and gone by the time Judge Pineda reached the heart of his statement. "Gloria de los Angeles Treviño Ruiz," he intoned, "is not legally responsible for the crimes of corruption of minors, kidnapping, or rape in regard to acts committed against Karina Alejandra Yapor Gómez. Therefore, it is ordered that she be freed immediately and absolutely." For a moment the entire courtroom sat in stunned silence; then, cheers and screams of joy erupted. "Gloria! We love you!" her fans shrieked.

It took several minutes before Judge Pineda was able to continue. Mary Boquitas and Marlene Calderon were also acquitted, he said, but added a warning note: "The proceedings against Sergio Gustavo Andrade Sánchez, who faces the same charges as apparent author of the crimes, remain open." Sergio would go on trial later in the year.

Gloria and Mary leaped into each other's arms. Soon after, they appeared outside the prison, free women for the first time in nearly a half decade. Gloria had, rather amazingly, thought to take a moment to change her clothes before leaving prison; instead of the sober red blouse and pearls she'd worn to court, she now appeared in a brilliant white sleeveless dress, perfectly highlighting her mane of red-and-gold-tinted hair, now swinging loose. The symbolism was too powerful to be coincidental, especially in the hands of an experienced showperson like Gloria: The scarlet tunic of the penitent had been replaced by virginal white as she emerged, reborn.

TV news microphones were shoved in front of Gloria, and as usual, she did not disappoint. Her freedom, she said, was a direct act of intervention on her behalf by none other than God himself. "Above all, I had faith in my God. That's why I knew he would touch the hearts of the judges," Gloria said. "It was something beautiful, marvelous. The day they had chosen to read the sentence, it began to rain, and a rainbow come out, and the moment they declared me free, the skies opened and became fiery, gorgeous, like the fiesta in my heart." And not only was the Almighty on her side, Gloria added, but the damned as well. "My friends behind bars were all shouting with joy and weeping with happiness.

"I am more innocent than any judge can say," Gloria continued, to the cheers of the rain-soaked crowd. "I got into this situation without having ever done anything wrong to anyone, and it took me years to get out of it." Gloria, of course, happily glossed over the fact that the reason it took her years to receive her acquittal was because she spent years developing strategies to dodge a trial. Or, as she put it to me when I interviewed her in a Brazilian hospital shortly before the birth of her son, "I will fight down to my fingernails to stay in Brazil."

And what very few people knew was that shortly before winning her freedom, Gloria had told a very different story to Judge Pineda in a closed session in his chambers. Previously Gloria had denied ever witnessing a single act of cruelty against any of her backup singers. Karina, Aline, the two Zuñiga sisters, the three de la Cuestas . . . all these girls who made accusations against Sergio, she angrily insisted, were liars. "It makes me sick," she had told me, "to see these girls showing up with new cars and beautiful manicures and television contracts, all because of the lies they're willing to tell about Sergio. He is the most gentle, wonderful man I have ever met." But in her last session with Judge Pineda, Gloria finally did something her lawyers had been begging her to do for years.

"I was also physically mistreated at the hands of Sergio Andrade," Gloria reportedly said. "I was never in agreement with the punishments and beatings he gave out, but I was afraid to speak up." Because of Sergio, she said, she had suffered bulimia and psychological terror. To this day, she reportedly added, she was still bulimic, and it was Sergio's abuse that caused it. Perhaps she was still too proud to use the word, but it was written between every line of her statement: For the first time in her tumultuous life, Gloria was calling herself a victim.

Karina Yapor wasn't buying it. Appearing on *Ventaneando,* the TV Azteca program that had made so many revelations in the case, she reacted bitterly to the verdict. "This is an international embarrassment," she said. "A failure of justice." And it wasn't over yet, Karina pointed out: There were still five days to appeal the acquittal, while prosecutors in Mexico City were still deciding whether to bring fresh charges against the trio. "The truth is, we have two very similar accusations of deprivation of liberty, rape, and corruption of minors," confirmed Mexico City's top prosecutor, Bernardo Batiz. One of them involved Aline Hernandez.

Batiz said he would decide very soon if Gloria and Mary Boquitas would be brought in for a new round of questioning and, perhaps, rearrested.

But the odds of Gloria seeing the inside of a cell again were slim. If prosecutors in Chihuahua hadn't been able to come up with enough evidence to convict her in four years of trying, it was doubtful they would in five days. Bernardo Batiz, meanwhile, had to be less than thrilled about building his case around Aline, who was then busy peddling her own unique line of thongs and lingerie. Aline's signature piece, according to one product description, "was a very unusual kind of panty which has jeweled straps which can be removed from the undergarment and worn as either bracelets or a necklace."

With the main witness against her in a sex case now the proprietor of a necklace-bracelet-panties business, Gloria knew she was out of danger. "I can't believe it," she gushed to reporters, right before she was whisked off to tiny Chihuahua airport and onto a private plane. "In the morning and throughout the day, I felt like I was in an old western movie, like my head was in the noose and I was waiting for a cowboy to arrive to save me."

"What about Sergio?" reporters shouted. "What do you want for Sergio?"

Gloria paused before answering. "Justice," she said, knowing full well what that could mean.

X   X   X

Within two hours, Gloria had arrived in Monterrey and was checking into a luxury suite at the Quinta Real, whose previous guests had included Prince Felipe of Spain and President George W. Bush. Her family and entourage filled five other suites, at six hundred dollars per night. Early the next morning, Gloria went to mass at Monterrey's Catedral Metropolitana, accompanied by her father and two of her brothers. Thousands of fans crowded into the cathedral as well, holding up giant posters of Gloria in bikinis. When Gloria stepped up to receive communion, her fans burst into cheers.

After mass, Gloria appeard briefly. "Wait till you hear my new album," she said. "It will prove I am a creative person, not a destructive one." And then, with a wink and a devilish grin, she added, "I can't wait to eat the world like never before." With that, she ducked into a waiting car and disappeared. But one member of Gloria's retinue lingered to speak with the press: Juan Osorio, one of Mexico's most successful soap opera producers and the man who had already crafted a TV series for Gloria before she had even been tried.

"The future is very exciting," Juan Osorio told the reporters. Gloria had already recorded an album's worth of songs behind bars, which were just then being mixed and orchestrated. The first single, "Tu nieve de mamey," was scheduled for release in a few weeks. But even bigger than the album, Osorio promised, would be Gloria's great big thank-you to her fans: In November she planned to fill all 104,000 seats at a massive concert in Mexico City's Azteca Stadium. Even Mary Boquitas was now finding the fame that had eluded her for decades; she would soon be starring in a movie called *Ángeles de Dios*.

"If Gloria Trevi used to be an idol," Osorios said, "she is now a phenomenon."